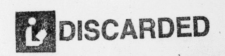

CHAPTERS ON
OLD ENGLISH
LITERATURE

16-17
175-176-7

218

225

Page from Genesis, MS. Junius XI, showing the
Translation of Enoch. (See p. 115.)

[Frontispiece

CHAPTERS ON
OLD ENGLISH
LITERATURE

By

E. E. WARDALE

M.A., Ph.D.

Hon. Fellow of St. Hugh's College, Oxford.

LONDON

KEGAN PAUL, TRENCH, TRUBNER & CO., LTD.

BROADWAY HOUSE: 68–74 CARTER LANE, E.C.

1935

PRINTED IN GREAT BRITAIN BY
STEPHEN AUSTIN AND SONS, LTD., HERTFORD.

CONTENTS

v

ABBREVIATIONS USED

Ags.	Anglo-Saxon or Angelsächsisch.
Anz.	Anzeiger.
Beit.	Beiträge.
Bibl.	Bibliothek.
C.C.C.	Corpus Christi College.
Cr.	Crīst.
Eccles. Hist.	Ecclesiastical History.
El.	Elene.
Engl. Stud.	Englische Studien.
Germ. Phil.	Germanic Philology.
Haupts Ztschr.	Haupts Zeitschrift.
J.E.G.Ph.	Journal of English and Germanic Philology.
Jul.	Juliana.
M.H.G.	Middle High German.
M.L.N.	Modern Language Notes.
M.L.R.	Modern Language Review.
Mod. Phil.	Modern Philology.
O.E.	Old English.
O.H.G.	Old High German.
O.N.	Old Norse.
O.S.	Old Saxon.
Pauls Grdr.	Paul's Grundriss der Germanischen Philologie.
P.B.B.	Paul und Braune's Beiträge zur Geschichte der deutschen Sprache und Literatur.
P.M.L.A.	Publications of the Modern Language Association of America.
Z.f.d.A.	Zeitschrift für deutsches Alterthum.
Z.f.d.Ph.	Zeitschrift für deutsche Philologie.

PREFACE

These Chapters on Old English Literature are intended to fill the gap between Professor Thomas's valuable, but all too brief account in his English Literature before Chaucer, and longer works, such as those of Stopford Brooke and the chapters in the first volume of the Cambridge History of English Literature. My primary object has, of course, been to make the works themselves known to my readers, but I have also tried to trace the development of prose and poetry during the period, showing in the poetry the modifications of the original Germanic character brought about by later influences of all kinds, and noting those forms or features which lead on to Middle English. In dealing with the many unsettled questions, I have given only the views which seem to me most important. Had I wished to do more, it would obviously have been impossible in the space which I have allowed myself; but references to other works are added for a student who may wish to make a more thorough investigation of such points for himself.

I have dealt at far greater length with the poetry than with the prose, for that is the form of literature which is characteristic of the period, and in it we see that particular form at its highest point of development. Important as Old English prose undoubtedly is, we see it at this time in its beginning only; its interest is rather that of promise than of performance.

My translations may, if they are thought worthy of it, call forth adverse criticism. In them I have endeavoured to give not only the thought of the original but, as far as I have been able, something of the manner in which that thought is conveyed. A polished modern rendering would have been useless for this.

I hope that I have in these chapters always acknowledged

my debts to others. They are heavy and various, and to all to whom I owe so much, I tender my thanks. My special gratitude is due to Professor H. C. Wyld for much valuable help and encouragement, to Miss Mary Loveday for many useful suggestions at the beginning and during the course of my work, and to Miss R. M. Marshall for much help in many ways, but especially in reading the proofs.

E. E. W.

CHAPTER I

OLD ENGLISH LITERATURE

Before entering upon a detailed study of individual works it would be well to consider briefly the general character of the vernacular literature of the Old English period, that is of the time between the coming of the Angles and Saxons to Britain in the fifth century and the Norman Conquest. The Latin writings, important as some of them are, do not concern us here.

In the first place it may be observed that all the earliest O.E. literature is in poetic form, and that it is to the poetry that we must look chiefly for the characteristics of the period. The prose arose later and shows such strong foreign influence that it is necessarily less individual in character. In the poetry we have achievement, in the prose chiefly promise. The ultimate source of the poetry is to be found centuries earlier on the Continent in the songs which the Germanic tribes composed in honour of their great men. Though, unfortunately, none of these lays have come down to us, their existence is proved by mentions of them in early writers, as when Jordanes[1] and Priscus[2] tell us that hero lays were sung among the Germanic tribes, extolling the deeds of their great men, and Tacitus[3] mentions such poems as having been made already in his day.

Further, some general knowledge of these songs, of the heroes thus honoured, and of the style of treatment in them may be gathered from extant poems, especially from those in Old English and Old Norse Literature. Such a knowledge, meagre though it must be, is valuable in helping us to distinguish between the native and foreign elements as we trace the development of the poetry through the various modifications it underwent during the O.E. period.

[1] Jordanes, De origine actibusque Getarum, C. V.
[2] Priscus, Fragmenta Historicorum Græcorum, IV, 92.
[3] Tacitus, Germania, II.

B

How soon these lays developed into epic form or into something more like that of the Northern Sagas, it is impossible to say. All that is certain is that epics were composed among the more westerly tribes after they broke off from the other members of the Germanic family, for we have an O.H.G. fragment, known as the Hildebrandslied, from an epic dealing with an episode from the story of the Gothic king Eormenric, and it seems certain from a passage inserted in the O.E. poem of Beowulf, that the story of the Frisian king Finn had been treated in a similar manner. In Beowulf itself, we have the epic in its later form after modification under Christian and classical influence.

Charms and gnomic verses must also have been composed in that early period, for the O.E. versions still retain traces of their heathen origin, and it may safely be assumed that love and marriage songs, drinking songs, and dirges were also made.

The stories which may be accepted as having come down from early times show that the Germanic tribes had a fine flair for a good tale and a keen appreciation of a telling situation. For instance a popular theme treated is that of the king who, having attained great power and fame, allowed himself to be led astray by this early prosperity and to degenerate from a mighty hero into a cruel tyrant, thus bringing upon himself his own punishment, in the vengeance taken upon him for his cruelty. This is one version of the story of Eormenric, king of the Goths,[1] whose name, " the very mighty one," speaks for itself.

A fine situation has been chosen in the tale of the faithful vassal, who, after the death of his lord in battle, is forced by stress of weather and other circumstances to remain for a time in the country of the conqueror and even to take an oath of allegiance to him. He has thus placed himself in a situation in which he is torn between the conflicting claims of his natural duty, that of avenging his murdered lord, and that which he has taken upon himself, of allegiance to the murderer. In the first case by failing he would incur the reproach of disloyalty and cowardice,

[1] Guðrúnarhvöt and Hamðismál.

both unforgivable sins at the time ; in the second, that of treachery. This is the story of Hengest the vassal of king Hnæf in the Finn epic.[1] An equally telling situation is that of Hildeburh in the same tale. A Half-Dane, she has been married to Finn king of Frisia, and when hostilities break out between the two peoples, she loses in one fight her own son and her brother, who are of course on different sides. She can neither rejoice in victory on the one hand, nor, on the other, can she obtain satisfaction for her loss by exacting vengeance, according to the code of the time, since each is a near kinsman. She too is torn between the claims of inherited and later accepted ties, between the ties of blood and marriage.

These and other stories like them, supplied magnificent material for the epic in the suggestion of their tragic happenings. It is to be noted that in England it was themes like these of individual tragedy and family strife which were preferred to larger subjects, but that, popular as these were, still greater prominence was given to more legendary material derived from folk tales, which was then treated with dignity in the epic manner.

These lays or epics were carried about from court to court, and from country to country by professional minstrels, the scops of O.E. poetry, and thus it could come to pass that of the historical characters introduced into Beowulf, only one, Offa of Mercia, is English, the others are all from foreign countries. The forms in which the names of those heroes are preserved show that the lays extolling their deeds must have reached the Angles and Saxons very early, in fact while they were still on the Continent, but even there it could only have been through these travelling minstrels that such lays became known outside their own countries.

Some of these minstrels, like a scop who calls himself Deor,[2] obtained regular posts at the courts and became personages of considerable importance. Though the actual poem of Beowulf must be dated about 700, the social life described is that of an earlier period and may be taken as

---

[1] Beowulf, vv. 1068.   [2] Deor's Lament, see p. 33.

giving us a good picture of the court life of some centuries earlier. From it we learn that the minstrel had his seat in the court at the foot of the dais ; elsewhere we are told that he was accustomed to receive liberal gifts of money or even of land for his songs. His duty was to entertain the lord and his courtiers with song and recitation, not only at banquets but also at the ordinary meals. Other minstrels, less fortunate in obtaining court posts, wandered from place to place, with song and recitation, sometimes composing new songs in honour of recent events, sometimes recounting lays and stories already known. How highly the art of minstrelsy was cultivated is shown by the strict rules which grew up for the metre in which the scops made their verses ; and in what high esteem the sister arts of poetry and music were held is clear from the fact that both were practised, not only by professional minstrels, but even by men of kingly rank. In Beowulf, king Hroþgar is represented as playing the harp and reciting hero lays, and when Gelimer,[1] the last king of the Vandals, was besieged by the Herulians on Mt. Papua in 534, he wrote to the commander of the besieging army to beg for a harp, as he had composed a poem on his own misfortunes and wished to sing it to an accompaniment on that instrument.

In O.E. times the custom of song-making lasted on, Biblical themes being added to secular ones, and peasants took their part in these performances. Hild,[2] from 657–680 Abbess of Streoneshealh, the modern Whitby, encouraged the servants as well as the monks of her monastery to make songs, and through this means the cowherd Cædmon discovered his gift. It remained for a later date to question the suitability of secular themes for the clergy. It was not till more than a century later, in 797, that Alcuin wrote to the Bishop of Lindisfarne to remonstrate, asking, " What has Ingeld to do with Christ ? Narrow is the house. It will not be able to hold them both. One king reigns eternally in Heaven, the other, the heathen, is damned and groans in Hell."

We have then to picture to ourselves the society of those

---

[1] Procopius, Vand. II, 6.   [2] Bede, Eccl. Hist. of Eng., IV, 24.

early centuries as steeped in legendary lore and as taking a very sensitive and critical interest in the form in which those legends were presented. We are specially told in Beowulf that the scop found words correctly bound together,[1] that is, perhaps, in correct alliteration ; and a few lines further on, that he related a tale expertly and with success.

When, however, certain of the Germanic tribes left their continental homes and settled in new surroundings in Britain, old contacts were broken, they came under new influences, and their literature, freed to some extent from tradition, developed on lines of its own.

The first external influence to be traced is that of Celtic, for the Romans seem to have left none behind them. The Celtic population, however, as far as it survived at all, was absorbed among the Germanic conquerors, and appears to have exercised some slight influence upon their mental outlook. This is seen in a certain lightness of touch in descriptions of nature. It appears especially in the North, but this may be merely because our earliest extant literature is of Northern origin. Far greater was the influence of Christianity and the classical learning which followed in its wake, an influence more subtle, more gradual, and more lasting. It was this superimposed on some original difference of temperament, modified by later climatic and other influences, which gave its distinctive character to the O.E. branch of Germanic literature. Probably, also, a key to a good deal of the history of that branch is to be found in the warning sent by Pope Gregory to the Abbot Mellitus [2] after his departure for England in 601. " There is no doubt," he wrote, " that it is impossible to cut off everything at once from their rude natures." At any rate the monks seem to have acted on this principle and to have shown great tact. They not only allowed their converts to retain some of their religious ceremonies, which indeed in Mayday and other customs may still be seen, but, far from trying to oust the native poetry because of its heathen character, they themselves actually preserved it by committing much to writing, and later by using the native metre for their

---

[1] Beowulf, vv. 870 ff.   [2] Bede, Eccl. Hist. of Eng., I, 30.

own paraphrases of the Bible and Lives of the Saints. It is significant of the way in which the clergy entered into the interests of their flocks that one of the first acts of the missionaries in Kent was to write down in English the Laws of Ethelbert. In Northumbria, where Christianity was introduced from Scotland, the missionaries appear to have shown the same sympathy with their converts. One result of this tolerance, which may be noticed in passing, is the curious jumble of Christian and heathen elements which is constantly met with in our oldest poems, as when one of the Gnomic verses tells us " the powers of Christ are great ", and then goes on to add " Fate is strongest ". It is also to be seen in the part played by " Wyrd " or Fate in the older O.E. literature generally, and by the difficulty in determining exactly what in its character is due to Christianity and what to native temperament.

As important is the encouragement thus given to literary activity. This can best be realized by comparing the fate of the native literature in England with that in Germany, where the Christian missionaries showed no such tolerance. There, in the ninth century, Otfrid a monk of Weissenburg, in Rhenish Franconia, set himself deliberately to stamp out the heathen beliefs and customs, as inimical to Christian teaching. For this purpose he chose for his theme the Life of Christ, and for this, in itself a foreign subject, he adopted a metre based on Latin, and a scholastic method of treatment.[1] The result is that all that has survived of native poetry is a fragment or two, just enough to give an idea of what has been lost. We have to wait till the thirteenth century in Germany for the stories of the Nibelungen and other old epic heroes.

Two periods of literature have to be distinguished in pre-Conquest England ; the first had its home in Northumbria and perhaps Northern Mercia, and flourished during the later seventh and eighth centuries. During these centuries Northumbria was a centre of learning, not for England only, but for all Western Europe and nearly

---

[1] Otfrids Evangelienbuch, herausgegeben von Oscar Erdmann, Halle, 1882.

all the great English monasteries were in that kingdom. It would be in them that the stimulus would have been given to the early Christian poems, and in their schools that the native poetry would have been written down, and naturally the poems thus copied were principally those by Northumbrians. This was an age of poetic activity; to it belong Beowulf and the early lyrics, as well as the poems of the Schools of Cædmon and Cynewulf, and many more works must have existed. It is generally conceded that the works written down must have represented but a part of those composed, while of them many must have perished in the raiding of the monasteries in pre-Conquest times by the Danes, as well as in the later days of Reformation zeal.

Later under Ælfred the centre of cultivation moved down to Wessex, and the second literary period arose. This may be said to have lasted from the middle of the ninth century till some time after the year 1000. It is the time of the O.E. prose writings and to it belong the works of Ælfred, Ælfric, and Wulfstan, and to it also we owe the MSS. of the old poems, which were copied then by W.S. scribes.

Another classification which cuts across this, but is, perhaps, more satisfactory, is to arrange O.E. literature in two classes, the first containing that which is of Germanic origin, which would include hero lays and epics, charms, gnomic verses, and early lyrical poems; and the second, that which grew up later on English soil. In this class would come all the religious epics, a few shorter poems, secular and religious, and practically all our prose. Speaking generally, the first class may be said to be essentially heathen, the second, Christian, but this division must not be taken too strictly, Hardly a single work is exclusively heathen, even the charms, and the heathen element is slow to disappear entirely from the early Christian works. All are, however, distinctively English in character, showing those qualities, which distinguish O.E. from O.H.G., O.S., or O.N. literature, and these qualities are very marked, for as time went on the old Germanic patterns got modified in the different countries, new features appearing in each.

In England, the warlike tone, the aristocratic colouring, natural to lays glorifying the victories or lamenting the overthrow of kings and heroes, lasted on, and with the power of vigorous description may be looked upon as part of the Germanic heritage.   But side by side with them appears a note of seriousness, amounting sometimes to melancholy.   Indeed almost all the lyrical poems are elegies. This may be due to the religious outlook of the Anglo-Saxons in pre-Christian days.   Whereas in Old Norse stories a mortal in trouble could always hope to find protection from one god or another, in O.E. nothing of the kind could be looked for.   The names of the old gods do occur and are indeed still kept in the names of Tuesday and other days of the week, but even then they were clearly nothing but memories.   The cheerful company of the gods and goddesses of the old Germanic mythology had been lost behind the one relentless figure of Fate, and the general tone of O.E. literature was coloured by this idea.   We are told over and over again that " Fate goeth ever as it will ", or that " Fate is full inexorable ".   How completely the old definite beliefs had been lost, as for instance, that in Valhalla, the hall in which the valiant feasted after death, may be gathered from Bede's account [1] of the speech of the noble at the court of Edwin of Northumbria, when the admission of the Christian missionaries was being considered.   " It seems to me, O King, that this present life of men on earth," he said, " is as if a sparrow should fly quickly through the house . . . So this life of men appears for a short while only, but what is to follow or what went before, we know not."   Hence if our ancestors delighted in nature, it was chiefly on the stormy sea, the mysterious dark forest, the solitary moors, the formidable mountains that their imagination dwelt, for here their love of fighting and their seriousness both found scope.   Even when we do get a brighter passage under Celtic influence, and the cuckoo is mentioned as the harbinger of spring, even then it is of his sad note that the poet speaks.

This high seriousness is, however, relieved from time to

[1] Bede, Eccl. Hist., II, 13.

time by touches of humour, so quiet, often so suggestive
only, that they have been overlooked by some critics.
In this point again O.E. literature stands in strong contrast
to that of O.N., in which the humour is very obvious ; it is
boisterous, even the gods can play practical jokes, as,
for instance, in the story of Ðrymr and Ðorr's hammer,
in which, when the giant Ðrymr has refused to give up the
hammer stolen from Ðorr unless the goddess Freyja will
marry him, Ðorr does not hesitate to dress himself up in
Freyja's garments and go as bride in her place to Ðrym's
home, where he astonishes all by his appetite.   Finally,
having by his ruse recovered his hammer, he makes short
work of Ðrymr and the other giants.[1]   No story of this
kind is to be found in the whole body of O.E. poetry, it
would have been impossible to an English poet.

Further with this seriousness and dignified quality of
humour there is combined, it must be confessed, a certain
tendency to moralize and that at considerable length.
The O.E. poet never quite got away from himself in
telling his story, or singing his song, as did his brother
in Scandinavia.   He was apt to interrupt his theme to
put in his own reflections on life in general, or on the
particular incident under consideration, and these reflections
tend to be of a didactic kind.

Such passages show, however, that our ancestors had a
lofty ideal and a stern outlook on life.   It might have been
expected that with a fate hanging over them, which was
neither to be conquered nor propitiated, men might be
justified in making the most of present possibilities of
enjoyment.   This was, however, far from being the doctrine
taught.   Over and over again the poets insist that the thing
most to be desired is to leave a good name behind after
death.   Thus Wiglaf says in Beowulf,[2] " Death is better
for every man than a life of reproach," and Beowulf himself [3]
declares, " Let him achieve who may, fame after death.
That is best for a warrior when no longer living."   And this
sentiment is expressed more fully elsewhere.[4]   To gain this

---

[1] O.N. Ðrymskviða.   [2] Beowulf, vv. 2890–1.
[3] Ibid., vv. 1387–9.   [4] Seafarer, vv. 72 ff.

good name the warrior must be bold and loyal, the king must be generous. Cowardice, ingratitude, and treachery are unforgivable." "It does not appear to me seemly," says Wiglaf,[1] "that we should carry our shields back to our homes, unless we may first fell the foe and protect the life of the lord of the Weders." His contempt for the followers of Beowulf who have forsaken him in his last fight is outspoken. "By no means had the folk-king," he says, "cause to boast of his comrades.[2] Lo! he may say, who will speak truth . . . that he (Beowulf) had thrown away in cruel fashion his (gifts of) armour when it came to him to have to fight."[3]

Out of keeping with this ideal character seems the habit of boasting which lasted on and appears as late as in the Battle of Maldon, at the end of the tenth century, though already in the earliest poems, such as the Wanderer, we get adverse criticism expressed of this custom. A man must wait, we are told, before he utters a boast, till that he, though bold in heart, can know thoroughly, whither the thoughts of his heart will lead him.[4] In fact it is deeds, not words, that really count. It is better to avenge a friend than to mourn too greatly.[5]

Indeed the virtues of moderation and self-control are constantly upheld by O.E. writers. The author of the little poem called the Wanderer, tells us that it is a noble virtue in a man to bind fast his heart and restrain his thoughts, let him think as he may.[6] Another passage which perhaps belongs to the same poem, is more explicit. A warrior, it tells us, must be patient, neither too passionate nor too ready of speech, too timid, nor too foolhardy.[7]

One wonders, in this connection, what is the true explanation of the small amount of lyrical poetry which we have before the Conquest. No doubt much has been lost, and it may be simply that by some chance a larger number of narrative poems happen to have been preserved than of lyrical, or again it may be that the monks to whom we

---

[1] Beowulf, vv. 2653 ff. [2] Ibid., vv. 2873–4.
[3] Ibid., vv. 2864 ff. [4] Wanderer, vv. 70–2.
[5] Beowulf, vv. 1384–5. [6] Wanderer, vv. 11–14.
[7] Ibid., vv. 65 ff.

owe our MSS. did not care to write down lyrical songs of a
secular and heathen character. But may it not also be due
in part to this feeling against indulgence in the expression
of emotion, with the result that the poets most in touch
with their times chose to make narrative rather than lyrical
poems ? When they did compose lyrics we find that they
gave in to the prevailing fashion by suggesting a story in
the background. It is, of course, impossible to decide.
What is certain is that we have very few O.E. lyrical poems.
Those we have are generally admitted to be of early date,
and may be taken as representing O.E. literature before
its special English characteristics, especially its restraint,
had fully developed. They have a great beauty of their
own, and from their very nature necessarily show a greater
emotional element than the lays and epics. But even so
they are less passionate than is O.N. poetry and it is often
just the restraint with which the emotion is expressed or
merely suggested in them, that gives the power. Anyhow,
whatever the cause may be, the fact remains that it is
chiefly narrative poetry which has been preserved to us
of that composed before the Conquest, and so general
is that character that most of those O.E. lyrics which
have come down to us, have narrative settings. The epics,
on the other hand, are distinguished from the O.N. Sagas
by a certain lyrical quality, in as much as the writers
frequently, as has been already said, disturb the progress
of the story by introducing their own feelings and reflections.
This is not so surprising in the religious poems since they
were avowedly meant for edification, but the habit is
found quite as much in Beowulf, where it has not the same
justification.

As Christian teaching came in new heroes and new themes
replaced those of Germanic origin, and as it penetrated
deeper we get modifications of the earlier type. The idea
of Fate disappears and a more cheerful note creeps in. In
Beowulf that idea is still prominent but by Cynewulf's time
it is gone. His two heroines, St. Juliana and St. Helena,
both show the old fighting spirit, but there is none of the
former hopelessness in the stories. The one-sidedness too

of the earlier poetry is beginning to disappear. The themes
treated no longer deal only with war and court life.
The older religious narratives are paraphrases of the Bible
and have to follow their originals, and Cynewulf's heroines
happen to be of noble birth, but in the Life of St. Guthlac,
written about the same time, it is the life of a saint of lesser
rank that is described. So again, in earlier times only the
Gnomic verses and the Charms show any recognition of
matters of everyday life ; later in the Riddles, indirect
results of the introduction of Christianity, every kind of
subject is found.

Classical influence, coming through the monastic schools,
followed that of Christianity, but its results appear as early
and are as widespread. The influence of Virgil has been
seen by some [1] already in Beowulf, in the slow sweep of the
movement and in the arrangement of the plot, as when the
poet goes on at once to his main theme and fills in
the details of his hero's earlier life incidentally only and as
opportunity offers, as well as in other points. A certain
classical influence can perhaps be seen also in the religious
narratives, though in metre and spirit they are true to the
native epic.

But the knowledge of Latin did more than provide new
models in the great classical writers, it gave England the
freedom of the literary movements of the Continent, it
brought her into touch with other branches of literature,
popular over Europe, but hitherto unknown to her. Not
only did Ælfred, in seeking the education of his people,
choose those Latin works to translate which were most used
in the monastic schools of Europe, but this new contact
led to the writing and collecting of Riddles, it produced a
Bestiary and introduced the form of the Debate. It also
made known to the English the story of Alexander the
Great and the magic tales of the East, and it is to be seen
in the pseudo-scientific works of the end of the period. As
in the sphere of religion, Christianity softened the gloomy
belief in a relentless fate, so classical influence on literature

---

[1] Alois Brandl, Geschichte der Altengl. Literatur.(Pauls Grdr., Abschnitt,
VI, p. 1008.)   See also p. 106.

modified the nature element in English poetry. The early delight in grand and wild aspects lasted on after the end of the O.E. period, but side by side with it the charm of sunshine and flowers made itself felt, first by translation as in the Phoenix, but also in due time it showed itself in native works as in the little poem on the Doomsday,[1] treated later. The influence of Latin hymns is also to be seen in the greater frequency of rhyme, which spread from its use in compounds like " word-hord " or in phrases like " hond and rond " to that of the linking together of the two halves of the long alliterative line.

The widening influence of classical learning is thus to be traced in the new matter introduced into branches of literature already cultivated, in new literary forms now made known and in the manner of treatment in all.

A later influence than that of the classics came from Old Saxon. It is to be seen in the interpolated passage of Genesis, known as Genesis B,[2] or the Later Genesis, and in the poem on the Day of Judgement,[3] which follows directly after Cynewulf's Christ in the Exeter Book. The first of these is certainly of O.S. origin and the second probably. The influence is to be traced in the larger emotional and psychological element, which makes these poems stand out in marked contrast to the narrative poetry of undisputed O.E. origin, in which the action is all-important. In Genesis B it is Satan's thoughts and feelings with which the poet is concerned, and these he has worked out with considerable subtility and at some length. Further he has adopted as more suited for the expression of emotion the longer line found in O.S., but rare in O.E. poetry.

Germanic poetry, of whatever kind, was all composed in one metre, the alliterative. This metre underwent certain modifications in England, but persisted as the only poetical form until the end of the period, the only difference in its use for epic or lyric being the position of the sense pause. In the lyric the thought generally ended with the line, in the epic it was carried on over the end of one line to the middle of the next and the pause came there.

[1] Chap. IX, p. 234.   [2] Chap. VI, p. 123.   [3] Chap. VIII, p. 190.

During the O.E. period rhyme began to come in, but only side by side with alliteration, never without it.

The rules which governed this alliterative metre were very complicated. Many scholars have investigated the subject and the conclusions at which they have arrived vary a good deal in many points.[1] It will be enough here, however, to mention the general features of the metre which are admitted by all, without attempting to enter into disputed points of detail. These characteristic features are its method of scansion, its principle of accentuation and its alliteration. Thus, in the first place, an O.E. line was scanned by feet and not by syllables, much variation being allowed within certain limits in the number of unaccented syllables. The accent fell on the most important syllable of the most important word, doggerel lines in which the accent is thrown on to an unimportant word for the sake of rhyme or metre being unknown. But the outstanding feature was the alliteration. The important words thus already emphasized by the accent were further stressed by the agreement of their initial letters, an obvious help to the memory in recitative as well as an ornament to the line. Possibly the importance of these words was further brought out in recitation by being chanted on a different note from the others, but of this we have no evidence.

During centuries of cultivation not only had strict rules been worked out for this metre, but a definite poetic diction had evolved itself and a distinct poetic vocabulary, enlarged greatly by the free formation of compounds. The most striking features of this diction were what are known as *variation* or the parallel phrase, and the *kenning* or descriptive term. By *variation* the chief thought of the sentence was further stressed by being repeated in a different form ; thus the subject or the object or the action could be expressed twice, or more frequently, or a whole sentence

---

[1] Cf. for instance, Sievers, Altgermanische Metrik, Halle, 1893. Sievers, P.B.B., Vol. X, p. 209 ff. Koegel, Geschichte der deutschen Litteratur, Bk. I, Ch. IV, 288 m. ff. Leonard, W.E., Beowulf and the Niebelungen Couplet. University of Wisconsin Studies in Language and Literature. No. 2. The Scansion of Middle English Alliterative verse, ibid., No. 11.

could be given in varied terms. For instance in the passage :—

> So that the traveller saw land, the sea cliffs glittering,
> the steep hills, the broad headlands—

only the object is repeated, but it is given four times. In the passage :—

> The sword had melted before, the engraved blade burnt up—

the whole thought is given twice.

Besides the possibility of thus giving emphasis when wanted, there must have been a practical gain in this device. There must always have been a chance of a word or a phrase getting lost in the clanking of armour in the hall and from many possible disturbances in the open, and such a loss would be remedied by this method ; it may even have arisen in part from this need.

This figure of *variation* is sometimes described as a use of synonyms, and called clumsy, but at its best it is more than that ; each term was chosen to add something fresh, to define the thought, or to represent it under a different aspect. Thus in the first example we are merely told to begin with that the traveller saw land, then that as he came nearer he could distinguish cliffs, and later that he could see that they were high and broad. In the second passage we have first just a general statement that the sword melted, and then we get the more definite picture when that sword is described as having had engravings on its blade.

In the same way in the description of the path traversed by Beowulf to the hag's mere we read :—

> Then the prince passed over
> steep rocky slopes, narrow ascents,
> where only one might go, and unknown tracks.

Here too, it will be seen that each phrase adds a new detail to the picture.

By this device, so admirably adapted for narrative, the poet could tell his story in a terse and picturesque manner, he developed his tale as a painter adds one stroke after another to his canvas.

It must, however, be admitted that not all poets were careful to make full use of the possibilities. As will be seen later, even Cynewulf is content sometimes to use mere synonyms.

The term *kenning* has been taken from Old Norse and many definitions have been given for it. Vigfusson in his Icelandic–English Dictionary describes it as a " Poetic paraphrase or descriptive name ". It would perhaps be better to say that the exact name of the object is not given, but a descriptive term is used by which it may be recognized, some characteristic attributive or activity being thus emphasized. A kenning may be a compound or a phrase. If a compound, the word which is the basic term will be defined or described by the other element. Examples of such kennings are " brōdenmǣl ", *engraved blade*, or " beadu-lēoma ", *battle-flash*, used for a sword ; " bēagabrytta ", *ring destributer*, or " gold-giefa ", *gold giver*, for a prince ; and " wǣg-hengest ", *wave steed*, for a ship. Examples of phrases used as kennings are the terms " ȳþa ful ", *cup of the waves* ; " ganotes bæþ ", *gannet's bath*, both used for the sea.

While many kennings are such compounds or phrases, this is not always the case. When a sword is called a " lāf ", *legacy*, or a prince a " helm ", *protector*, these words are just as much kennings as are " beadu-lēoma " and " gold-giefa ", whether or not they are looked upon as elliptical forms of " fæderes lāf ", *father's legacy*, and " folca helm ", *protector of the people*.

The O.E. kennings were usually very simple, unlike those of Old Norse, which were often more fanciful, There, for instance, the tip of the sword's sheath was called the dew shoe, and a man was named the son of the day, while others were more far-fetched still. But simple as the O.E. kennings were, their poetic value was great. By them the poet was able to suggest a vivid picture without interrupting his narrative ; he had no need for the simile, for why stop to say that a sword flashed in battle like lightning, when it could be called once and for all, " a battle-flash ". The value to the poet of these terms in working out his variations is obvious, for from their very nature, by their use they emphasized one particular aspect of the object, which was the exact function of variation. A series of parallel phrases may contain a succession of kennings, though this is not necessarily the case.[1]

For his alliteration the poet made full use of the ease with which compounds could be formed, though it can hardly be, as has been suggested, that a practice so characteristic of the language arose only out of the need for alliterating terms.

O.E. has traces of strophic formation in a few of the lyrical poems. In O.N. it was more common. How far its appearance in O.E. is a survival of an older, more general, practice cannot be proved, but the poems in which it is found are taken by most scholars to be of early date.

Pictorial as O.E. poetry is, and it excels in the drawing of vivid and vigorous pictures, there is little mention of definite colour. Objects may be described as white, which often does not mean more than shining, they may be black, wolves are grey, grass is green, a woman may be fair, a man grey-haired, but with the exception of the red roofs mentioned in the Ruin and the blue sky above the sea in Exodus, it is the general effect only that is depicted. We have to wait for classical influence to get an exact description of colour, as in the Phoenix. On the other hand sound plays a great part. As a warrior walks, his sword clashes against his corslet, the floor resounds under his tread. It is what the Seafarer hears in his exile, the dashing of the waves against the cliffs, the screaming of the birds, that is so terrifying and so greatly intensifies his loneliness. It is noticeable also that inanimate objects are constantly represented as actors; swords are not merely weapons, they are battle-friends, the helmet is not a protection but a head-protector. This insistence on sound and on activity in every object gives an extraordinarily virile character

[1] For discussions of the Kenning see Bode, Die Kenningar in der angelsächsischen Dichtung, Darmstadt and Leipzig, 1886.
Rankin, A Study of the Kennings in Anglo-Saxon Poetry, J.E.G.P., vol. VIII. Van der Merwe Scholtz, The Kenning in Anglo-Saxon and Old Norse Poetry, B. H. Blackwell, Oxford, 1929.

to O.E. poetry, and is in harmony with its great concernment with scenes of battle and storm.

In early Germanic days the only written documents were inscriptions carved in runic letters on some hard substance such as ivory or stone. Each of these letters had its own name, that of some word beginning with the letter. Thus " þ ", our " th " was called thorn ; " ƿ ", our " w " was known as wynn, *joy*, and so on. The runic alphabet used in England was not absolutely identical with those of other countries, for after the Anglo-Saxons broke off from the other Germanic tribes their language underwent certain modifications, new sounds arose and new symbols had to be introduced to represent them.

These runic inscriptions are on various kinds of objects. Some sixteen have been found on crosses or stones in south Scotland and the northern counties of England, of which some have been removed to the British Museum. The most important of these monuments is the Ruthwell Cross, of which a brief account may therefore be given here. It stands now in the church of Ruthwell in Annandale, 8 miles from Dumfries, but it has not always been there. In 1642 it was turned out by the General Assembly of St. Andrews and left lying in the churchyard, where it became much dilapidated. In 1823, however, it was restored and taken into the manse ; now it is again in the church. It is of sandstone, 17½ feet in height and ornamented with designs of foliage, flowers, and dragons, besides the inscription in runic letters mixed with Roman characters. This inscription consists of three short passages in the Northumbrian dialect, almost identical with lines in the poem known as the Dream of the Rood and evidently from the same source, and another sentence, which Stephens and others have read as " Kadmon (or Kedmon) mæfaueþo (or mæfauœþo)". This has been translated, though without any authority, as " Cædmon made me ", and the inscription assigned to the Whitby poet. But while the language, which is not later than the seventh century in which he lived, would allow this, the Kadmon on the cross must surely refer to

the maker of it, rather than of the poem, and no word
" fauœþo " is known.[1] Plaster casts of this and other
crosses are to be seen in the Victoria and Albert Museum in
South Kensington.

Besides these inscriptions on stone, runes are also to be
found elsewhere. While many are on small objects such
as knives and rings, of which several may be seen in the
British Museum, by far the most important set is on the
whalebone casket presented by Sir Augustus Franks to
that Museum. The history of this casket is interesting
and may therefore be given shortly. At one time it was in
the possession of a family in Auzon, by whom it was used
as a work-box. By them, apparently, the silver fittings
holding the casket together were removed, so that it fell
to pieces and one side got separated from the rest.
After various vicissitudes the top and three sides were
bought by Franks in 1857 and given to the British
Museum, and the remaining side, when eventually discovered, was purchased by a M. Carrand, of Lyons, who
bequeathed it with the rest of his antiquities to the Bargello,
or Museo Nazionale, at Florence, where it now is, its place
in the casket being supplied by a copy. The whole casket
is richly carved with scenes from the stories of Weland,
Romulus and Remus, and the taking of Jerusalem by
Titus, besides other scenes not so easy to decipher. The
runic inscriptions which explain the carvings are found
bordering the sides, but runes occur among them which are
not known elsewhere.[2]

When, however, the Roman missionaries introduced the
use of parchment, the angular letters of the old alphabet
were replaced by the more flowing Latin symbols for
ordinary purposes, though runes continued to be used for
special effects, this artificial survival of them lasting on
throughout the O.E. period. Cynewulf used them to sign
his works, they are to be found in many of the Riddles,
and they are the subject of the Rune Song. This is a little

---

[1] Die Northumbrischen Runensteine, Wilhelm Vietor, Marburg in
Hessen, 1895.
[2] The Franks Casket by Arthur S. Napier, Oxford, 1900.

poem which will be treated later in more detail, in which the runes are taken in turn and described in two or three lines. Thus of " þ " it is said :—

The thorn is cruelly sharp, its point is evil for every thane, exceedingly fierce for every man who rests upon it.

While much of O.E. prose has been preserved in two, three or even more MSS., O.E. poems are to be found, with hardly an exception, each in a single one only. Most of the poems were early collected and copied into four large composite MSS., some containing poetry and prose, others poetry only. It may be convenient here to mention these with the works to be found in each. When poems or prose works occur in separate MSS., these are given in speaking of the work.

The four great MSS. collections are :—

I. MS. Vitellius A. 15 ; a MS. of the Cotton Collection in the British Museum.

This includes poetry and prose, and contains the great epic of Beowulf, which comes after the following prose works : Ælfred's Blooms ; the Gospel of Nicodemus ; the prose dialogue between Salomo and Saturn ; a fragment from the Passion of St. Quintinus ; the Legend of St. Christopher ; the Wonders of the East and the Letter of Alexander the Great to Aristotle. It is followed by the fragment left us of the epic of Judith. There is an autotype copy of Beowulf, with transliteration and notes by Professor Zupitza, in the publications of the Early English Text Society.

II. The Codex Exoniensis or Exeter Book.

This was presented by Bishop Leofric to Exeter some time after 1050, when he transferred his see from Crediton to Exeter. It contains poems only. In it are Crist ; Guþlac ; Azarias ; Phoenix ; Juliana ; Widsiþ ; the Gnomic Verses ; the Physiologus ; Riddles ; all the lyrical poems and some short didactic ones, e.g. the Gifts, the Moods and the Fates of Men ; Counsels of a Father ; the Wonders of Creation ; Address of the Soul to the Body, and Doomsday, with one or two more fragments. A facsimile reproduction has recently appeared, with introductory chapters by R. W. Chambers, Max Foerster, and Robin Flower.

III. The Codex Vercellensis or Vercelli Book at Vercelli near Milan. How this MS. came to Vercelli is unknown, but it may possibly have been taken there by the Cardinal Guala, who was in England in the reigns of John and Henry III, and who built the church at Vercelli, dedicating it to St. Andrew.

This MS. contains : Andreas ; Fates of the Apostles ; Address of the Soul to the Body ; the Dream of the Rood ; Elene ; a prose Life of St. Guþlac ; with many homilies at the beginning and interspersed among the poems.

There is a facsimile reproduction of the whole MS. edited by Professor Foerster.

IV. MS. Junius XI in the Bodleian Library, presented to the Library by the Dutch scholar Francis Dujon or Junius, Librarian to the Earl of Arundel. It contains the poems : Genesis ; Exodus ; Daniel ; and three short works : the Lament of the Fallen Angels ; the Descent into Hell and the Temptation, classed together by Grein under the title Christ and Satan.

There is a facsimile reproduction of the whole MS. by Sir Israel Gollancz.

All four MSS. may be dated roughly about 1000.

CHAPTER II

GNOMIC VERSES, CHARMS, AND EARLY LYRICAL POEMS

Not only was every form of early O.E. Literature, whether narrative, lyric, or didactic, for convenience' sake thrown into poetic form and written in the general alliterative metre, but we have subjects treated in verse in O.E. which have little literary quality of any kind. Foremost among such are the Gnomic Verses. In them moral truths are inculcated or facts of general knowledge stated ; they correspond to the proverbs of later times and represent the experience or wisdom of centuries.

Two sets of these verses have been preserved, one in the Exeter Book, the second in a Cotton MS. in the British Museum.[1] As a rule the verses are trite and commonplace, and such bare statements as these : " a king shall rule the kingdom," or " cities are seen from afar ", may be taken as fair representatives of the ordinary type, especially in the set in the Cotton MS. In the Exeter Book, however, we find a few expanded into something more attractive, as in the advice to travellers : " Well must a man hold fast to a friend on every road. Oft he may journey far where no friend is waiting for him. Friendless and wretched he takes wolves for his comrades, full treacherous beasts, and these comrades rend him." Or in the account of the return of the fisherman to his wife : " Her beloved is welcome to the Frisian woman when his boat comes to anchor. She invites him in, washes his seaweed-stained garments and gives him fresh raiment."

The real interest of these verses is, however, in their popular origin, and in the glimpses which they give us, therefore, of the everyday life and thought of the people, of their amusements and beliefs. For instance, one tells

[1] Cott. MS. Tiber, B. 1, fol. 113.

us that " the hawk must be on the glove ". Elsewhere we read " the dragon shall be in his cave and exultant over his treasure ", proving that the existence of dragons was no mere literary tradition but a fully accepted article of faith. Another point of interest in these Gnomic Verses is that, while they contain references to the old gods and preserve their names, they also illustrate the tentative way in which the early missionaries sought to insinuate the new doctrines and with what surprising results. Thus they tell us that " Wodan created false gods, but the All-ruler the gloriously wide heavens ". Elsewhere we read that, " Wind is swiftest in the air ; thunder at times loudest ; the powers of Christ are great ; Fate is strongest."

It is impossible to date these verses. Originally they must have been not only pre-Christian but pre-English. How popular they continued to be may be gathered from the adoption of them by the poets. Thus the writer of the little poem, the Wanderer, has inserted a whole passage of them in his work, and they occur elsewhere.

Further and more attractive survivals of Germanic days are the Charms, of which O.E. possesses eight, directed towards various ends. While most are for healing different evils, some have other purposes. One, for instance, is to help take a swarm of bees, another is to secure fertility of crops, a third to find strayed cattle. Unlike the Gnomic Verses, the Charms have received literary cultivation and there seems to have been a standard form for them. In its fullest form the charm consists of three parts, first the naming or description of the means to be used, secondly a short narrative, telling how the evil arose or some former occasion on which the remedy worked, and lastly the charm itself. Considerable elaboration of the second part is found in some, giving distinct artistic merit.

The O.E. charm, which best illustrates this full form, is one to cure a sudden attack of stitch in the side. The malady is represented as a wound from a spear, sent down from the sky, apparently by a Walkyrie, and the middle part is worked out in four scenes of unequal length with a refrain at the end of each.

The first part with the recipe in prose runs thus :—

Against a sudden stitch. Feverfew and the red nettle, which grows in through the house-wall, and dock. Boil in butter.

After this comes an account of the occasion of the wound :—

Loud were they, yea loud, when they rode above the hill !
They were resolute when they rode above the land !
Shield thyself now, if thou wilt escape this attack.

Then follows the refrain :—

Out, little spear ! if thou art herein !

The next scene is not so clear. The occasion is still that of the wounding, but the speaker may be an onlooker merely or the victim. It goes :—

I stood beneath my linden shield, beneath my bright shield,
where the mighty women were arraying their forces,
and sending their whistling spears.
I will send another weapon back against them,
an arrow flying forth towards them.

Then comes the refrain again :—

Out, little spear, if it be herein !

The third scene has two lines only. It shows us the making of the knife with which the ointment is to be spread :—

A smith sat, he beat a little knife
[till it was] badly wounded with his iron tool.
Out, little spear, if it be herein !

The fourth, of one line only, shows us the spears being made :—

Six smiths sat, wrought battle spears.
Out, spear ! not in, spear !

Finally comes the charm itself, with all the repetition on which its virtue depended. We can follow the movement of the hand backwards and forwards as the ointment is rubbed in :—

If there be herein any piece of iron,
the work of a witch, it shall melt.

If thou wert wounded in the skin, or wert wounded in the flesh,
or wert wounded in the blood,
or wert wounded in a limb, never shall thy life be injured.
If it were the shot of giants, if it were the shot of elves,
or if it were the shot of a witch, now will I help thee.

This is a remedy for thee against the shot of giants, this is
a remedy for thee against the shot of elves,
This is a remedy for thee against the shot of a witch. I will
help thee.
Flee to the mountain head.
Be thou whole. May the Lord help thee.
Take then the knife and put it in water.
(That is—let none of the healing ointment with its magic
power be left on the knife.)

Obviously the term " Lord " is an addition of the scribe's.
A charm against giants and elves must be heathen in its
origin and the foes who rode above the hills, throwing
down spears on those below, can only be the " Walkyries ",
(choosers of the slain), the war maidens of Germanic
mythology. These are represented as riding through the air
or hovering over the battle-field, deciding under Wodan's
direction who should conquer and who should be slain.
They come a good deal into O.N. literature, but in O.E.
they are, of course, only found in their original function in
the earliest writings, which are still practically heathen.
They are alluded to in other charms. Thus an O.H.G.
charm, if we may be allowed the digression, tells us that :—

Formerly settled goddesses, settled down hither.
Some wove fetters [for the prisoners taken from the opposite
side].
Some held back armies [of the advancing foe].
Some broke up fetters [of the prisoners taken by the foe].
Escape from thy fetters, flee from thy foes.

So again they occur in another O.E. charm, one for taking
a swarm. In it the bees are called triumphant women
(sigewīf). That is, the bees and their stings are represented
under the figure of the Walkyries and their spears.

No other charm is so complete as that just given. Sometimes the three parts are merged together. For instance in

that for taking the swarm, to which we now pass on, there are two scenes only, one in which the swarm is found, the other in which it is taken. It runs thus :—

> Against a swarm. Take earth and throw it with thy right hand under thy right foot and say :—
>
> I hold it [the swarm] under my foot. I have found it.
> Lo ! earth may prevail against every creature,
> and against anger and against forgetfulness,
> and against the mighty tongue of man (slander).

Then in the second scene :—

> Throw dust over them, when they swarm, and say
> [Settle] ye triumphant women ! sink to earth !
> never wildly fly ye to the wood !
> Be ye as mindful of my good
> as is every man of food and home.

Here not only are the three parts not kept distinct, but the repetition of the formula is wanting. That is still found, however, in another later charm for securing fertility of crops in which Christian influence is prominent. It is for freeing bewitched land, and the passage in question runs as follows :—

> Erce ! Erce ! Erce ! Earth mother ! (probably the Harke, who flew through the air in the shape of a dove, making the fields fruitful).
>
> May the Allruler, the eternal Lord grant thee
> fruitful and flourishing fields,
> giving increase and gaining strength,
> the bright fruits of the stalks of millet,[1]
> the fruits of the broad barley,
> the fruits of the white wheat,
> all the fruits of the earth.

Or in another O.H.G. charm, if we may again be allowed to digress :—

> Phol (Baldor) and Wodan journeyed to the wood.
> Then the foot of Baldor's horse was sprained.
> Then Sinthgunt chanted a charm, and Sunna her sister.
> Then Frija chanted a charm and Volla her sister.
> Then Wodan chanted a charm as he well knew how.

---

[1] The meaning of the word in the MS. is doubtful.

After this comes the charm itself also with the repetition

> Be it injury to bone, be it injury to blood,
> be it injury to limb,
> bone to bone, blood to blood,
> limb to limb, as though it were glued.

These examples are quite sufficient to illustrate the character of this class of poetry. That it goes back to Germanic days is clear from the references to the figures of the old mythology and the resemblance between its representatives in different countries. Another proof of its early date is probably the strophic form which some examples show. Those given above have been little interfered with by scribes; others show a greater modification in thought and terminology from the later influence of Christianity and do not, therefore, represent the class so truly.

It has been pointed out in the preceding chapter that one of the features which distinguish O.E. narrative poetry from the Saga literature of O.N. is the lyrical element which the O.E. poet has allowed to creep into it, by obtruding his own personality in the reflections which interrupt his story. All the more surprising is it, therefore, that not a single pure lyric and very little of what may be termed lyrical poetry have been preserved. We do not, for instance, possess a single love song though such poems must have been composed at least as early as the hero lays, and judging by the passion and pathos of the Lament of the Wife, O.E. love poetry cannot have been lacking in force and beauty of sentiment and expression. But whatever the reason for this lack may be, it is in harmony with the general development of Germanic literature among the Anglo-Saxons, for the love "motif" is hardly to be found in O.E. poetry. The epic is curiously business-like in its wooings and marriages; indeed, we only know that our ancestors had any marriage songs at all from the two words "brȳd-lēoþ" and "brȳd-song" which are found in the vocabulary and can mean nothing but *bride-song*.

That there were dirges is clear, though no independent ones of early date have been preserved. Only later do we get those on the deaths of Edgar and Edward the Confessor, which were inserted in the Chronicle. The existence of them in early times is, however, proved by passages such as that at the end of Beowulf,[1] in which the funeral ceremonies are described. As they rode round the funeral pyre, the warriors told how Beowulf had been the most generous of men, ever desirous of fame, the most gentle and gracious to his people. So, too, in the Finn episode,[2] inserted in Beowulf, Hildeburh laments with songs (giedds) at the burning of her brother and son, and in the Dream of the Rood,[3] the disciples are represented as singing a song of sorrow (sorgléoþ) after placing the corpse of the Saviour in the tomb. The nature of these dirges may be further inferred from other passages, such as that in Beowulf in which the last of the owners of the treasure commits it to the earth. " Hold, now O earth! now heroes may not, this treasure of nobles. Lo! valiant ones gained it in former days upon thee, but now death in battle, cruel life-bale has carried off each of my race. They have all departed hence . . . the hard helmet, adorned with gold, shall lose its platings, the armourers sleep, who should polish the battle mask, the war coat rusts, left behind its wearer."[4]

Akin to these dirges are what may be called the death songs, that is songs purporting to contain the last words of the dying hero. Of these, as of the dirges, no independent early example exists, and when later, in recorded times we get Bede's Death Song, it cannot be taken as illustrating very closely the usual character of this class of poems. It runs :—

> Before that enforced journey none shall be
> wiser in thought than he shall have need,
> that he may ponder e'er his going hence
> what for his soul of good or evil,
> after his day of death shall be decreed.[5]

That such death songs were composed in early times can be inferred, however, as in the case of the dirges, and their nature better seen from passages in other works. Thus

---

[1] Beowulf, vv. 3180 ff.   [2] Ibid., vv. 1117-8.
[3] Dream, vv. 67 ff.   [4] Beowulf, vv. 2247 ff.
[5] Earliest version in Northumbrian in St. Gall MS. 254.

Beowulf, when mortally wounded, is made to review hi former life. " I have lived my appointed time in the land," he is made to say, " I have held well what was mine. Not in treachery have I sought battle, nor sworn many oaths in falseness. For all this may I now rejoice, because the Ruler of men may not reproach me with the death of kinsmen now when my soul must leave my body."[1] Later in the Battle of Maldon, Byrhtnoþ says in the same spirit, " I thank Thee, Ruler of the nations, for all the joys which I have known on earth. Now I have, O gracious Lord ! the greatest need that Thou shouldest show mercy to my spirit, that my soul may pass into Thy keeping and the fiends of hell not harm it."[2]

Thus, while the existence of songs celebrating happier moods can only be known from the vocabulary, we have ample proof that those of a more mournful nature were common, and while many of those which were composed have doubtless been lost, we do possess a certain number. Such lyric poetry as has been preserved deals with the darker aspects of life, with its hardships and sorrows, and, apart from the Charms (if they may be included under the term lyrical), which from their nature were unlikely to show this quality, almost all O.E. lyrical poems are elegiac in character.

There are in the Exeter Book seven short poems of great beauty, worthy representatives of this class of literature. They are generally known by the titles, Deor or Deor's Lament, Wulf and Eadwacer, The Lament of the Wife, The Message of the Husband, The Ruin, The Wanderer, and The Seafarer. All, in spite of their differences of theme and treatment, show certain marked points of resemblance, and they may therefore be treated with advantage as a group before passing on to consider them individually.

All must be early, for all are essentially heathen in character. This is seen in the kind of fatalistic acquiescence which runs through Deor's Lament, in the belief in the irresistible power of Fate which pervades the Wanderer, and in the absence of any Christian thought in the others.

[1] Beowulf, vv. 2736 ff.   [2] Battle of Maldon, xv, 173 ff.

A later scribe has occasionally substituted a Christian for a heathen term, and probably it is such a scribe who has added a long passage of didactic nature at the end of the Seafarer, but such words or passages betray their later date by being out of harmony with the rest of the matter.

The early date of these poems appears also in points of vocabulary,[1] metre,[2] and syntax [3] and perhaps less definitely in the strophic form in which some of them are written. Deor's Lament and Wulf and Eadwacer are in strophes with a refrain, and it has been suggested that traces of a similar formation are to be seen in the Lament of the Wife, the Seafarer, and the Wanderer.[4] The only other instance of this is in the Charms, which from their very nature must be pre-Christian and therefore early, and it seems likely that all poems showing this particular feature are of the same period.

From these various tests, one or more of which apply to each of these seven poems, it may be assumed with fair certainty that the group belongs to the earliest period of our literature ; that is, they may be dated not later than the eighth century and probably before the end of the seventh.

All appear to have been composed in Northumbria and therefore to have been the fruits of that first literary period to which we owe the Beowulf ; all depict a state of society in which men were constantly at war either

[1] Vocabulary. The Ruin contains words, such as " hreorge ", *in ruins* ; hwætred (meaning unknown), not found elsewhere, having apparently died out later.

The Wanderer uses the word " Wyrd " in the plural, in "wyrda gesceaft " *the shaping of the Fates*, v. 107. We know that the Germanic mythology included three of these goddesses, those of the past, the present, and the future, but as a rule in O.E. they have been merged into one. This use of the plural suggests, therefore, an early date, at which the older belief had not quite died out.

[2] Metre. This requires the poems to have been composed at some early date before the loss of medial h, j, w, and the subsequent contraction of the two syllables into one, or at any rate before the use of the traditional forms had died out in poetry. Thus in the Lament of the Wife, v. 28, we must read " under actrēowe " not " actrēo ", as in the MS.

[3] The omission of the definite article with the noun and of " mid " with the dative is frequent, as in " winter wunade ", *inhabited through the winter*, " calde geþrungen ", *oppressed with the cold*.

[4] Dr. Rudolf Imelmann, Wanderer und Seefahrer im Rahmen der altenglischen Odoaker-Dichtung, pp. 15, 18, 51.

with their fellow-men or with the hostile forces of nature, though in one case, in the Message of the Husband, the dangers have been overcome, and in another, in the Seafarer, there is as much enjoyment as sorrow in the strife.

There seems to have been something of a standard form for poems of this kind, for three begin with almost the same line, " I may relate a true tale about myself " or " I may say about myself ".[1]

These lyrical poems stand in strong contrast to the epic as represented by Beowulf in their absorption in emotion, their passion, the universality of their appeal and in the part played by women. In Beowulf much expression of emotion is rare, great though the depth of feeling implied may be, especially in the relation between lord and thane ; self-restraint is the foundation of the heroic character and the hero must express himself in actions rather than in words. " Better is it for every man that he avenge his friend than that he greatly mourn." [2]

The Wanderer certainly knows that it is a noble custom in a man that he bind fast his secret heart,[3] but he does not practise it, and in general in these little poems, not only may the man express his natural feelings, but the woman also may have her part. In Beowulf, always excepting the Finnsburg episode [4] and the allusion to Thyth in the Offa passage,[5] which are taken from other sources, woman is not much more than a lay figure, though a dignified one. She may hand round the drinking cup, she may at times

---

[1] From the fact that all are concerned with the account of hardships or sorrows which the speaker has experienced, it has been suggested that their origin is to be sought in the old funeral rites and that they arose from the custom of friends collecting at the burials of the dead and showing their sympathy with the mourners by reciting tales of suffering through which they themselves have gone and survived. It is possible that at first some magic formula followed the tale, the object of the whole being to secure the departure of the soul of the dead man, and prevent its returning to earth, just as in the Charms we get first the story of some former occasion on which the remedy had worked, and then the formula to ensure its acting again. Such an origin would account for the usual introductory line, but if it is really the true one, the O.E. poems had travelled a long way from their starting point. Sieper, Die altenglische Elegie. Strasburg, 1915. Einleitung, p. 13. Other scholars have thought that they deal with definite situations in the hero legends, but this is a subject which is treated in the following chapter.

[2] Beowulf, 1384-5.   [3] Wanderer, 12.
[4] Beowulf, 1068 ff.   [5] Ibid., 1931 ff.

even offer advice, but she plays no real part, she is always in the background, whereas in these lyrical poems, she and her emotions may be the poet's theme. This contrast in subject and treatment is not due merely to the differences in the requirements of epic and lyric. Beowulf is of its time and country; the matter of the lyrics is of all time and every country. These poems are nearer in spirit to the Finnsburg passage and to the O.H.G. Hilde- brandslied, as far as we can judge from the few lines left. May this not be the spirit of the older Germanic literature ?

From these general remarks on the group as a whole we may pass on to the study of each poem, beginning with that usually known as Deor, or Deor's Lament, since it stands somewhat apart from the others. It is more obviously connected with the old hero lays and epics than are they, though it is in itself essentially lyrical in character.

It is in six strophes of unequal length, as they stand in the MS, though an attempt has been made to equalize them. It is possibly autobiographical. In it a scop, named Deor, is represented as lamenting a sorrow which is not defined, and consoling himself with the reflection that others before him have suffered as much and so has he himself in earlier days; yet those sorrows have passed and so may this present one. Indeed, Deor's Consolation, as it is called by German writers, is a better title than his Lament. Thus he alludes to the sufferings of Weland, maimed and captive at the court of King Nidhad ; of Beaduhild, ravished by Weland ; of an unknown Mæþhild ; of Theodoric in exile for thirty years in the city of the Mærings ; of many a man bound in sorrow under the cruel rule of Eormenric and finally of his own grief, having been once a favoured scop (minstrel) at the court of the Heodenings till his place was usurped by Heorrenda. After each allusion comes the refrain : " the sorrow of that passed, so may the sorrow of this " :—

Weland among the Wermi [1] tasted of misery,
a resolute man, he endured hardships,

[1] Or among his serpent-engraved weapons. The MS. has clearly Wurmi.

he had for companions sorrow and longing,
exile, cold as winter. Oft knew he woe
after Nidhad had laid upon him by force,
slender fetters on him [who was] the better man.
The sorrow of that passed, so may the sorrow of this.

To Beaduhild her brothers' death was not
such grief of heart as was her own distress,
as soon as she for certain had perceived
that she was with child ; never could she,
with all her courage, think how this might go.
The sorrow of that, etc.

We have many of us heard of Mæþhild.
The wooing of Geat was without bounds,
so that love-longing deprived him of all sleep.[1]
The sorrow of that, etc.

Theodoric possessed (inhabited ?) for thirty winters
the city of the Mærings ; that was known to many.
The sorrow of that, etc.

We have heard of Eormenric's
wolfish mind. He ruled widely over the people
of the kingdom of the Goths ; that was a cruel king.
Many a man sat bound in sorrow,
expecting misery, often wished
that the [power] of his kingdom might be overcome.
The sorrow of that, etc.

Then follow seven lines which may not belong to the
original, and finally a strophe which should probably have
come first, since it begins with an introductory line found
in others of these poems :—

I will say about myself
that for a time I was " scop " of the Heodenings,
dear to my lord and my name there was Deor.
For many winters I had a good service,
and a gracious lord, till Heorrenda,
a man skilled in song received the rights in the land
which the protector of men had before given to me.
The sorrow of that, etc.

The other lyrical poems are not so closely connected
with hero lays, but they all have narrative settings and in

---

[1] Translation of strophe doubtful. See p. 47.

the case of many of them, especially of Wulf and Eadwacer
and the Ruin, and, less markedly, in that of the Lament
of the Wife and the Message of the Husband, one is struck
with the vividness of the pictures presented ; one has at
once the impression of a story or scene behind. While it is
true that they deal with the universal themes of love and
fear and regrets for past happiness, yet one feels that it is
in each case with a definite situation that one has to do,
with some episode out of a once well-known story, which,
if it were known, would explain many details, now obscure.

The first of these, Wulf and Eadwacer, is in the Exeter
Book between Deor's Lament and a set of Riddles, of which
it was long believed to be the first. It may still be found
in older works in O.E. literature under the title The
First Riddle, though now it is generally called Wulf and
Eadwacer, or sometimes Signy's Lament. Like Deor it is
in strophic form, with a refrain.

The modern English version which follows is, with one
or two slight alterations, that of the late Dr. Bradley.[1]
The story, much of which is obscure, seems to be that of
the eternal triangle ; a woman is the speaker and two men
are mentioned ; one named Wulf appears to be her lover,
and the other, called Eadwacer, is probably her jealous
husband.

The poem begins in the middle, not only of a strophe,
but of a sentence, or perhaps the lacking verses should be
between the first and second lines :—

Is to my people as though one gave them a present.
Will they give him food if he should come to want ?
It is otherwise with us.

Wulf is on one island, I on another.
The island is closely surrounded by fen.
On yonder island are fierce and cruel men.
Will they give him food if he should come to want ?
It is otherwise with us.

I waited for my Wulf with far wandering longings,
when it was rainy weather and I sat tearful.

---

[1] Permission has been courteously given for its use.

When the brave warrior clasped me in his arms,
it was joy to me, yet was it also pain.
Oh Wulf! my Wulf! it was my longing after thee,
that made me sick ; it was thy seldom coming,
it was a sorrowful heart, and not the want of food.
Dost thou hear Eadwacer ? the bold [1] whelp of us two
shall Wulf carry off to the wood.
Easily can that be broken asunder which never was united,
the song of us two together.

The many suggestions which have been made for the
background of this striking little poem, for the particular
story from which it is taken, will be considered in
Chapter III.

Another lyric as passionate as Wulf and Eadwacer is
that known as the Lament of the Wife. Here, too, we get
the same skilful suggestion of conflicting emotion and
effective restraint in the expression. In this poem of fifty-
three lines we have the heart's cry of a woman, cut off from
her own friends, whose husband has had to leave her,
though we are not told why. She is left alone, persecuted
by his kinsmen and banished by her lord's orders to a
solitary place among caves and ruins overgrown with
briars. But all along her grief is not only for her own
sorrows, but also for his sufferings.

The poet begins in what was apparently the orthodox
way :—

> This tale I tell concerning my full sad self,
> my own wanderings. I may recount
> what miseries I have endured since I grew up,
> both of old and new, but never more than now.
> Ever have I suffered from my exile journeys.

Then she goes on to explain her present sorrow and the
straits in which she is left :—

> First my lord departed hence from out his people,
> over the dancing waves. I had care at dawn
> as to where in any land my prince might be.
> Then I turned me to go to seek service,
> a friendless exile, because of my dire need.

---

[1] Bradley, *cowardly*.

The man's kin began to plot
with secret thoughts, how to divide us twain,
that we most widely in the world apart
might live as foes. (and yet I longed).

They have apparently succeeded in poisoning his mind
against her for she goes on :—

My lord, the stern one, bade me be brought hither.[1]
I had few dear ones in this place,
few gracious friends. Therefore is my mind gloomy.

The next passage is ambiguous but probably refers to her
husband :—

I had found me a man full sympathetic,
unfortunate, gloomy of heart,
concealing his thought though meditating violence,[2]
while gay of bearing. Full oft we two have vowed
that nought should sever us save death alone,
nought else. That is changed once more,
it is now as though it never had been,
this love of ours. Now must I far and near
endure the hatred of my dearly loved one.

After this she goes on to describe the place to which she
has been banished. It is a cave, under an oak-tree in a wood,
round her the valleys are dark and the hills are high, the
ruined city walls are overgrown with briars. But through
it all, " all am I filled with longing," is her cry, " full
oft hath come upon me the departure of my lord." Then
she compares her lot with those of happier ones. While she
is wandering solitary at dawn, under the oak-tree, among
the caves, or sitting bewailing her sorrows through the long
summer day, others are living in happiness together, but
" Never may I find rest from my sorrow of heart ", she
cries. The next passage has given much difficulty, but
from its similarity to the earlier one in which she is describing
her husband, it seems best to take it as also referring to
him and not to the man who has come between them, as
has been sometimes suggested.

---

[1] *Or* take refuge here.   [2] *Or* thinking on death.

Ever should a young man be serious-minded,
stern the thoughts of his heart, so also should he have
a cheerful bearing, even if also grief of mind,
a host of lasting cares, whether all his joy
depends upon himself, or whether it be exiled
far in a distant land that my friend sits
under a rocky cliff, rime-covered from the storm,
in a gloomy hall. He remembers too oft
a happier home. Woe to him who shall
in longing wait for a loved and absent one.

The Lament of the Wife may be aptly followed by the
Message of the Husband, since they are thought by some
to be connected and the Message to be a sequel to the
Lament. Anyhow this poem strikes a happier note than
any of those already considered. In it earlier difficulties
have been overcome and we have a follower arriving in
a boat with a message graven on a piece of wood, sent
from a husband to his wife, asking her to join him. A feud
has obliged him to flee his own country and leave her behind.
Now, however, he has overcome his troubles and has no
lack of riches or pleasures. She is to cross the sea to join
him as soon as she hears the note of the cuckoo :—

Now (the messenger says) I am come hither
in my boat and must know
how thou about my lord's love
dost think in thy heart. I dare promise
that thou shalt find in him a fast and noble faith.
Lo ! he bade me pray thee, he who carved this (stave)
that thou, the ring-adorned, shouldest call to mind
within thyself the spoken vows
which ye in days of yore oft uttered,
while ye might in the mead cities
dwell in your home, inhabit one land,
live in friendship. Him hostility drove forth
from his victorious people. Now he bids thee
be instructed that thou shouldest " disturb " the deep,
as soon as thou mayest hear at the cliff's edge
the mournful cuckoo singing in the grove.
Let nothing after that prevent thy voyage,
no living man delay thy journey.
Set out to seek the sea, the seamew's home.

> Sit thee in thy boat, that thou south hence,
> over the ocean's path mayest find thy man,
> where now thy lord is waiting, hoping for thee.

Then omitting a few lines which have been too much damaged for translation, we go on :—

> Now the man has
> overcome his woe, he has no lack
> of steeds or jewels, or of joys of mead,
> or any noble treasures upon earth.

The next passage introduces five runes, which are here distinguished by capitals, "EA" representing a single rune.

> I put together S, R,
> EA, W, and D to declare on oath,
> that he, the covenant and pledge of love,
> the while he lives, will carry out,
> which ye in former days oft vowed.

While the general sense of the poem is clear, many problems have arisen over the interpretation of details to be taken later.

The next of these lyrical poems to be considered is a very interesting, but unfortunately a very much damaged one of forty-eight lines in which is described a ruined city with fallen towers and roofs and lichen-covered walls. It is generally known as the Ruin, and the poet must have had some definite background for his vivid picture. While belonging to the group in general character, it stands apart in the exactness and detail of the scene described, and in having a scene, not an episode of human life for its theme. Many lines are defective, in others the words are obviously miswritten. Allowing for a few emendations which may be accepted as fairly certain, the poem runs as follows :—

> Glorious is its cornerstone ; the Fates have broken,
> have destroyed the city ; the work of giants decays,
> the roofs are fallen in, the towers are in ruins,
> rime-covered enclosures, of lime deprived ;
> jagged roofs, slashed and fallen,
> eaten into with age. The clutch of earth has
> destroyed, gathered in the owner-makers,

the hard grip of earth.   For a hundred generations
the peoples have passed away.   Often its walls have seen,
lichen-covered and grey and red-stained, one kingdom after
    another,
they have stood firm under storms ; tall, spacious, it has fallen,
there remain yet . . .

The remainder of this line and the following six are too
defective to be translated, but after that the poem goes on :—

        Nor did he throw the swift one,
the bold in heart into chains, stern of thought he bound
the wall planks wondrously together with wires.
Bright were the houses of the city, many the halls of the
    springs,
lofty the assemblage of gables, great the clamour of the army.
Many a mead hall was there, full of social joys
until that Fate the Mighty changed this.
The slaughtered fell far and wide ; then came days of
    pestilence.
Death, the sword-bold, destroyed wholly the men,
the ramparts became desert places,
the foundations of the city crumbled.   The restorers had
    fallen,
the multitudes to the earth.   Therefore the courts stand
    desolate,
and the red-stained roofs.   From its tiles parts
the top of the " roost-beam " ; with a crash it has come to
    the ground,
broken into heaps, where formerly many a warrior,
glad of mood and gay with gold, with beauty adorned,
proud and wine-flushed, shone in trappings of war,
gazed on the treasure, on silver, on cunningly wrought gems,
on riches, on possessions, on precious stones,
on this bright city of a broad kingdom.
Stone-built courts stood there, the stream spat out heat,
in a wide gush ; the wall enclosed all
in its bright embrace.   That was pleasant.

The remaining lines are defective but they clearly speak
of hot streams pouring out over grey stone, a hot round
pool, and baths.

The two remaining poems, the Wanderer and the Seafarer,
differ from those already discussed in being more general in

character. With them the reader feels no such need, as with the poems just considered, of a story in the background in order to be able to understand either fully. Many a wanderer and many a seafarer must have had similar experiences. They are, however, the best known of the set, and on the whole, the finest. While they are little behind the Lament of the Wife, and Wulf and Eadwacer in their delineation of the human passions of love and fear and in the conflict of emotion depicted, their stories are framed in magnificent nature settings, unsurpassed elsewhere in O.E. literature.

The Wanderer recounts the sufferings and privations of one whose lord's hall has been overthrown and who has in consequence been obliged to wander far in search of another service, apparently crossing the sea to seek it. This must have been no uncommon situation in those days, the poet may even have had some experience of the sort himself. The Wanderer does not seem, however, to have been successful, for the poem gives a powerful picture of an utter solitude and desolation, which even exile, by itself, could hardly explain.

As it stands now in the Exeter Book, the poem begins with an introduction which has a strong Christian flavour :—

Often the solitary one lives to find grace,
the mercy of the Creator, though he, troubled in mind,
across the paths of ocean must long
" stir with his hands " the ice-cold sea,
wander o'er tracks of exile. Fate is full inexorable.

After this the poem goes on in a very different strain, in one which is entirely non-Christian :—

Thus the Wanderer, mindful of hardships,
of cruel slaughters, told the fall of his kinsmen.
Oft must I alone at every dawn
lament my cares ; there is now no living man
to whom I may dare clearly
tell out my mind. I know of a truth,
that it is in a man a noble custom,
that he bind fast his secret heart,
keep close the casket of his thoughts, think as he will.
Nor may a weary heart withstand Fate,
nor a gloomy mind bring help.

Therefore the glory-eager oft bind fast
their sad thoughts within their breasts.

And so has he been forced in his misery, cut off from his
native land, far from his kinsmen, to bind his thoughts in
fetters, since in days of yore the darkness of the earth
covered his gold-giver and he has had to wander, wretched
and chill of heart, over the chain of the waves, has sought
the hall of some distributor of treasure, wherever he could
find one who had known his lord and would now comfort
him in his distress.

Here the Wanderer goes on to reflections on the sorrows
of exile in the abstract, though he has obviously his own
sufferings in mind all the time. Much of the pain is due to
the memory of earlier and happier times :—

When sorrow and sleep together
oft bind the solitary wretch,
it seems to him in his heart that his liege lord
he embraces and kisses and on his knees he lays
hands and head, as when he before
in days of yore enjoyed the throne.
Then awakens again the friendless man.
He sees before him the grey waves,
sea birds dipping, spreading out their wings,
rime and snow falling mingled with hail.
Then are the more grievous the wounds of his heart,
they are sore for his beloved one, his sorrow is renewed
when the memory of his kinsmen floods his mind.
He greets them with songs of joy, eagerly he scans them.

At this point come three lines very difficult of exact
interpretation though the general sense is clear that these
visions fade away and no one brings him real tidings, so
desolate is he. One may hazard as a possible translation,
allowing for a bold rendering of a kind of idiom found
elsewhere. These comrades of men (memories) float away
again :—

No living sailors (lit. life of floating ones) bring there
many well-known sayings. Trouble is renewed
for him who must send very often
over the chain of the waves his weary soul.

Here, at verse 58 of the poem the whole tone changes. Hitherto the poet has been treating a definite theme, his own sorrows and sufferings, if in one passage thinly veiled under those of any exile. Now he passes on to general reflections on the sadness of life. He speaks now again in his own person :—

> Therefore I may not think in all this world
> why my soul should not be darkened,
> when I consider the whole life of man ;
> how they suddenly forsook the hall,
> these bold retainers. And thus this middle earth
> every single day falls and decays.

A set of gnomic verses follows here, to the effect that a man should be temperate in all things, and especially that he must not utter boasts after the fashion of the epic heroes, unless he is sure he can fulfil them. Then the poet goes on :—

> A wise man should understand how gloomy it will be
> when all the dwellings of this world lie desolate,
> as now here and there throughout this region
> stand walls blown upon by the wind,
> covered with rime, ramparts in ruins.
> The wine halls decay, the warriors lie
> cut off in their joy, all the valiant band has fallen,
> the proud ones beneath the ramparts.

Some battle bore away, others suffered other fates.

> Thus the Creator of men hath ravaged this region,
> until the ancient works of giants stood empty,
> void of the sounds of inhabitants.

One who has experienced this and remembers much bloodshed in times past speaks these words :—

> Whither has passed the steed ? Whither has passed the
>   retainer ? whither the giver of treasure ?
> Where are the seats at the banquets ? where the rejoicings
>   in the hall ?
> Alas for the bright goblet ! alas for the armed warrior !
> Alas for the glory of the prince ! How has the time passed
>   away,
> vanished beneath the covering of night, as if it never had
>   been !

There remains now behind the beloved band of valiant ones
a wall wondrous high, bright with serpent shapes.
The might of the spears has borne hence the warriors,
weapons eager for slaughter, Fate the glorious!
      Storms beat upon the rocky cliffs,
frost falling binds the earth,
that terror of winter, when darkness comes,
the shades of night descend, from the north is sent
a fierce storm of hail to the injury of men.
All the kingdom of earth is full of hardship.
The decree of the Fates changes the world beneath the
      heavens.
Here possessions pass away, here the friend passes,
here man passes, here the kinsman passes,
all the foundations of this earth shall be destroyed.

Five lines end the poem, lines of little poetic value and
of a marked didactic and Christian character. They end,
" Well shall it be for him who seeks favour and consolation
from his Father in the heavens, where there is safety for
us all."

From the Wanderer to the Seafarer the transition is easy.
The two poems come together in the Exeter Book and both
differ from the other lyrics in treating general themes
which require no special explanation. They showed marked
resemblances in vocabulary and phraseology, and on this
account they are often ascribed to one author. They certainly
belong to the same school. But with the outward form
the resemblance ends. In matter and style they are very
different. While in the Wanderer the hardships described
are a source of unredeemed gloom, and the speaker's mind
is filled with bitterness, in the Seafarer there is no gloom.
The hardships and dangers are fully recognized but so is
their fascination. The poem breathes the true spirit of
adventure. It is, too, more realistic in detail than the
Wanderer, and shows a greater variety of mood and subtility
in its delineation.

The poet begins with the conventional introduction :—

I may relate a true tale about myself,
tell my journeys, how in days of toil
a time of hardship have I oft endured,

bitter sorrow of heart have I lived through,
explored in my keel many abodes of care,
the dire tumult of the waves. There was oft my lot
a close nightwatch at the prow of my boat,
while it was beating along beside the cliffs.
      O'erpowered with cold
were my feet, bound with the frost,
in icy fetters.

The speaker goes on to give a realistic picture of solitude, which it would be hard to surpass. The man, he says, to whom fate is kind on earth, does not know how he lived out on the ice-cold sea throughout the winter, in exile, far away from his friends and kinsmen, hung round with icicles, while the hail drove in showers :—

There I heard nought but the booming of the sea,
of the ice-cold waves, or at times the song of the swan.
For revelry, I took to me the note of the gannet,
the voice of the curlew in place of the laughter of men,
the song of the seamew in the stead of the mead-drinking.
Storms there beat upon the rocky cliffs where the tern
    answered back,
the glittering-feathered, full oft the eagle screamed,
the dewy-feathered. No protector was there
to cheer my solitary soul.

    .   .   .   .

The shades of night fell, from the north came snow,
rime bound the earth, hail fell to the ground,
coldest of grains.

But now, after this vivid picture of the hardships of the sailor's life, the poet turns to the other side of it, to the joy of adventure, the thrill of fighting the sea :—

          And yet now
the thoughts of my heart urge me on
that I myself should seek out the deep streams,
the play of the salt waves.
The desire of my heart drives me at every moment
to fare forth, that I should seek far hence the dwellings of
    strangers.
And yet there is on earth no man so proud,
so richly gifted nor in his youth so keen,

so valiant in his deeds, so favoured by his lord,
who shall not ever yet have care before a voyage.
For him there is no thought of the harp or giving of rings,
no delight in woman, nor joy in the world,
nor in aught else but the tossing of the waves ;
ever has he this longing who hastens to the sea.
Groves put forth their blossoms, cities grow fair,
fields become gay, the world revives,
all these urge on the eager heart,
the ready soul to journey forth, of one thus minded.

Even the cuckoo, the harbinger of summer, urges him on with its sad note, though boding sorrow to the breast. The prosperous man does not know what those endure whose wanderings take them farthest :—

And yet (he goes on) my thought o'erflows my breast,
my soul roams with the flood over the home of the whale,
urges my unresisting heart on to the ocean.

Here the original poem is usually admitted to end. What follows is of a very different character, to be discussed later.

For the purpose of giving the contents of the poem, it has been assumed that it has to do with one speaker, who is balancing in his own mind the fascinations of the sea against its terrors. But this is not the universal interpretation. It is thought by some [1] that two speakers are involved, an old man who is warning a young sailor against the dangers of the sea and the young man who points out its fascinations. [2]

[1] See p. 60 for various views.
[2] For a recent modernization of this poem, see " The Seafarer ", by Gavin Bone in Medium Ævum, vol. iii, No. 1, Feb., 1934.

LYRICAL POEMS (*continued*)

The whole subject of these lyrical poems is full of difficulties. We have the poems, but we know nothing, and we have no means of finding out anything, about the poets or the circumstances of their lives. From our knowledge of Old English literature in general it seems unlikely, in spite of the form in which some are cast, that they are autobiographical, as has been suggested, and still less likely is it that the writers were treating purely imaginary and independent situations. The more general view now is that most, at any rate, do deal with epic characters and situations well known at the time, though not so obvious to-day, but scholars differ greatly in the associations they suggest for them. The matter of these backgrounds has therefore been left for a separate chapter, since the views advanced are too important, and the controversies raised too interesting to be passed over shortly, and any adequate account earlier of each would have interfered too much with the consideration of the group as a whole.

In Deor's Lament the only obscure allusions are those to Mæþhild and the Mærings, but though the other personages are known, their stories may not be so familiar to readers to-day as they were to an audience of that time and a brief explanation of each reference may be useful.

The story of Weland, from which the matter of the first and second strophes is drawn, is not told anywhere in O.E. literature, though it must have been well known from the frequent allusions to it, not only in pre-Conquest times but afterwards, and by the survival of the name in place-names, as in Wayland's Smithy in Berkshire. It is, too, one of the subjects treated on the Franks casket. Our authority for it is the O.N. Völundarkviða, from which the following outline is taken.

Weland, the famous smith, and his two brothers married three swan maidens but after some years their wives flew away. While the two brothers had gone out to seek them, Weland, who had been left at home, was seized by soldiers of Nidhad, king of the Níarar, who were perhaps the Neriki, a tribe living in South Sweden. In our poem Weland's captors are called Wermi (if we accept that emendation), through confusion with another tribe living in the same district. These men carried him off to Nidhad who wished to secure for himself Weland's skill as a worker in metal. By him he was maimed and imprisoned, lest he as the " better man " should escape.

For this, Weland took a terrible revenge. Having enticed Nidhad's two sons to him, he killed them and made of their skulls drinking cups for the king, jewels of their eyes for the queen, and a necklace of their teeth for their sister, Beaduhild. Then, when the last took him a ring to mend for her, he ravished her and, making himself wings, flew away.

The translation of the third strophe is doubtful ; in Chapter II it has been made as close as possible to the original, but much is obscure, and many suggestions have been made for the interpretation of it. The difficulty is that we have no mention anywhere in O.E. or O.N. literature of a Mæþhild, and all attempts to identify her have been so far unsuccessful. They are either too far-fetched to be acceptable or require too much emendation of the succeeding lines. All that can be said for certain is that " sorglufu ", given here as *love-longing*, must mean some sort of love and have to do with a love story, rather than with a tale of revenge, as in some of the translations offered, and that " frige " is therefore better taken as the plural of " frigu ", *love*, and translated as here, *wooing*, than as that of the adjective " frēo ", *freeborn*, and translated as sometimes, *nobles*.[1]

---

[1] Mæþhild has been taken by Sieper, (Die altenglische Elegie, p. 156) as another name for Svanhildr, the young wife of Eormenric, whom out of jealousy he had put to a cruel death (see below). In Widsith his wife is called Ealhhild, which seems to indicate that the first syllable of her name did vary in the different versions of the Eormenric Saga.

Tupper, (Mod. Phil., VIII, Oct., 1911) reads Mæþ Hilde, as two words,

The legend of Theodoric the Great has twisted his invasion and conquest of Italy into a return from thirty years exile at the court of Attila. Who the Mærings were is unknown. Here, according to the legend, they seem to have been Huns, the followers of Attila, but the only reference to them elsewhere makes them Goths. The O.H.G. writer, Notker, in the introduction to his translation of Boethius calls Theodoric Rex Mergothorum. This may be another form of the legend. A connection with the Tyrolese Meran has also been suggested.

Eormenric, the Hermanaricus of classical writers, whose kingdom extended from the Baltic to the Black Sea, was, no doubt, of historical origin, but he is remembered in Germanic legend chiefly for the cruel acts of his later years. Thus, according to an O.N. story, the treacherous councillor Bikki, having been sent by the king with the latter's son Randver to woo the maiden Svanhildr for him, incited the prince to win her for himself, and Jörmanrekr, as his name appears in O.N., in vengeance had her trampled to death in the gate of his capital, and according to a later High German legend he caused his two nephews, the Harlungs to be put to death in order to gain their treasure.

Heorrenda, the successful minstrel, may be the Horant of the M.H.G. story of Gudrun, and is no doubt the O.N. Hjarrandi, not mentioned, however, till later in O.N.[1]

With Deor, however, our certain knowledge of the stories referred to ends. The three following poems, Wulf and Eadwacer, the Lament of the Wife, and the Message of the Husband, read as though they were treating of well known personages or episodes, but it is by no means clear whether they are from any stories which have come down to us, though many attempts have been made to fit them

---

connecting Mæþ with the O.N. meiða, *to injure*, and translating, " the violation of Hild." He thus links this verse to the preceding ones. But both these readings require considerable emendation or unusual renderings of the following lines. They cannot belong to a love story.

Stevanovič, (Anglia, XXXIII, p. 397 ff.) takes the line as "the fate of Hild ", identifying her with a Walkyrie wooed by Wodan, for whom one of the names found is Geat.

[1] For a recent edition of the whole poem, see Deor, ed. by Kemp Malone in Methuen's Old English Library.

with backgrounds. The need for a setting for the last two poems, the Wanderer and the Seafarer, is less obvious, since they are more general in character. The Ruin speaks for itself, it may describe a scene which the poet has seen for himself and is complete without any background of legend being necessary to explain it.

An ingenious suggestion has, however, been made that all six poems belong together and that we have to do with a lost epic in prose and verse of which these few verse passages are all that have survived. Dr. Imelmann [1] has brought them all together as follows : The speaker in Wulf and Eadwacer is the same as in the Wife's Lament ; the Seafarer describes the sufferings endured by the Husband in his exile ; the Wanderer is a faithful follower who has fled with his lord and who in the Message of the Husband returns to summon the Wife to join him, while the Ruin describes the forsaken home. There are difficulties in accepting this view. Though no doubt the old stories were told in prose among the people themselves as well as sung by the minstrels, such an epic would imply an early cultivation of a literary prose which is certainly not to be gathered from the crude character of the documents we possess from the period, the late seventh or early eighth century.

That the poem of Wulf and Eadwacer represents a scene from some definite story, well known at the time, is now generally admitted, though for a while, as has been said, it was believed to be a riddle, for which solutions were offered which differed widely. They ranged from the answer " Cynewulf ",[2] a sort of charade on the name of the supposed author, to others such as " a Christian Teacher " [3] and " a riddle ".[4]

An entirely new direction was, however, given to the

---

[1] Die altenglische Odoaker-Dichtung, Berlin, 1907, and Wanderer und Seefahrer im Rahm der altenglischen Odoaker-Dichtung, Berlin, 1908.

[2] This was Leo's fantastic solution in his Quæ de se ipso Cynewulfus, sive Cenewulfus, sive Cœnewulfus, tradiderit, Halle, Program, 1857, regardless of the fact that for it he had to take as alternative forms cyne, *royal* ; cēne, *bold* ; cwēn (North. cōēn), *woman* and cēn, *torch*, according to requirements.

[3] Morley, English Writers, II, 225.

[4] Trautman, Anglia, VI, Anz., p. 158.

E

study of the poem when Dr. Bradley in 1888 declared it to be not a riddle at all, but a fragment of a dramatic soliloquy, like Deor's Lament or the Lament of the Wife, and pointed out its resemblance to the latter. It was, he said, the lament of a woman captive in a foreign land. Wulf was, he thought, her lover and Eadwacer her tyrant husband, but whether the story was taken from history or from Teutonic legend he declared himself unable to determine.

Since then, this general interpretation has been universally accepted and the only question has been to find the definite background which it is felt there must be, and which would clear up what is vague. Dr. Bradley [1] and Professor Gollancz,[2] who had arrived independently at much the same conclusion, both, guided apparently by the agreement of the name, suggested the widely spread story of Theodoric the Great, identifying Eadwacer with the Odoacer or Odovacar overcome by him, though they differed in their allotment of the rôles of husband and lover.[3]

Later Dr. Imelmann [4] found his original in another Odoacer, the Saxon king who invaded France in 463, and Professor Brandl [5] suggested, as an alternative background, the story of Wolfdietrich. We have, however, no proof that the doings of either the Saxon king or of Wolfdietrich were known in England, whereas allusions to Theodoric the Great are common.

Very interesting in its general direction is the theory of Professor Lawrence [6] who in the same year, 1902, which saw the publication of the interpretations of Dr. Bradley and Professor Gollancz, expressed his conviction on metrical and linguistic grounds that Wulf and Eadwacer was a translation from some lost O.N. poem and an almost literal translation. His view was further worked out by Professor Schofield,[7] to whom he showed his article, and

---

[1] Academy, Vol. XXXIII, p. 197 ff.
[2] Ibid., Vol. XLIV, p. 572.
[3] Athenæum, 1902, pp. 551 and 758.
[4] Die altenglische Odoaker-Dichtung, Berlin, 1907.
[5] Geschichte der Altenglischen Literatur, § 20.
[6] P.M.L.A., XVII, pp. 247–261.
[7] Ibid., XVII, pp. 262–295.

the situation was identified by him with an episode in the Völsunga Saga, which was certainly well known in England at the time,[1] though the extant O.N. versions of it are later.

The story is as follows : The whole family of Wæls has been treacherously destroyed, except Sigemund and his sister Signy, by the latter's husband Siggeir. The two bide their time for vengeance. After Signy's two elder sons have shown themselves unfit, the third, called Fitela in Beowulf, Sinfiotli in O.N., who is the son of Sigemund and Signy and so wholly a Wælsing, comes through the imposed tests of courage triumphantly and is taken off by Sigemund for further training. This is the situation which Schofield suggested as here represented. Signy is the speaker, Wulf is Sigemund, lurking in exile, and the whelp is Fitela, carried off by Wulf to be trained in the forest in endurance, for the furtherance of their plan of vengeance. "Eadwacer," which he took as an adjective, *ever wakeful*, is a term applied to Siggeir. He called the poem Signy's Lament.

While the poem fits into this background strikingly well in many points, all Lawrence's conclusions cannot be accepted unreservedly. Though the undoubted resemblances in vocabulary, idiom, and especially in the metrical form of the refrain,[2] do suggest a closer connection with O.N. literature than that of common origin only, it is not easy to say what that connection is. The theory of a translation implies a written literature for O.N. then, for which there is certainly no proof. Could the suggestion of a Scandinavian settlement in Yorkshire in the sixth or seventh century [3] be accepted as proved, a possible explanation might be that we have an O.N. poet having lived in England long enough to use English but remembering his native idioms and metre. But this cannot be taken as proved and the question must be left uncertain.

---

[1] The story of Sigemund the Wælsing (O.N. Völsung) is referred to in Beowulf, vv. 874 ff., and told in part.

[2] This form is not uncommon in O.N. It is the Ljóðaháttr, and consists of one long line on the ordinary type and another with two, or according to some, three feet and no cæsura. At the end of the poem this form is repeated.

[3] Moorman, F. W., English place-names and Teutonic sagas. Essays and Studies by members of the English Association, Vol. V, pp. 75–103.

The interest of this little poem is, however, enhanced rather than diminished by the uncertainty of background. If Deor suggests tragedy in outline, Wulf and Eadwacer affords us a picture of a definite moment of mental conflict, touched in with a skill which is all the more effective for the restraint of the artist.

As in the case of Wulf and Eadwacer, so also in that of the Lament of the Wife, to which we may now pass on, a good deal of misunderstanding obtained at first over the import of the poem.

Since it was first published by Conybeare in 1826 in his Illustrations of A.S. Poetry, much has been written upon it, but a few only of the views expressed can be mentioned here.

At the beginning a woman is clearly indicated as the speaker by two distinctively feminine adjectives: " geomorre ", *sad* and " selfre ", *self*. These were a stumbling block to earlier scholars,[1] whose views may be passed over lightly, but more lately Schücking[2] has declared the speaker to be a man—the young man who must always be sad and serious-minded, his thoughts stern—and the introductory lines in which these feminine forms occur, a later addition.

Ettmüller[3] was the first critic to accept the MS. reading and since then almost all scholars have followed him, directing their efforts largely, as with Wulf and Eadwacer, towards trying to find the background which would explain those points in translation which are at present uncertain. It is, of course, possible that the poet has treated an abstract theme, but it is far more likely that he had a definite subject before him. The best suggestion yet offered is that brought forward tentatively by Wülker,[4] already in 1885, that the poem has to do with Offa I, the great king of the Angles in the fourth century, while they were still on the Continent. This has been taken up and worked out by Miss Rickert[5]

---

[1] Thorpe (Codex-Exoniensis), unable to accept a woman speaker, corrected each word to the corresponding masculine form. Taine (Littéra-ture Anglaise) missed both grammar and the note of passion, when he described the poem as depicting the deep feeling between two friends.
[2] Z.f.d.A., XLVIII, pp. 436 ff.
[3] Scopas and Boceras, pp. 214 ff., Quedlingburg, 1850.
[4] Grundriss zur Geschichte der Angelsächsischen Litteratur, III, S.173.
[5] Mod. Phil., II, pp. 29 ff., 365 ff.

and Professor Lawrence,[1] who have shown how admirable a background the legends about him afford.

Moreover it is certain that he was a well-known character in England at the time. The Widsiþ tells us how as a boy he gained for himself the greatest of kingdoms in fight against the Myrgings near Fifeldor (the Eider), and he is mentioned in Beowulf.[2] Later his story continued to be sufficiently popular in England for a monk of St. Albans in the twelfth century to write from current legends, as he says, a Latin version in his Vitæ Duorum Offarum, or St. Albans Book, as it is often called. By that time modifications had crept in, and the story had become located in England.

In this twelfth century account we are told that Offa while hunting came across a beautiful maiden, the daughter of the king of York, who had been turned adrift by her father. Offa rescued her and, when later pressed by his subjects to marry, made her his wife. After children had been born Offa left her to go on a warlike expedition to help the king of Northumbria ; the messenger whom he sent back to report his success had to pass through York, and while there the king contrived to substitute for the real letter a false one, in which Offa was made to admit defeat and to command that the queen, as having brought about the misfortune by her witchcraft, should be abandoned in the woods with her children, who were to have their hands and feet cut off. They were, however, found and healed by a hermit. After a time Offa came across them in the forest and all ended well.[3]

The earlier mentions of Offa tell us nothing of this marriage. It must be a later addition from another source, and this source Miss Rickert [4] has found in a folk-tale spread all over Europe, which she calls the tale of the exiled princess . Details differ, of course, in the various forms of legend so widely spread, but the essential incidents

---

[1] Mod. Phil., V, pp. 387 ff.   [2] v. 1959.
[3] Grein's connection of this story in his Bibliothek der ags. Poesie, S. 363, with the Genoveva Saga, need not be more than mentioned, since he himself withdrew the suggestion later.
[4] Mod. Phil., II, pp. 338 ff.

in all are the same. In all a daughter is banished or sent away for some reason from her home, and in most she goes across the sea. Having reached another country, she marries the prince. He leaves her either of necessity or for some warlike purpose, and his kinsmen or her old persecutor make mischief, and by some means, often a forged letter, contrive to separate the two. She has to flee a second time, but eventually husband and wife are brought together again and all ends well.

It will be observed that Chaucer's story of Constance is based on the same folk-tale. Indeed from that important version of it the name Constance is sometimes given to the whole saga. What the point of contact was ; why this particular folk-tale should have been drawn into the story of Offa is not clear, but the points of resemblance are so obvious that the theory deserves careful consideration. It will be seen that we have here all the material for an epic, in the combination of historical with legendary elements ; we have, however, no proof that there was ever an Offa epic, one can only speak with certainty of an Offa saga.

This background, if it be accepted, certainly helps, by supplying the explanation of lines otherwise difficult to understand, to bring out the pathos of this story of misunderstanding and apparently rejected love, in, for instance, the exile journeys which had ever been a source of misery to the heroine and her fears for her husband if she believes him to be defeated and captive.[1]

In the Message of the Husband we are faced with a different kind of difficulty than that of background, for the question here is where the lyric begins. Preceding it (as given in

---

[1] Stevanovič (Anglia, XXXII, p. 399) prefers to identify the story with another widely spread folk-tale, the Crescentia story, of which versions are to be found as far east as Persia. The outlines of this story resemble those of Constance in many points. In it a man goes away over the sea for some reason leaving his wife behind. His brother seeks to gain her love, but she repulses him. In revenge he accuses her to her husband, of unfaithfulness, and when she goes out to meet the latter on his return he has her driven away and murdered. This he thinks more likely than the Constance legend to be the source since it has no mention of the children which play an important part in the latter, and there are no children in the Lament. Is it too daring to suggest that two folk-tales, with so many features in common, may be, in spite of points of divergence too, variants developed from a common original ?

Chapter II) in the MS. come some lines in which an object
is represented as speaking and describing how it had grown
up in a desolate spot near the sea, and how the point of the
knife had shaped it till it was able to convey a message in
such a way that none but the person addressed could
understand. This some scholars take to be the first part
of our poem, in which the envoy, the rune stave, is explaining
its origin and supplying its credentials.[1] Others believe it
to be a riddle with no connection with the poem.[2] The
latter was the view taken in Chapter II, and the poem assumed
to begin with the arrival of the messenger, who is probably
a man bearing a message,[3] not as has been thought by some,
a personified piece of wood with the runes engraved upon it.

Secondly, the meaning of the runes in the last passage
is not clear. While Dr. Bradley [4] has explained them as
spelling the name of the husband, who thus signs his letter,
and reads them as Sigeward with S standing for the whole
of Sige, which may be perhaps an alternative name for the
S rune, Miss Kershaw [5] suggests that they are the initials
of the five oath-helpers required by English law, who are
here supporting the husband's declaration of loyalty.[6]

A connection between the Message of the Husband and
the Lament of the Wife has often been suggested [7] and many
arguments have been brought forward in favour of this

[1] Blackburn, Journal of Germ. Phil., Vol. III, pp. 1–13.

[2] Tupper, Riddles of the Exeter Book, p. 43, includes it among the
Riddles. See also Sieper, Die altenglische Elegie, p. 211. The description
does not fit any tree from whose bark rune staves could be cut; the object
is clearly a reed; moreover it closely resembles a riddle of Symphosius
to which the answer is a reed.

[3] Brandl, Geschichte der altenglischen Literatur, § 21. Stopford Brooke,
English Literature from the beginning to the Norman Conquest, p. 156.

[4] M.L.R., Vol. II, No. IV, p. 365.

[5] Anglo-Saxon and Norse Poems, p. 42, n. 2.

[6] Other interpretations are that they spell Eadwacer, the name of the
husband, with the vowels given once only and the S and C confused. See
Imelmann, Die altengl. Odoaker-Dichtung. Sieper, Die altengl. Elegie,
p. 214, suggests Sigerun and Eadwine, reading " to Sigerun pledges himself
Eadwine (as husband) ". See also Trautmann, Anglia, XVI, p. 220.

[7] Trautmann, Anglia, XVI, pp. 222 ff. Imelmann, Die altengl.
Odoaker-Dichtung, p. 40. Brandl, Geschichte der altengl. Literatur, § 21.
But Schofield, English Literature from the Norman Conquest to Chaucer,
pp. 201 ff., allows of no connection. He suggests that the Message may
be an early form of the Tristan story in which Tristan and Isolde com-
municate with each other by means of linden twigs inscribed with runes.
Sieper, Die altenglische Elegie, p. 216, also denies any connection.

view. It is curious that among the few lyrical poems which have been preserved to us, we should have one telling of the sorrows of a wife whose husband has left her, and another describing the troubles of a husband who has had to flee and leave his wife behind him. It is natural at first sight to suggest a connection between them. Moreover, the objections made to the theory on the ground of points of dissimilarity in the stories and in the tone of the poems, do not seem conclusive at first sight. There are points of difference no doubt.

In the Lament there is no mention of a feud which has driven the husband away, and there does seem to be some kind of misunderstanding between him and his wife, though its cause is vague, while in the Message there is certainly a feud and no kind of misunderstanding. But these differences are capable of explanation. That in the story would be natural, if the misunderstanding is on the wife's side only and in consequence of a forged letter of which her husband knows nothing, and if the cause of his flight was really a feud of which she, however, had no knowledge. So, too, the difference in tone can be accounted for. In the Lament the wife is separated from her beloved one and is torn with anxiety for his safety, moreover she is being persecuted by his family and herself living under difficult conditions ; naturally the tone is one of passion and fear. In the Message, on the other hand, whatever sufferings and hardships the exile may have endured, he has now conquered them and his position at the moment is one of contentment except for her absence, which he hopes soon will be ended.

If, however, an origin in the Offa Saga be accepted for the Lament, it would be difficult to fit in the Message. In it, it is the hero who comes back to the heroine ; not she who joins him. And in any case a real objection is in the style of the two poems. The subtle delineation of emotion, the note of restrained passion which distinguish the Lament are wholly lacking in the Message. In it the sentiment and the expression of it are straightforward and simple. There is no suggestion of any subtle psychological insight, as in the Lament.

The Ruin, which comes next, has been placed between the Message and the Wanderer, because while, unlike all the other poems of the group, its subject is a scene and not a human experience, yet, as in the preceding poems, that subject is definite and not of general application as in those which follow. It will be seen that hot springs and baths are spoken of among the ruins. Attention was called to these details in 1863 independently by two scholars in different countries ; by Professor Earle of Oxford in a paper read before the Bath Natural History and Antiquarian Field Club, and by Professor Leo in Halle, and both suggested Bath as the city described, though the poem is written in the Northumbrian dialect. The old Roman city of Acamanna Ceaster (later Akmanchester) was taken by the Saxons in 577 and probably destroyed since no further mention of it is found till 676. In that year Osric founded a monastery there. Our poem may well describe the ruins of the former buildings, though the term " burh " applied to them is something of a difficulty. It is used more generally for a fortress than for a city.[1] But the ruins must have been those of a Roman city from the mention of baths and hot streams of water and Sieper has more recently emphasized the Bath theory.[2] This identification would date the poem in the first half or middle of the seventh century, since the poem must have been written before the founding of the monastery, but the lichen-covered walls and completely crumbling towers point to a date some considerable time after the destruction of the city.

Such a date makes the poem among the earliest preserved, and this is borne out further by the words which occur here and nowhere else. Certain metrical intricacies, found but rarely outside this poem, might in themselves suggest a later date. Such, for instance, would be the use of rhyme within the half-line, as in " scorene gedrorene ", *slashed and fallen* ; forweorene, geleorene, *destroyed, gathered*

---

[1] Sweet in Warton's History of English Poetry, ed. by Carew Hazlitt, p. 18.

[2] He points out that recent excavations bear out many details in the poem.

in; but the same peculiarity is found once in Exodus, which is known to be early.

A noticeable feature in the Ruin is the feeling for colour, as shown in the mention of the red stained walls, contrasted with the grey stone. This is another point of resemblance between this poem and the Exodus,[1] whereas early O.E. poetry speaks in general of very little definite colour.

The two remaining poems, the Wanderer and the Seafarer, may be from some story well known at the time, or they may simply tell independently of the experiences of travellers. They may even be autobiographical. Neither would gain much by being fitted into a lay or epic, and criticism of them has concerned itself much more with the poems themselves than with finding a setting for them. Thus, in the case of both, it has been doubted whether they, as usually accepted, are really to be looked upon as one poem, or whether the scribes have not joined together in the MS. two or even more works. For instance, in reading the Wanderer, one is at once struck with the difference in spirit between the opening lines and final passage which are clearly Christian, and the rest which is essentially heathen in its unrelieved gloom and its belief in fate, in spite of a Christian term interpolated here and there. Moreover, the beginning lines do not agree with what follows in another way. They speak of the hardships endured by one who is long tossed about on a stormy sea, while the rest of the poem is on the sorrows of exile and solitude. It is true that a sea journey is mentioned, but not as one of the causes of suffering, and it is not dwelt upon. If one could imagine a poet so overwhelmed himself by the gloom of his own picture as to wish to soften the effect by assuring the reader that everything will be right in the end, he would surely have made his consolation apply to that picture and not to an entirely different situation. Most scholars [2] agree therefore that a certain number of lines at the beginning and the last five are later additions by a Christian scribe, though they differ as to the number of lines which should

[1] See Chapter VI, p. 131.
[2] But see Lawrence, J.E.G.Ph., IV, p. 460.

be allotted to the Prologue. The same scribe probably inserted the few Christian terms which occur in the body of the poem.[1]

Less clear is the question as to whether all that comes between the Prologue and Epilogue is the work of one man.

As pointed out, there is a definite pause in the sense after the verse " over the chain of the waves his weary soul ". What follows is more general and of unequal quality in itself. While some good lines occur, some are very weak, and the whole is inferior to what has gone before. It may be that the difference in tone is due simply to that of subject.[2] Hitherto the poet has been describing a definite situation, in the second part he is making general reflections upon the sorrows of life. The forte of the Anglo-Saxon poet was in the depicting of scenes or events more or less within his own experience, he was less happy in treating more general themes or in reflective passages. This would account for the lower level reached in the later part, which is, however, too closely connected in many places with what has gone before to have been added afterwards by someone else. It is possible, too, that the weaker lines were inserted by a scribe, it may be by the same who added the Prologue and Epilogue,[3] and that the bulk of the poem, therefore, is by one man.

The pagan outlook and in especial the reference to the Fates, make it difficult to accept a third explanation offered, namely that the whole of the later part was added by the Christian scribe, and that the occasional good lines were from some fine poem which seemed to him to fit.[4] It is hardly likely that he would have quoted anything so markedly heathen in character, as are most of the lines.

With the Seafarer the situation is more complicated.

---

[1] It may be suggested that the second half of verse 4, " Fate is full inexorable ", must belong to the original poem. The sentiment is purely heathen and the scribe's object in his addition was to introduce some Christian element. The poem cannot, however, have begun in the middle of a line. The scribe may have worked over an existing passage, leaving, in a surprising way, this definitely heathen half-line.

[2] Rieger, Z.f.d.Ph., I, pp. 324–330.

[3] Boer, Z.f.d.Ph., XXXV, pp. i ff.

[4] Sieper, Die altenglische Elegie, p. 198.

Not only has it been questioned whether it is to be considered as one poem or more, but, as mentioned in Chapter II, some critics have seen in it a dialogue in which a young man is praising the fascination of the sea and the joy and excitement of the sailor's life, while an old man is trying to dissuade him from it by pointing out the hardships and dangers to which he is exposed.

The difficulty about accepting this view is that its supporters do not agree among themselves upon the distribution of the speeches, one putting down to the youth [1] what another divides between him and the old man.[2] Indeed one critic, Boer,[3] makes two independent poems of the passage, taking the first part down to verse " to cheer my solitary soul ", as a description of an actual voyage with its hardships, and the second part, which he points out is more general, as a dialogue. But, as one might conclude from this divergence of opinion, there is no real contradiction between the views expressed, we have merely the seaman's life considered from different angles.[4, 5] Great though the hardships may be, yet the speaker cannot resist the fascinations. At the prospect of a voyage his mind is filled with anxiety, it is true, but also with longing.[6]

The poem as given in Chapter II, is followed in the MS. by a long passage of varying degrees of excellence or weakness, of which the general tenor is to extol the joys of heaven. It begins " therefore more ardent for me are the joys of the Lord, than this dead life, transitory on land ". This cannot mean, as ten Brink has interpreted it, that the contrast between the joys of heaven and sorrows of earth is greater than that between the fascination and the terrors of the sea, which has been the subject hitherto. The O.E. poets understood well the value of contrast in getting their effects,

---

[1] Rieger, Z.f.d.Ph., I, p. 330.

[2] Kluge, Engl. Stud., VI, pp. 322 ff. ; VIII, pp. 472 ff.

[3] Boer, Z.f.d.Ph., XXXV, pp. i ff. See also Sieper, Die altenglische Elegie, pp. 191 ff.

[4] See Lawrence, J.E.G.Ph., 4, pp. 460 ff.

[5] Sweet, AS. Reader, 9th ed., Notes to Seafarer.

[6] In this connection it may be noted that the different aspects are joined by " for þon ". This usually means " for this, because or therefore ". Here it must be translated, however, by some phrase like the modern English " for all that ". See M. Daunt, M.L.R., XIII, p. 474 ff.

but this can be no instance of it. It is agreed by most critics that this passage is a later addition. It is entirely different in character from the Seafarer proper. While the latter shows an unusual flight of imagination for those times in the description of the soul escaping from its bodily prison and roaming free over the world, and a vivid realism in other passages, as in the picture of the winter storm at night at sea or in the account of the birds, what follows shows nothing of those qualities. Moreover, there is no coherence in the thought. Sometimes the construction is faulty, at others it is the thought that is confused. A few lines seem to be from an old dirge :—

> Those days are passed away,
> all the pomp of the kingdom of the earth.
> There are now neither kings nor emperors,
> nor givers of gold, as formerly there were,
> while they wrought the mightiest deeds of fame,
> and lived in the most noble glory.

At other times we have nothing but prose. " Nor may the body, when the life departs from it, swallow what is sweet, or feel pain, stir the hand, or think with the mind," thus passing into a didactic vein quite out of harmony with the tone of the Seafarer.

If the view is accepted that the Prologue and Epilogue of the Wanderer are later additions and that the real Seafarer consists of the first sixty-four lines only, it is clear that the outlook on life in both is purely pagan. Any Christian touches which appear in either are quite out of character and must be looked upon as later insertions, probably due to the scribe who added the continuation of the Seafarer. A striking passage in the Seafarer is that of the description of spring, with the cuckoo calling, the leaves coming out on the trees, and the flowers in the meadows. Such a description of nature in her brighter aspects is rare in O.E. poetry, and may be due to Celtic influence, coming in either from the many Celts left in the North of England or from the Celtic missionaries in that area. The cuckoo as a portent of sorrow or death is a distinct Celtic touch.

Chapter IV

THE EARLY EPIC: BEOWULF

The Lyrics just considered have been taken first because they may be said to belong wholly to the earlier period of O.E. literature, later influences, such as that of Christianity, having had no essential effect upon them ; but better known and far more important is the Epic. Indeed, the outstanding feature of O.E., as apparently of Western Germanic literature, is the Epic. For the origin of both we must go back to Germanic days, but, unlike the Lyric, the Epic shows a gradual development in character under the influence of Christianity and classical learning.

The terms Germanic and National have both been given to the earlier epic, or fragments of epics, which treat of Germanic heroes, but neither name is satisfactory. Germanic is unsuitable, because while there is ample proof that the Germanic peoples sang or chanted poems in honour of their great men, there is no evidence of these having been expanded into epic form before the separation of the various tribes. Indeed the epic would seem to have been a special development among the West Germans. Rich as Old Norse literature is, it did not produce this particular form.

The term National is equally unsuitable since the heroes whose deeds were sung by the Old English and Old High German poets were not specifically English or German. They go back to the later fourth, the fifth, and sixth centuries. They belong to the Migration Age, and are a common inheritance of all the Germanic races.

During those three centuries, while the tribes were spreading and fighting their way to new territory in order to satisfy the needs of their increasing numbers, and the Huns were in their turn advancing from the east upon the Germans, the great leaders naturally came into prominence. To this period belongs the dramatic story of the death of King

Eormenric, the Jörmunrekr of Old Norse, the Ermenrich of Middle High German, and the Hermanaricus or Armanaricus of Latin writers. The fame of his magnificence, valour, and cruelty was well known far and wide, and his death was such a subject for story that we have more than one version of it. According to contemporary authority [1] he died by his own hand, on the eve of a battle with the Huns, terrified at their menace. According to legend, [2] his death was largely due to the attempt of the two brothers Sörli and Hamðir to avenge his cruel murder of his queen, their sister, Svanhildr, a vengeance " motif " which, in varying forms, is found in several of these early tales. To this period also belongs the figure of the great Hun leader, whose deeds were so familiar to the Goths, that he has come down to history under a Gothic name, Attila or Little Father, O.E. Ætla, O.H.G. Etzel, O.N. Atli. Again we have more than one account of his death.

According to Latin writers, [3] he died from the breaking of a blood vessel on the night of his marriage to a certain Ildico, but in the O.N. version he is represented as having been murdered by his wife Gudrun to avenge the death of her three brothers. [4] Further this period saw the conquest of Italy by Theodoric the Great, the O.E. Đeodric, the M.H.G. Dietrich, and at its close the establishment of a Lombard kingdom in Italy under the Alboin of Latin writers, the Ælfwine of O.E. legend. Now Eormenric died about 375 ; Attila in 453 ; Alboin in 572 ; Theodoric reigned from 489 to 526. All these great events are to be placed, therefore, between 350 and 600. Meanwhile, while these great happenings were agitating all Western Europe, others were making a deep impression within a more limited area. Such an event was the unsuccessful attempt of a Scandinavian invader, the Hygelac of Beowulf, on the kingdom of the Frankish king Theodoric between 512 and 520 ; others were the constant struggles in Scandinavia between the various tribes of the Swedes, the Geats (O.N. Gautar),

---

[1] Ammianus Marcellinus, XXXI, 3, 1.
[2] Völsunga Saga, Ch. 42, Guðrúnarhuọt and Hamðismál.
[3] Priscus and Jordanes.
[4] Atlakviða.

and the Danes. These centuries formed the heroic age of the Germanic tribes, they supplied the material and gave the impetus for a great literary activity, to which the name Romantic Movement has been not unaptly given.

The fame of these great leaders and their doings was sung at first no doubt in lays, then as time went on these lays absorbed into themselves episodes from folk-tales and thus a superhuman element crept in. For instance, the killing of a dragon who is guarding a great treasure was a popular incident in folk-tales, and one which is often found attached to hero lays, if not actually attributed to a historical character. Later, since these stories were handed down by word of mouth, variations in the telling inevitably arose, leading sometimes to contradictions within the one story, and sometimes to more than one version of the same event, as we have seen in the accounts of the deaths of Attila and Eormenric.

But not only did these lays take to themselves elements from folk-tales, they tended also to overlap and to make the hero of one attract to himself stories of others, and thus cycles of lays arose, collected round some outstanding figure. In this way, with a fine disregard for chronology, in the M.H.G. epics, Theodoric the Great, from being the principal character in his own story, becomes a warrior at the court of Attila, a prince and hero still, indeed, but in a subordinate position. Or into the story of Hroþgar, Beowulf is introduced from a folk-tale and the stories of Hygelac and the various Geat and Swedish princes are linked on.

Now it is certain that the Anglo-Saxons were familiar, as will be shown later, with many such tales, and that at any rate some of them had been developed into epics. While we actually possess one only that is complete, Beowulf, traces of others remain. Two fragments exist from the story of Waldere, or Walther of Aquitaine, the Waltharius of the Latin version, and these from their style of treatment would seem to be passages from a lost epic on the subject. We also possess a short passage dealing with one episode in the tragic story of the Frisian king Finn and his queen. It is apparently from a lay only ; the subject would seem, however, to have been worked up also into epic form, for the court poet in Beowulf is represented in one place as entertaining the king and his court with an account of part of the same story,[1] and from the style one must conclude that he is drawing from an epic rather than from a lay. It may be pointed out in passing that the stories which can be proved to have been treated in England, have been brought from regions not far removed. Hroþgar, to whose aid Beowulf came, reigned in Zealand, Hygelac met his death at the mouth of the Rhine, Finn was king of the Frisians and Waldere's great fight was in a pass in the Vosges.

While these are all the epics of which we have actual remains in Old English, others must have existed and been well known. In other passages in Beowulf the scop tells of Sigemund,[2] the father of the better known Siegfried of the M.H.G. Nibelungenlied, of Weland the Smith,[3] and of the Mercian king Offa [4] already mentioned. The writer of the little poem known as Deor's Lament [5] speaks, as we have seen, of Weland, Eormenric, Theodoric, and others, all of whom were evidently as well known in England as in Germany or Scandinavia, where their stories have been preserved in full, in epic or saga. But our most important source of information is the poem called the Widsiþ, or Far Journey. In this the poet gives a long list of the kings and countries he has visited and, as far as he is speaking of Germanic princes, his list probably affords a fairly complete index to the hero lays familiar to the Anglo-Saxons at the time.

That they were all familiar must be inferred from the fact that neither the writer of Widsiþ nor those of the other poems named make any attempt to introduce the characters they mention, they assume that all are as intimately known to their hearers as to themselves. Their deeds must have been told in lays or epics.

Though neither a lay nor an epic, the Widsiþ belongs

---

[1] Beowulf, v. 1068 ff. [2] Ibid., v. 874 ff.
[3] Ibid., v. 455. [4] Ibid., v. 1957 ff.
[5] See chap. II, p. 33.

F

from its subject matter to the chapter which deals with them, and must be considered briefly here.[1] It purports to be the account given by a gleeman or professional minstrel, well named Widsiþ, of the places he has visited, the people he has met, and especially of a journey he took in the following of the lady Ealhhild, sister of Ælfwine, apparently for her marriage to Eormenric. The second syllable of her name must have led to her confusion in some version with Svanhildr, his wife in other stories, and caused her herself and her true bridegroom to be swept into the Eormenric cycle, in spite of differences of date. It is possible that the nucleus of the work is autobiographical ; the story is told with a simplicity and directness which suggests its truth, though of course these may be nothing but a proof of the poet's art. The same claim might be made for other O.E. poems, as, for instance, Deor's Lament, as well as for the later Mandeville's Travels or for Robinson Crusoe. In this case, if it is true, it would prove the original poem, of which our version is a later recension, to be amongst the earliest products of O.E. literature, for Ælfwine lived in the sixth century. The poem, as we have it, is, however, undoubtedly a compilation in which later writers have inserted freely names of kings and peoples of countries ranging from England to India, and of different ages, whom it is obviously impossible for one man to have met, since he would have to have lived for some centuries. Thus the writer has no scruple in making Eormenric of the fourth century and Ælfwine of the sixth, contemporaries.

The work begins with nine lines in which the poet introduces himself.

He was of the race of the Myrgings, and had wandered widely among many nations. With Ealhhild, the dear peacebringer, he for the first time sought out the palace of Eormenric, the fierce traitor. Then after a few lines to explain that a king must live rightly if he wishes his kingdom to prosper, as did Alexander, the mightiest of monarchs, and others, he goes on suddenly to give a list of kings and heroes,

---

[1] For a full treatment see Chambers, Widsith, A Study in Old English Heroic Legend.

which includes, of those mentioned elsewhere in O.E. poems, Breca, Finn, and Hnæf, besides Eormenric. A Cæsar who ruled the Greeks is also found in it.

After this follows a passage of some interest. We read :—

Offa ruled the Angles ; Alewih, the Danes.
He was the boldest of all these men (in the list).
He could not, however, work deeds of manliness above Offa,
but Offa [1] gained in battle, first of all men,
while still a boy, the greatest of kingdoms.
None wrought greater deeds than he of courage
in the fight. With his single sword
he enlarged his boundaries towards the Myrgings,
by Fifeldor. Angles and Swabians
held it afterwards as Offa gained it.

Then the poet goes on to speak of Hroþulf and Hroþgar [2] :—

For long they held
peace between themselves, uncle and nephew,
after they banished the race of the Vikings,
and humbled the pride of Ingeld in war,
cut down at Heorot the might of the Heaþobeards.

Because he has wandered so much, the poet can, he says, tell many tales, recording how helpful (that is, how generous) the noble ones have been to him. Another catalogue of names follows after this, but this time it is chiefly of peoples among whom he has wandered, not kings, and as far as they have been identified, all are Germanic. However, among the names of peoples, he mentions the Burgundian Guþhere,[3] who gave him a splendid jewel, as a reward for his songs, and Ælfwine, son of Eadwine, who had the readiest hand in doing praiseworthy acts, the openest heart in distributing rings.

Then follows the third catalogue, also of peoples, and this time including Greeks, Israelites, Egyptians, Hebrews, and Persians, as well as Picts and Scots, after which the poem goes on :

I was with Eormenric the whole time,
where the king of the Goths was generous to me.

---

[1] Cf. Chap. III, p. 53. [2] Cf. Chap. V, p. 90 ff.
[3] Cf. p. 70 ff.

He gave me a necklace, this prince of citizens,
on which six hundred shillingsworth of pure gold
had been expended.
This I gave into the possession of Eadgils,
my own lord, when I returned home,
as a reward to the beloved one, because he had given me land,
my father's heritage, this lord of the Myrgings.
And Ealhhild gave me a second one,
the noble and virtuous lady, daughter of Eadwine,—

whose praises he continues to sing for some lines.

Finally comes a list of the nobles forming the household of Eormenric. This, though of great value to the student of O.N. or O.H.G. literature, contains no names found elsewhere in Old English. The Epilogue which follows gives us the comforting assurance that the gleeman in the course of his wanderings generally finds someone not niggardly in his gifts and the poem ends, " He who works praiseworthy deeds (presumably in his gifts to minstrels) shall have glory and fame under the heavens."

It will be observed that the heroes dealt with here at greatest length are just those who are the subjects of special poems, Hroþgar,[1] Finn,[2] Guþhere,[3] and Eormenric.[4] The only name not found elsewhere is that of Ælfwine. The Widsiþ, therefore, not only enlarges our knowledge of the lays known to the Anglo-Saxons, but it corroborates very definitely what may be inferred in other ways as to which were the most popular. Incidentally, it shows how widely the minstrels *did* travel, if such a list of countries could have been accepted for a moment, and explains how the lays were carried from one country to another, making it possible for an O.E. poet to make a great epic about Scandinavian heroes. The early date for the poem, to be assumed if any part is autobiographical, is borne out by traces of strophic formation. The lists of kings occur at intervals of varying length and are certainly, at any rate, for the most part later insertions. It has been thought that they may be elaborations of an earlier refrain, or they may be independent additions, put in wherever there was a pause

---

[1] pp. 90 ff.   [2] p. 73.   [3] pp. 69 ff.   [4] p. 48.

in the original poem. Certainly such pauses are noticeable. Of more value from the literary point of view than Widsiþ, are the passages from the Waldere and Finn epics, to which we may now pass on.

The two fragments of the Waldere epic contain sixty-five lines only. They were discovered by Werlauff in the Royal Library at København in 1860, and published in the same year by G. Stephens under the title " Two Leaves of King Waldere's Story ". The MS. cannot be earlier than the year 1000. The scribe seems to have copied with great care from an imperfect original, which metre and language show to have been composed in Anglia, before the eighth century. As in the case of Beowulf, it is probable that the epic arose in Northumbria, the home at that time of learning and culture, rather than in Mercia. The fragments treat of a story told at length in 1,456 hexameters in a Latin poem by a certain Ekkehard, a monk in the Swiss monastery of St. Gall, who lived about the year 930, and named his work Waltharius manu fortis. A brief outline of the story, as told in this Latin version, will make our fragments more comprehensible.

At the court of Attila were three hostages of royal blood : Hiltgund of Burgundy, Waltharius of Aquitaine (the later M.H.G. version locates him at Langres near Chalon), and Hagano of Worms. Hiltgund and Waltharius are betrothed. After a time Hagano's king dies and his son Guntharius, who succeeds him, refuses to continue to pay the tribute demanded by Attila. Hagano's position becomes in consequence difficult, and he contrives to flee. A little later Waltharius and Hiltgund also succeed in making their escape, carrying away with them much treasure. When they reach the Rhine, Guntharius hears of them and sets out to intercept them and obtain their treasure, taking with him the unwilling Hagano and eleven others. Waltharius takes up his position at the entrance of a narrow pass in the Vosges, where he defeats his opponents, one after the other, in a series of single fights, till at last Guntharius and Hagano alone are left. They attack him together, on the plain this time ; the fight is terrific, finally all three are so severely wounded that they can fight no more and they come to terms, everything ending in peace and friendliness. During the nights Hiltgund has kept watch while Waltharius slept, singing to keep herself awake.

The lost O.E. epic must have been drawn from the same source as this version, though details differ in the two. Kœgel,[1] because of certain points in vocabulary and idiom, has suggested that the English poem is a translation of an O.H.G. original. The story was evidently widely spread. Our two fragments can be better fitted into it as told in the Latin version, if we reverse the order in which they appear in the MS.[2] Then, taking the second passage first, the position would be that Waldere (Waltharius), worn out with all the preceding fights, has tried to propitiate Guþhere (Guntharius), or perhaps only to gain some respite, by offering him a valuable sword. He is certainly now about to begin his last fight with Guþhere, for the passage opens in the middle of a speech of the latter, in which he is refusing the proffered sword. " (I know) no better sword," he says, " except the one which I possess, hidden away in its sheath. I know that Þeodoric thought to send it to Widia with much treasure besides, as a reward, because he (Widia), Nidhad's kinsman, Weland's son, had let him out from the power of the giants."

Upon this Waldere, seeing no escape, makes his challenge in the correct epic fashion. Hagena has already fought him and been defeated, or, more probably, has managed to withdraw and avoid attacking his old comrade, for in the O.E. version he and Guþhere are not allowed to do anything so unheroic as to fight two against one. " Dost thou indeed deem," he says, " friend of the Burgundians, that Hagena's hand would have offered me battle and cut me off from movement ? Fetch, if thou dost dare, the grey corslet from one thus battle-weary. On my shoulders rests the heirloom of Ælfhere, good and broad, adorned with gold, a garment without blemish for a prince, as long as his hand defends his life. It will be no foe to me if unnatural

---

[1] Geschichte der deutschen Litteratur, Bd. I, p. 239.
[2] Brandl, Geschichte der alt.-eng. Literatur, § 24.

kinsmen should fain meet me with swords as ye have done."

The first passage of the MS. contains Hildȝyþ's (Hiltgund) heartening words to Waldere, and follows on quite naturally here. She is encouraging him to persevere in this last effort, and tells him that Mimming (his sword), the work of Weland, will never fail any man who can wield it. Oft in battle before it one man after another had fallen, stained with blood and wounded with the sword. " Champion of Ætla," she cries, " let not thy courage droop to-day, thy valour fail ! The day is come when one of two fates shall be thine, either to lose thy life or, thou son of Ælfhere, to gain eternal glory among men." Never has she, she goes on, known him through the twitting of any man to refuse fight or take refuge behind ramparts to save his life, though many might be slashing at his corslet with their swords. Rather she fears for him that he would seek fight too rashly. Then she bids him " have no fear for the sword ; that best of treasures shall be a help to the two of us. By it thou shalt humble the boast of Guþhere, because he first, unjustly, began the conflict. He refused the sword, now without treasure shall he turn from the strife and seek his old home, or sleep here ".

Here the first fragment of the MS. ends. After it should perhaps come some lines of pious reflections interpolated in the second passage, in which the scribe, after the manner of the monkish copyist, tried to reconcile the old stories with the new teaching, and some which must have ended the original poem. " Then should the proud distribute their wealth, make use of their possessions." These lines proclaim the poet to have been of the professional minstrel class, such as sang loud and clear in Heorot.

Since it is evident that Waldere is the work of a minstrel who was not above reminding his hearers to be liberal, it may be taken as a more genuine type of the Germanic epic than Beowulf. There is no Christian influence to be traced in the sentiments, for the few Christian lines have clearly been added later, and there are no digressions for reflections. At the same time, the slow movement, the length of time allowed for speeches whether of challenge or encouragement, and the richness of parallel phrase justify us in considering these fragments as portions of a lost epic, rather than of a lay. What part Hagena played in this O.E. version cannot of course be known, but in any case his position, torn between his duty to his king and his faith to his friend, must have provided good epic material. Even in these short fragments we get a glimpse into the hero's mind and motives. We see him worn out and doubting his power of further resistance, but undaunted still and twitting Guþhere with having believed that Hagena would have taken part against his old comrade. Hyldgyþ, too, has an important part to play.

The Waldere epic, like Beowulf, as we shall see later, is made up of a mixture of historical and legendary elements. Historical are the figures of Ætla or Attila, the famous king of the Huns in the fifth century, and Guþhere, king of the Burgundians, the Gundicarius, defeated according to contemporary authorities in 435 by the Roman general Aetius.[1] The legendary element is supplied by Hildgyþ. The first part of her name brings her into connection with another heroine, also called Hildr, in the Old Norse story of Hogni, as told by Snorri in the Skaldskaparmál. Hogni has a daughter Hildr, who is carried off by Heðinn in her father's absence. Hogni pursues the fugitives and catches them up by the Orkneys. Hildr tries to bring about a reconciliation, offering her father a necklace as a peace offering ; this he refuses and the fight begins. Every morning Hildr awakens by magic chants those who were slain during the previous day, in order that they may resume the battle. The connection is, however, not only, or indeed so much, in the similarity of name, as in that of activity, for Hildr is a common enough form whether as first part of a compound or by itself. In both stories the function of the heroine is to rouse the warrior or warriors to new life in the morning. Scholars are chary now in admitting mythical sources for these old stories, but without too great rashness the sun myth may perhaps be suggested as ultimate origin

[1] Chadwick, The Heroic Age, p. 22.

for this particular touch. It may be pointed out that in one case the heroine's activity is on the seashore, and in the other on the spur of mountains overlooking a plain, both situations in which the sunrise can be observed to advantage.

The second of these early epics which must have existed and been well known to the Anglo-Saxons, is the Finn epic, telling the story of the death of Finn, king of the Frisians, and the events leading up to it. But in this case we have nothing left of the original epic. That the story was well known is proved by the casual way in which the Beowulf poet introduces the characters, when he tells how the scop entertained the king and his court with the tale. The episode treated in Beowulf will be touched on in speaking of that poem, but the whole story deserves a separate study on its own merits. Besides the passage in Beowulf we possess fifty lines of a fragment of a lay on the same subject. The MS. has been unfortunately lost since Hickes found it in the Lambeth Library and published it in 1705. The lines are sometimes imperfect, sometimes corrupt, the mistakes being due probably sometimes to Hickes, sometimes to his MS. This fragment tells of a fight in a hall which lasted for five days and in which was the leader Hnæf with his follower Hengest and other warriors. It must therefore be placed before the episode in Beowulf, for in that Hnæf has already been killed. The passage begins in the middle of a sentence, but we may reconstruct the story thus : Hnæf and his followers are in the hall at night and someone appears to have caught sight of the approaching attackers, from the glittering of their armour. He says :—

(Those are) never gables that burn.
Then spoke the battle-young king (Hnæf).
This is no dawn from the east, nor does a dragon fly here, nor are the gables of this hall burning.

Then after a gap the poem goes on :—
                    birds are singing,
the greycoated one (the wolf) howls, the battlewood resounds, the shield answers back to the shaft. Now appears the moon

fitfully (?) among the clouds ;   now shall deeds of woe arise,
which will work evil for this folk.
Awaken ye, my warriors !
Take your spears, think on valour !
. . . in the front, be resolute !
Then arose many a gold-adorned thane, girt his sword upon
   him.
Then to the door went the noble warriors,
Sigeferþ and Eaha ;   their swords they drew,
and at the other doors were Ordlaf and Guþlaf,
and Hengest himself followed behind.
Then Guþhere (one of the enemy) would have restrained
   Garulf,
that he should not thus, for the first time, bear his noble life
to the doors of the hall, and his armour also,
now that those fierce in fight would fain destroy it.
But he asked clearly above them all,
this valiant-hearted hero, who might be holding the door.
" Sigeferþ is my name," he (the door-keeper) said, " I am
   lord of the Secgas,
a warrior widely famed.   Much woe have I endured,
hard fights.   For thee is ready here
whichever (of good or evil) thou wilt seek from me."

And so they continued fighting for five days until one
warrior fell back because his corslet was broken and his helmet
pierced.   We may continue the story from the Finn episode.
From it we learn that Hnæf, Hengest, and their followers
were Half-Danes or Scyldings, and that Finn, king of the
Frisians, had married Hnæf's sister Hildeburh, daughter of
Hoc.   It must be inferred that in the preceding fight the
Danes were on the whole the losers, for Hnæf had been
killed.   But the Frisians had also suffered greatly, since
the son of Finn and Hildeburh had also fallen, and the
Frisians had lost so many men that they could not pursue
their advantage.   It was also too late in the year for the
Danes to be able to return home, since, as we learn, they
had to cross the sea :—

By no means without cause did the daughter of Hoc
lament her destiny, when morning came,
and she beneath the sky could see
the slaughter of her kinsmen.   Death had carried off

all the thanes of Finn, except some few alone,
so that he could not there gain aught by fight with Hengest,
nor screen by battle the sorry remnant
from the thane (Hengest) of his lord (Hnæf).

An agreement was therefore made, by which the Danes
should be provided for in honourable fashion through the
winter. Any Frisian should be put to death who twitted
them with their position that they now, lordless, were
following the murderer of their ring-giver, since necessity
forced it upon them.

This treaty having been made and confirmed with oaths
and presents of gold, preparations for the burials were
undertaken :—

Of the warlike Scyldings
the noblest warrior was ready on the pyre.
Then at the burning it was easy to see
the bloodstained corslet, the boar all golden,
the boar hard as iron, many a prince
sent to his fate by wounds, for some had fallen in the fight.
Then Hildeburh at the funeral pyre of Hnæf
bade her own son be given to the flames,
the two bodies burnt, when placed upon the funeral pile.
Sadly the woman mourned. . . .
Then wound to the welkin the greatest of slaughter fires,
it crackled in front of the mound.
Fire swallowed up all,
that greediest of foes, of those whom battle had destroyed,
of both the armies. Their glory was passed.

Unwillingly Hengest remained in Friesland for the winter
while

the sea tossed with storm,
fought against the wind or winter locked the waves,
in fetters of ice,
till the new year came. . . .
Then was winter passed,
the bosom of the earth was fair ; the exile longed,
the stranger, to depart from the palace.

The interpretation of the next few lines is very uncertain,
but the general sense must be that against the custom of

warriors Hengest, having sworn fealty to Finn, failed to
keep his oath ; the unnatural truce came to an end and
hostilities broke out again. The Danes attacked the palace,
Finn was slain on his own hearth, and his queen carried off
back to her people. However the earlier part of the Finn
story be reconstructed, we have here material indeed for
tragedy. We may take it with Professor R. W. Chambers [1]
that Finn was not himself guilty of the treachery of attacking
his own guests, but that it was the act of the Eotens, a
subordinate tribe, and probably due to some private feud ;
that Finn only took part when his own son was slain and that
it was therefore possible for Hengest to come to terms
with him. Or we may agree with Professor Klæber [2] that
the quarrel centred round Hildeburh. It may be that she
had been given in marriage, according to the custom of the
times, to confirm a treaty between Danes and Frisians
after some war, but that the enmity was too deeply rooted
and broke out again after many years. It may possibly have
been some quarrel over the marriage ceremonies, as in the
story of Signy, which broke out into active hostility even
after such a lapse of time. Again we may accept the suggestion of Professor Williams [3] that Hengest is the evil genius
of the tale, suspicious of Finn's hospitality and ready to
incite to strife on the slightest provocation. There are
close parallels in Germanic literature for all these possible
interpretations. In any case we have a type of epic unlike
that of Beowulf, and resembling more that from which
the Waldere fragments have come, or to which the Eormenric
and Theodoric stories must have belonged. In these the
historical element was more prominent than the legendary,
(Finn is generally supposed to have been mainly historical),
and some moment of human tragedy has been chosen.
Indeed here the whole story is full of tragic situations. We have Hildeburh living many years of happy
married life with Finn, evidently a mighty and prosperous
king. Then, when her brother and his followers come to

[1] Beowulf : An Introduction, pp. 248 ff.
[2] Beowulf : The Fight at Finnsburg, pp. 219 ff.
[3] The Finn Episode in Beowulf.

visit her, for some reason a quarrel arises and her happiness is destroyed in one night, and she can take no side for she is divided between the rival claims of husband and brother. The more the character of Finn is cleared from the charge of treachery, as in the view of Professor Chambers, the more the tragedy deepens for him. He is entangled in the net of fate, borne along by the actions of those around him till he has to countenance a great act of treachery and his death is the outcome. He too has to find a way to reconcile his duty to guests and followers.

Hengest is an equally tragic figure, even if we accept Professor Williams's interpretation of the story. For him the conflict is between fidelity to his oath and the paramount duty of avenging his murdered lord, and according to one reading he, like Finn, paid the penalty with his life.

Then again the Finn epic is in marked contrast to Beowulf in its treatment of its subject, as far as it can be gathered from what has survived. There is plenty of action in the Finn fragment, but in it and in the Waldere passages the story is carried on entirely be means of speeches, and in both therefore that story is told from the point of view of the actors, not from that of the onlookers. This last is the case in the Finn episode, and as a result perhaps we get in all three an attempt at a subtler delineation of character than in Beowulf. In Waldere we do not get the hero going with no misgivings to the fight, whatever may be the result ; we have him, instead, so worn out by his previous efforts, that he distrusts his power to meet his last foe and tries to propitiate him, but still with spirit enough left to twit him with having expected help from Hagena. So in the Finn fragment it is the hostile attitude of the combatants that stands out more than the actual fights. In the Finn episode this subjective treatment is still more marked. The emotions and passions of the characters are the theme, the sorrow of Hildeburh and the struggle in Hengest's mind between conflicting duties. Indeed the episode in this respect is more like the interpolated passage in Genesis B, or what is left of the O.H.G. epic, the Hildebrandslied. Again we have a point of difference between what may be called the typical O.E. epic as seen in Beowulf and these fragments in the prominence of the parts played by women. This and the greater emotional element bring us into touch with the lyrical poems already considered, in which, as we have seen, women play important, sometimes even the chief, rôles.

We have little knowledge of what the common Germanic literature was like, but it may be suggested that the Finn and Waldere epics and the lyrical poetry from their resemblance to the O.H.G. remains are nearer to it than is Beowulf.

From the study of these fragments of epics which certainly did once exist, and the consideration of others which probably existed, since the stories were well known, we may pass on to the only complete example of this class of poetry which has come down to us. This is Beowulf, not only the most important epic of Germanic origin, but by far the most important poem of pre-Conquest times. Ever since its transcription by Thorkelin, Beowulf has engaged the special attention of all students of Old English literature, and the reader's appreciation of the beauty and charm of the poem itself has certainly not been diminished by the discovery that most of the characters in it, with the one exception of the hero, are almost certainly historical. To follow the results of the researches of scholars during the last fifty years or more makes thrilling reading as detail after detail becomes cleared up. Gradually one after another of the characters mentioned has been identified with some historical personage, or found in some genealogical table, until the whole composition of the poem has been laid clear, while a possible background for Beowulf himself has been discovered in a widely-spread folk-tale. It is even thought that the burial mounds of three of the Swedish kings may be identified near Upsala.

But before discussing its subject matter further it will be well to begin with an outline of the poem itself.

The poet starts with a short account of the prosperous reign of Scyld Scefing, king of the Danes, telling how he increased his fame and extended his territory till, at the appointed time, he departed in a ship loaded with treasures

Passage from the Beowulf MS., showing the two handwritings.
The second begins with l. 4

and arms, in the same mysterious way in which he had
come to the Danish shores as a child.   His son Beowulf,
who must be carefully distinguished from the hero of the
poem, succeeded to Scyld's lands and fame ; his son was
the lofty Healfdene, who had four children, of whom the
eldest, Heorogar, succeeded him for a short time only,
the second son, Hroþgar, being king of the Danes at the time
of the events dealt with in our poem.   The poet then goes
on to tell how Hroþgar wished to build himself a magnificent
meadhall :—

> It came into his mind,
> that he would bid men make
> a mighty meadhouse, greater
> than the sons of men had ever known,
> and there within would deal out all
> to young and old, which God had given to him,
> all save the " folkshare " and the lives of men.
> Then I heard far and wide the work proclaimed
> to many a race throughout this middle world
> to adorn the folkstead.   To him in due course came,
> quickly as men count time, that it was all complete,
> this mightiest of hall dwellings.   He gave it Heorot for a
>   name,
> whose word had power far and wide.
> His vow he broke not, rings he gave,
> treasure at the banquet. . . .
> There was the sound of the harp,
> the clear song of the bard.

But in the moors and fens near dwelt the monster Grendel
and his mother, and these sounds of revelry in the hall
stirred him to anger only.   Night after night he made his way
to Heorot, carrying off the thanes to be devoured in his den :—

> This thing of evil,
> grim and greedy, soon was ready,
> fierce and angry, and from their beds
> snatched thirty thanes ; thence back he turned,
> exulting in his booty to fare home,
> with that full slaughter sought his dwelling-place. . . .
> Nor was it a longer space
> than till the next night that he wrought again

yet greater fatal ill, not shrinking from it,
from open harm and hidden, he was too set on them.

This went on for twelve years till none would sleep in the hall, and Grendel, this foe of mankind, this dire and lonely wanderer, as he is called, took up his abode in it by night, working all kinds of wickedness, though he might never do injury to the throne, " that precious object he despised, he knew no wish for it." This story of the woes of the Danes spread far into the surrounding countries. It reached the ears of Beowulf, the son of Ecgþeow, in his home at the court of the Geats and led him to resolve on the rescue. With fourteen chosen comrades he set sail and after a prosperous journey arrived with them in the land of the Danes. When they had declared their race and explained their purpose, they were guided to the court and well received by Hroþgar whom Beowulf addresses :—

Hail to thee Hroþgar ! I am of the kin
of Hygelac, and his thane. Many a deed of fame
have I attempted in my youth. To me the affair of Grendel
within my native land was clearly told.
Sea travellers relate how this hall stands,
this noblest dwelling, for every warrior
empty and useless, as soon as evening's light
beneath the vault of heaven has been hid.

.   .   .

Therefore I from thee,
O ! Prince of Bright-Danes ! will now beg,
thou Shield of Scyldings ! for one single boon,
that thou wilt not refuse me, lord of warriors !
the people's noble friend, now I am come thus far,
that I alone, with but my band of men,
with this bold troop, may cleanse this Heorot.

Unferþ, however, the spokesman of Hroþgar was jealous of Beowulf and, as they sat together in the hall, began to taunt him with what he called his failure :—

Art thou that Beowulf, who did strive with Breca
in the wide ocean didst contend in swimming ?
where ye for pride explored the waves,
and for a foolish boast ventured your lives
in the deep waters . . .

seven nights ye toiled, he in the sea outswam thee,
he had the greater strength.

Now, he went on, Beowulf will have a yet harder task before
him. The latter, however, put aside the scoff with dignity,
explaining that it was he who had won, but would not
leave Breca till the force of the current and the wind drove
them apart, and how, being fully armed, he had been able
to defend himself from the sea beasts which attacked him, and
to destroy them, until he was finally carried on to the shore
of the Finns. At this point Hroþgar's queen, Wealhþeow,
entered the hall and filled the goblets of the warriors according to custom, and thus the day passed away till nightfall.

That night Beowulf with the other Geat warriors lay down
to rest in Heorot, but not undisturbed. Again Grendel
approached the hall :—

Then came the " warrior " journeying to the hall,
outcast from joy ; the door at once fell open,
though fast with fire-forged bands, when he touched it with
  his hands,
intent on ill he swung it open, since he was swollen with rage,
the dwelling's mouth. Quickly then
along the bright paved floor the demon stalked,
wrathful of mood he went ; from out his eyes there gleamed
a hideous light most like to fire.
Within the hall he saw then many warriors,
the band of kinsmen, sleeping there together,
the company of thanes. Then his heart rejoiced,
he thought how he would sever, ere the day should come,
this direful monster, in each of these,
body from soul, since now had come to him
the hope of an abundant feast.

By no means did the monster think to delay,
but he seized quickly in the first place
a sleeping warrior, tore him unawares,
bit into his body, drank his blood in streams,
swallowed him in large mouthfuls. Soon he had
devoured the whole of the lifeless one,
even his feet and his hands. Further in and nearer he came,
seized in his grasp the doughty-hearted
warrior on his couch.

G

But he (Beowulf) was ready for him. Propping himself up on his arm, he seized the evil-minded one and closed with him.

A fierce fight followed, in which even the benches were wrenched away from their places, but at last Beowulf succeeded in tearing off a hand, arm, and shoulder of the monster, though he failed to hold him altogether, and Grendel escaped away thus wounded to the fen to die there. Great were the rejoicings in the morning, the day was spent in racing and feasting while minstrels sang of Sigemund and Finn and their glorious deeds, and Hroþgar rewarded Beowulf with rich gifts of armour and steeds. But the joy was short-lived. Grendel had been killed but his mother, a monster too, and almost as terrible, still lived, burning to avenge her son. That very night while the Danes, with renewed confidence, were sleeping in Heorot, and Beowulf had been given a place within the palace, she broke into the hall and killed and carried off Aeschere, an old and trusty councillor of Hroþgar, though the other warriors perceived her approach in time to defend themselves. Thus sorrow was renewed in Heorot.

Having been aroused, Beowulf at once offered to go in search of the hag in order to avenge Aeschere, and was directed to the mere at the bottom of which she and her son lived. He is told that :—

> They (the monsters) o'er hidden regions
> range, wolf-haunted slopes, and wind-blown cliffs,
> wild fen tracks, where the mountain stream
> under the darkness of the headlands passes down,
> a flood beneath the earth. It is not far from here,
> as marked by miles, that the mere lies,
> over which hang rime-clad groves,
> a wood fast rooted leans above the water.
> There may be seen each night a fearsome wonder,
> fire on the flood. None lives so wise
> of the sons of men, that he may know its depth.
> Though the heath ranger, hard pressed by hounds,
> the hart mighty of antler, should seek the woodland grove,
> put to flight from afar, sooner will he give up his life,
> his breath upon the shore than he will enter in

to hide his head. That is no canny place
whence rises up the tumult of the waves,
dark to the heavens.

And it is here that Beowulf may find the hag.

Accordingly with his company of Geats and an escort of
Danes he went forth over narrow paths and solitudes to where
the mere lay. Armed as he was, he leapt in, but the depth
was so great that it took him a good part of a day to
reach the bottom :—

> Then the warrior perceived
> that he was in some unknown hostile dwelling
> where the water could do him naught of harm,
> nor, for the hall's roof, could it reach him,
> the deadly touch of the flood. A light as of fire he saw,
> a white gleam shining brightly.
> Then, valiant, he perceived the outcast of the deep,
> a mighty sea-wife.

He gave her a tremendous blow with all his force with his
sword, but—

> then the stranger found
> that the gleam of battle (his sword) would not bite,
> do injury to life, but its blade gave way
> at the need of its lord. Oft before had it endured
> fight, hand to hand, had often pierced the helm,
> the armour of one doomed ; now for the first time
> for the costly treasure did its virtue fail.

Finding the sword he has brought useless (one lent him by
a repentant Unferþ [1]), Beowulf seized a gigantic one from
the wall and at length overcame his foe, though this
second sword was melted by her blood.

On his return to the surface he found that the Danes,
deceived by the blood-stained waves, had given him up
for dead and gone home. His own Geats were, however,
still there and received him with great joy. All set out for
the court, four men being hardly able between them to
carry the head of Grendel, which Beowulf had cut off when
he found the monster lying dead below. Once more Heorot
was full of joy, till night drew on and all went to rest.

---

[1] Or perhaps lent in malice, as known to be of no use against magic.

Beowulf's mission was now accomplished, and he and his companions were eager to leave. The parting was cordial on both sides, Beowulf promising the friendship and help of the Geats if needed again by the Danes, and the aged Hroþgar presenting his with fresh gifts, and embracing him with tears :—

> The man was so dear to him
> that he could not restrain the trouble of his breast,
> but in his heart, fast in the bonds of thought,
> for the beloved one a secret longing
> burnt in his blood.

Beowulf and his followers then set sail and arrived in due time in the country of the Geats where they were well received by King Hygelac, Beowulf's uncle, and by his queen, the youthful Hygd, famed for her queenly and womanly virtues. To these Beowulf related in full his adventures since he set out, and presented many of Hroþgar's gifts.

Here the first part of the story ends. In the second the poet goes on to tell how some years passed in peace and prosperity till Hygelac died and was succeeded by his son Heardred, whom Beowulf served as faithfully as Hygelac. But Heardred's reign was a short one ; the Geats were frequently at war with their neighbours, the Swedes, and Heardred was therefore willing to afford a refuge to Eanmund and Eadgils, the nephews of the Swedish king Onela, when having rebelled against their uncle they were obliged to flee the country. Onela pursued them and, in the battle which followed, Heardred and Eanmund were killed, and Beowulf succeeded to the throne of the Geats, over which he reigned fifty years. But now in his old age his kingdom was disturbed by the inroads of a fiery dragon.

Some hundreds of years before men had collected an immense treasure and the last survivor had buried it in a cavern near the seashore, singing the following dirge :—

> Do thou hold now, O earth ! since men may not
> these treasures, once of nobles. Lo ! in earlier days upon thee,
> these, valiant ones attained ; death in fight has seized them,
> dire life-bale, each one of the living
> of my people, who have given up this life.

They had known joy in the hall. Now have I no one who
    may bear the sword,
or polish the golden plated flagon,
the costly drinking cup. The valiant ones have passed else-
    where.
The hard helmet, adorned with gold,
must lose its ornaments, the armourers sleep
whose duty was to tend the battle mask,
so shall the warcoat, which in fight withstood,
over the crash of shields, the bite of iron blades,
rust, left behind the warrior ; nor may the corslet's rings
with the war leader travel far
upon the hero's side. There is no joy from the harp,
nor melody from the wood (the harp). Nor does the bold
    hawk
swing through the hall. Baleful death has
driven far hence many living races.

The treasure had remained in the cave after his death
till discovered by a dragon with poisonous fiery breath,
who had guarded it ever since. But one day a slave, escaping
from his lord, stumbled upon the place and, venturing in,
found the dragon asleep in it amidst his treasure. Though
terrified at the sight, he yet had presence of mind to carry
off one costly goblet as a peace offering to his enraged lord.
When, however, the dragon awoke he scented the intruder
and presently missed the goblet. His anger was roused and
the whole neighbourhood made to suffer. Scouring round in
search of his foe, he set fire to farms and homesteads, even
to Beowulf's own palace, till the whole countryside was
filled with consternation. News of this was brought to
the aged king, into whose possession also had come the
stolen cup. Old as he was, he determined on one last adventure to punish the dragon and to secure the treasure for
his people. He set out therefore with eleven followers and
the serf to guide them to the place. They reached the cave
beneath the cliffs close to the rolling sea, and Beowulf called
loudly on the dragon. In answer came first a blast of fiery
breath from out the cave ; then he himself came writhing
along the ground towards them in tortuous coils and the
fight began. Beowulf's iron shield, made expressly against

the dragon's fiery breath, helped him, but his sword splintered
on the monster's hard hide, and he was for a moment in
deadly peril. His followers, terrified at the dragon, had fled
into the wood for safety, all except one, the bold Wiglaf,
who made his way through the flame and smoke to his
lord's side, at the same time calling upon his companions
to do their duty and show their gratitude for Beowulf's
past generosity :—

> I recall the time when we received the mead cup,
> when we vowed to our lord
> in the hall, when he gave us these rings (coats of mail),
> that we would repay to him this battle gear,
> should need like this e'er come upon him,
> these helmets and hard swords.
>   Now is the day come
> that our lord has need of the strength
> of bold warriors. Let us go up,
> to help our warrior prince, while this may last,
> this grim fire-terror. God knows of me,
> that to me t'were liefer that my body,
> with my gold-giver's, flames should seize.
> Unmeet it seems to me that we should bear our shields
> back to our homes, unless we first may
> fell the foe and guard the life
> of the Weders' lord.

When Wiglaf's own wooden shield was burnt by the hot
breath of the dragon, he continued to fight behind Beowulf's.
But not till Beowulf drew his short sword and cut the
monster in two could they overcome him, and then Beowulf
himself was wounded to the death and died, giving thanks
to God for the life granted to him :—

> Now I would give my son
> my battle weeds, if had been granted me
> an heir to my inheritance, to follow me,
> of my body. I have held this people
> for fifty winters ; there was no king,
> not any one of those around
> who durst approach me with his battle friends (swords),
> or threat me with his terror. I have lived in this land
> my appointed time. I have held well what was mine,

nor sought hostility with craft, nor sworn many
oaths in falsehood. For all this may I now
when sick with mortal wounds have joy,
because the Ruler of mankind shall have no cause
to reproach in me the death of kinsmen, now that
my soul must leave my body.

A magnificent funeral pyre was prepared for him by his
people, and afterwards a lofty mound erected on the spot
as a memorial of his deeds, while the dragon and treasures
were pushed together over the cliff into the sea, where
neither could bring evil to mankind in the future.

CHAPTER V

BEOWULF (*continued*)

The subject matter of Beowulf contains both historical and fabulous elements. It has grown up out of a union of history and folk-tale. As had already been said, most of the persons and many of the events dealt with have a historical basis. They are mentioned by independent Latin writers or in O.N. documents which may be considered reliable for the main facts, or in later Latin writings based on such documents. The figure, however, of the hero Beowulf himself cannot be traced, and his feats against Grendel, the hag, and the dragon, as well as some other incidents, are obviously taken from folk-tale. In fact the main story is fiction, the epic of the Deeds of Beowulf is really a glorified folk-tale, given substance by the introduction of historical characters as background, dignity by the beauty and sincerity of the telling, and further possessing all the fascination of tales of high adventure. In the first part of Beowulf two tribes play the chief rôles, the Geats and the Danes. Attempts have been made to identify the Geats with the Jutes, but it is more probable that they were the Gautar of O.N. records, the modern Götar. The name corresponds exactly and the position assigned to them is right. We know that the Gautar occupied at that time the southern part of Sweden, except a small district along the southern extremity of the peninsula, which was inhabited by Danes. Their country would correspond more or less to the modern Gottland.[1]

The Danes were scattered. They lived in this southernmost tract of Sweden, the modern Skaney, called in Beowulf Scedenigge, on the islands of the Danish Archipelago and in the northern part of the present Danish peninsula. The

[1] See R. W. Chambers, Beowulf: an Introduction, pp. 8 ff., for a summary of the arguments.

terms, East, South, and West Danes, given them in Beowulf, are rather from a general sense of their scattered position than used with any definite geographical application. The site of Heorot, the banqueting hall built by king Hroþgar, is now usually identified with the modern village of Leire, in the island of Zealand, the old Danish capital, the name of which appears first in O.N. literature as Hleiþr and later in Latin texts as Lethra. Of the Geat princes mentioned in Beowulf, Hreþel and his three sons, Herebeald, Hæþcyn, and Hygelac, Beowulf himself, and perhaps his father Ecgþeow, the only certainly historical character is Hygelac. He must have been a personage of some importance, for he is undoubtedly the king whose fatal expedition is mentioned by three Latin authors. Gregory of Tours, writing in the later sixth century, tells us in his Historia Francorum [1] that a certain Chlochilaicus invaded the realm of the Frankish king Theodoric and, after overrunning it, returned to his ship laden with booty; but, before he could set sail, he was overtaken by Theodoric's son Theodobert with fresh troops, overthrown, and the booty recovered.

Our next authority is the Liber Francorum, of about 727. Here Theodoric is called king of the Attoarios, who must be the Hattuarii of other Latin writers and the Hetware of Beowulf, which gives another point of connection. In this account the name occurs as Chlochilaico and Chochilago. Thirdly comes the Liber Monstrorum, somewhat later. This corrects one point which is wrong in the other stories. While they both make Hygelac a Dane, this third authority says he ruled over the Geti, and adds that his bones are preserved on an island in the Rhine and shown as marvels. The king's name also is nearer in this third version. One MS. has it as Huiglaucus, which may easily be a miswriting for Hugilaicus, the Latinized form of an earlier Hugilaic, which would be exactly the O.E. Hygelac. This expedition took place about 520; it must evidently have made a considerable sensation, for besides these mentions it is referred to four times in Beowulf, at vv. 1202 ff.; 2354 ff.;

[1] p. 110 in Monumenta Germaniæ Historica.

2501 ff., and 2913 ff., and it is told with some fulness. Though Beowulf is not mentioned by any of the Latin writers, there is probably a slight foundation for him in some warrior who escaped from the general destruction. But the Beowulf who appears in our poem must be mainly from another source. Not only does his name not occur elsewhere but, as Professor Chambers [1] has pointed out, it does not alliterate with those of the other Geat kings mentioned, as it would have done had he belonged historically to that dynasty. Moreover the absorption of the Geats into the Swedes, which is known to have taken place later, would hardly have followed a prosperous reign of fifty years as that of Beowulf is described to have been. It is much more likely to have happened after the ineffective reign of the weak Heardred. Both these considerations point to Beowulf having been introduced among the historical figures from another source, and that source may well have been a folk-tale. The reason for the connection of the folk-tale with the story of the death of Hygelac can only be conjectured. If some warrior did distinguish himself by a conspicuous feat of swimming he might gradually have been made the hero of other tales of similar deeds of prowess, and been merged finally in the figure of the folk-tale hero, who performed his great feat under the water.

For the Danes the Saga of Hrolf Kraki, and the Latin history of Saxo Grammaticus, written about 1200, and based upon Danish and Icelandic tradition and records, helped out by occasional mentions in other sagas and elsewhere, are our chief authorities.

For the members of the Danish royal family we have more historical background. Those mentioned in Beowulf are Scyld, the founder of the dynasty, Healfdene, Heorogar and his son Heoroweard, Hroþgar and his two sons, Hreþric and Hroþmund, and Halga and his son Hrothulf. Nearly all these are mentioned in one source or another, though differences occur between the various accounts. Thus in Beowulf the prominent member of the family is Hroþgar, whereas in the Hrolf Kraki Saga and in Saxo it is his nephew

---

[1] Beowulf: An Introduction, pp. 10 ff.

Hroþulf, Saxo's Roe, who plays the chief part. In Beowulf Hroþulf's importance is only vaguely hinted at in one passage in which he is represented as sitting on the high seat beside Hroþgar, while the king's own sons only occupy places among the other young warriors in the body of the hall.

Scyld was probably a historical character originally, but what we are told of him in the poem is obviously legendary or even mythical.

It is significant that the Danes begin to be mentioned by Latin writers in the sixth century ; the increasing importance of the tribe thus implied would explain Hroþgar's need for a new hall and a larger one. This must have been built at the very beginning of the century, to allow for the twelve years of Grendel's ravages and for Beowulf to have had a year or two at home after killing the monsters before Hygelac's fatal expedition.

In the second part of the poem the historical element is greater in proportion to the fictitious. This part deals with the constant quarrels between the Geats and the Swedes.

Among the Swedes are mentioned Ongenþeow, his sons Onela and Ohthere, and Ohthere's sons Eadgils and Eanmund, most of whom are found in Old Norse stories, though not always in the same connection. Here our chief source of information is the Inglinga Tal which is considered fairly reliable. In this the name of Ohthere occurs in the form Ottarr, that of Eadgils as Aðils, and that of Onela as Ali, though by this time the story has become obscured and Ali is no longer Aðils's uncle, but a Norwegian prince. Aðils, or Athileus as he is called there, is also mentioned by Saxo in connection with Hrolf Kraki, but the story told of him is different. Saxo seems to have confused two characters of the same name.

But this is not all. Not only are most of the principal characters, as we have seen, historical, or at any rate, with some historical foundation, but the same may be said of many of the minor personages.

When the poet is describing Beowulf's return home and wishes to emphasize the virtues of Queen Hygd, he does so by contrasting her with Þryþ, the fierce wife of Offa, who is certainly historical. He is the fourth century king of the Angles while they were still on the continent. Further in the same scene Beowulf is made to say that he had met at Hroþgar's court Ingeld the son of Froda. These are personages found in Saxo and in O.N. stories and, while the tales show a good deal of diversity and much of what is said is untrustworthy, there must be some common source for these versions and probably a historical background. Then earlier in the poem after singing the deeds of Sigemund, the poet introduces a certain Heremod by way of contrast. This name occurs in W.S. genealogies where he is called the father of Scyld, and it has been suggested that it may have been given to a certain Lotherus, son of Dan, of whom Saxo tells a story somewhat similar to that told in Beowulf of Heremod. Both were at first welcomed by their subjects, but both failed to fulfil the expectations of the people and were dethroned for their cruel tyranny. Finally it is generally supposed that there is some historical foundation for the figures of Finn, son of Folcwalda, and of Breca, though no definite background has yet been found for either.

But numerous as the historical characters in Beowulf are, and important as are the rôles they play, it is the fabulous or folk-tale element which has come to be the main theme of the whole work. Again it is better to take the two parts separately. In the first part the essentials of the story may be said to be the fight of a young hero, who has come across the sea from a distance, first with a man monster who has been working havoc in a hall, and later with a female monster in a hall which is under the water and full of treasure. The origin of this story has been a subject of much discussion and cannot yet be said to be finally settled. Former scholars endeavoured to explain it as having been developed out of a nature myth, and various interpretations have been given. Perhaps the most widely accepted theory was that of Müllenhoff.[1] He took the story to represent the conquest of the destructive forces of the sea along the coast of the North Sea. Beowulf he explained

[1] Beowulf: Untersuchungen, pp. 3–4.

as a divine helper who came to the rescue of the people against the inundations which occurred in spring along that low-lying coast before the construction of dykes. Grendel was the inundation, the hag the bottom of the sea whence came the inundating waves. The dragon fight was the autumn counterpart, in which the hostile force triumphed. Sarrazin,[1] on the other hand, saw in the various monsters fatal exhalations rising at night from the surrounding swampy ground, from which the hero saved the people.

But however ingenious and sometimes suggestive these explanations may be, it is now the general opinion that we have to look to folk-lore for our source rather than to nature myth. Now Old Norse literature offers us several stories which have a marked resemblance to the fights as told in Beowulf. In the Grettis Saga, Grettir kills two trolls, one a woman and the other a man, and the account is strikingly like that in Beowulf. Elsewhere in the same story he overcomes the destructive ghost of the shepherd Glam, and again certain points in the narrative recall forcibly the Beowulf adventure. In the Hrolf Kraki Saga the figure of a certain Böðvarr Bjarki shows remarkable points of resemblance with that of Beowulf. The tale of Orm Storolfsson is less close, but it is yet important enough to deserve consideration.

The story as told in the Grettis Saga goes as follows :—

The bonder (or small farmer) of Sandheaps remained at home one Yuletide while his wife went to service at the neighbouring town of Isle-dale River. During the night a great disturbance was heard round his bed and in the morning he had disappeared. The next year the good wife went again to her service, leaving behind in charge an excusably reluctant servant. In the morning he too had disappeared and bloodstains were found about the door. The third year the outlaw Grettir, having heard the report, came to the farm, giving his name as Guest, and undertook to lie in wait. He shut himself alone in the hall and lay down without taking off his clothes. At midnight a great din arose outside and in came a huge troll wife

---

[1] Beowulf Studien, p. 65.

carrying a trough in one hand and a chopper in the other. Grettir sprang up and they wrestled together till even the cross panelling of the room gave way and the fittings of the outer door, as the troll tried to carry Grettir away towards the river. When, however, they reached the bank Grettir managed to swing the troll round and draw his short sword with which he cut off her arm. Upon this she fell into the water and was carried down into a whirlpool. Grettir rested for a while and then went home all swollen and blue as he was. The farmer's wife on her return thought that her hall had been much mishandled! After resting some days Grettir took the priest Steinn with him to the point where the troll had disappeared and, giving him a rope with which to draw him up again, leapt off the rock into the water, lightly armed and girt with his short sword only. Behind a waterfall in the river he found a great cave and in it a terrible giant. They fought and Grettir cut in two the giant's sword and obliged him to reach out for another, a magic one hanging on the wall. Seizing the moment of this diversion, Grettir struck him in the breast and killed him. The priest seeing the water stained with blood, concluded that it was Grettir who had been killed, dropped the rope and went home. Grettir stayed for a time to examine the cave in which he found much treasure and the bones of two men, then, managing to climb out unaided, he returned home with these in a bag. The points of resemblance with the Beowulf story are so obvious that one need only notice the differences. In the Grettis Saga the attacks are yearly, in Beowulf nightly; in the Saga the female monster attacks and the male is found in the hall, in Beowulf it is the reverse. In the Saga the part played by the followers is taken by the priest, a later Christian touch, and the giant has to find the second sword, not the hero. Grettir goes to look for the two men who have been killed, he knows nothing of a second monster, Beowulf knows definitely of her existence, and goes to find her, incidentally returning with the head of Grendel.

The story of Glam comes earlier in the book and has only one monster, but in it the resemblance to the fight

in Beowulf comes out strongly in the details.   Grettir,
having heard of the ravages of the ghost of the thrall Glam,
who was wont to haunt a certain farmhouse, riding the
house-top at night and making a great disturbance,
volunteered to watch for him. When he went in to the farm
he observed traces of former attacks in that the fittings
were all broken away from the outer door, the partition
panelling injured and the beds torn from their places.
" An uncouth place it was." Now when men should go to sleep
Grettir would not put off his clothes, but lay down on the
seat against the bonder's bed, wrapped himself up in his
cloak and set his feet against the seatbeam, which was
a very strong one." Glam came as usual. As the door opened
Grettir saw how the thrall thrust in his head which seemed
to him monstrous big and roughhewn.   The monster fared
slowly when he got inside the door, turning and looking
along the hall and glaring over the place. Grettir lay still,
and Glam seeing that some bundle lay on the seat, stalked
up along the hall and gripped at the bundle wondrous hard,
but Grettir set his foot against the beam and moved in
no wise.   Glam pulled again much harder but still the
wrapper moved not.   With a third attempt, however, he
drew Grettir upright off the seat and they struggled together,
wrecking the hall, driving the seatbeams out of place, and
breaking all that was before them till Glam was fain to
get out. He tried to drag Grettir with him but the latter
resisted seeing that if it was ill to deal with him indoors,
it would be worse outside. On the threshold Grettir fell
and in his fall broke asunder roof, rafters, and frozen thatch.
Finally Glam was killed and his head cut off. Here again
the points of resemblance need no comment.

The story of Böðvarr Bjarki is less like in general but
has certain touches in which the similarity is striking.
It goes thus :—

Böðvarr Bjarki was the son of the Norwegian prince Biorn
(or the Bear) and the peasant maiden Bera. His father
died early and he was brought up at the court of King
Hring of Updal. One of his brothers, Ðorir, was king of
Gautland (Geatland of Beowulf). While on a visit to him,

Böðvarr heard of the condition of things at the court of King Hrolf Kraki at Lethra (identified with Heorot) in Denmark and went to help him. Having arrived, he went into the hall and sat down at one end of it and when the other warriors jeered at the timid Hottr and threw bones at him, Böðvarr took his part. He thus got involved in a quarrel in which a warrior was killed. The king, however, when told of it, upheld Böðvarr and eventually took him into his service. As the Yuletide approached Böðvarr observed that the courtiers were becoming anxious and asked the reason. He learned that for two years past a winged monster, huge and horrible, had appeared at that time and done much damage. No weapon could wound it ; in fact, it was really not a beast but a troll. When Christmas came the king forbade his men to venture against this monster, the cattle must take their chance. All promised to obey, but, when night was come, Böðvarr crept out with the unwilling Hottr, carrying him when he was too frightened to walk. The monster appeared, Hottr screamed and ran, but Böðvarr drew his sword and killed him with one stroke, making Hottr drink the blood to give him courage. Then follows an incident which would have been impossible in an Old English story with its grave dignity. Having killed him, Böðvarr and Hottr set up the dead monster to make it appear alive. In the morning the cattle were found unharmed, but the herdsmen were terrified when they saw the beast. When the king came with his courtiers, Böðvarr, to the astonishment of the king, made Hottr go up and attack it. Of course, at the first blow it fell down and all supposed that Hottr had killed it, and the coward was henceforward looked upon as a hero. Here the points of resemblance are chiefly in detail. Like Beowulf, Böðvarr comes from the land of the Gautar or Geats, having heard there of the misfortunes happening in Lethra or Heorot. Like Beowulf he gets at once into a quarrel, though here it is not the hero who is twitted but another warrior. The ravages are yearly and not nightly, a variation which we have seen in the Grettis Saga too. Hrolf Kraki belongs to the same Danish family as Hroþgar, he is the Hroþulf of the Beowulf. It is impossible not to be struck by the similarities.

In the story of Orm Storolfsson, Asbjorn and Orm were sworn brothers. Asbjorn was killed in a cave beside the sea by the giant Brusi, and many of his followers were killed and devoured by Brusi's mother, a monstrous black cat. Orm was in Iceland whence he came two years later to avenge his friend. It was the cat which attacked him first, and the fight was desperate. Orm used a bow and arrows, but she bit all in two. In his extremity Orm prayed to God and St. Peter, vowing to go to Rome if they would help him. After this the power of the huge cat diminished and Orm succeeded in breaking her back. Next he attacked Brusi and killed him in horrible fashion. Here we have two of the essential points in the story. There are two monsters, male and female, and the conqueror comes across the sea. Otherwise the resemblance is not so marked. Still the similarity in outline or in detail in these stories suggests that they all go back to a common source and that the points of divergence are of later growth.

In 1910 an extremely interesting theory was brought forward by Professor Panzer,[1] in which he identified this source with a widely spread folk-tale, which he called that of the Bear's Son. He has collected variants from almost all parts of Europe and even from Asia, tracing the tale back to a time before the Christian era. In all versions the common features are that the hero has been brought up by wild beasts or is only half of human parentage. He defends a hall or castle from a demon which always comes at night, succeeding when others (usually his elder brothers) fail by being unable to keep awake. Two monsters are involved, one a man and the other a woman, they live underground and the hero tracks the one first wounded down to his lair by blood-stains, leaving companions or a companion above to wait for him. In the lair he finds great treasure and kills the second monster, succeeding in making his escape with his booty, though his companions have given him up and gone away. Most of these features

---

[1] Studien zur germanischen Sagengeschichte : I, Beowulf, München.

occur in the versions given above, and it is possible that the North-West of Europe had evolved a special form of the tale for itself, emphasizing the features shown in these Old Norse and Old English forms.

Many more analogues exist, all dealing with fights with monsters under or behind waterfalls, and some with further details not found in Beowulf, showing how widely the story had spread. But these given are the most important.[1]

To return to Beowulf.

>This is not the work of an unsophisticated gleeman. Conscious skill is shown in the development of the theme as a whole, as well as in the treatment of individual episodes. There is a definite framework to the poem ; it does not perhaps show out very clearly, but it is there, indeed it seems to have been taken as a model by later writers. The structure of the Andreas is very similar and may well have been influenced by it.

Thus the poet begins with the genealogy of the Danish kings up to Hroþgar, passing on to the building of Heorot, and thus leading the way to his main theme. The need of the larger hall suggests a state of prosperity for the Danes and thus throws into stronger relief by contrast the distress caused by the ravages of Grendel. The fact also of the tale of his depredations spreading so quickly to the Geats living inland on the Scandinavian peninsula, helps further to heighten this effect. Little is actually told us about Beowulf at this stage, but his heroic quality is to be inferred from the promptness with which he comes to the rescue.

Having thus introduced his subject and set his stage, the poet begins his real story. But the movement is slow at first. The ceremonious reception of Beowulf by Hroþgar is told at some length, with the account of the swimming match between Beowulf and Breca, and Beowulf's dignified rejoinder to the twitting of Unferþ. Even when the poet has got Beowulf and his Geats into the hall for the night, he still holds the action back. It has been pointed out that he seems to make three attempts to begin the narrative of

---

[1] For a suggestion for the origin of these monster folk-tales, see an article by Gustav Hubener in Eng. Stud., 62, 3.

Grendel's inroad. We have at v. 710 " Ða cōm of mōre " ; at v. 714 " Wōd under wolcnum " ; and at v. 720, " Cōm ða tō recede." But the criticism is not quite fair, for each so-called beginning marks a different stage in the action and was probably intentional, and when the poet has stimulated the interest of his audience sufficiently by these feints, and lets himself go, the movement is swift and vigorous and he gives an extraordinarily vivid picture of the noise and confusion in the hall while the fight is raging. Doubtless the poet has weakened the effect of this climax by adding the second fight with the hag, but the two were in his original and he could not help himself. Moreover he has saved himself from the reproach of repetition by differentiating the two entirely in treatment. While the first fight is a real rough and tumble struggle between two men, monstrous but human, in the second we have a large supernatural element. Beowulf takes several hours to swim down to the cave, and when he gets there it is full of treasures, among which is a magic sword, and the destruction of the hag can only be brought about by the help of magic. In spite of the wealth of detail in the description of the second fight, the poet seems to imply that he intended that with Grendel to be his climax, since he expressly tells us that the hag was less terrible than her son. The cutting off of Grendel's head and the whole scene in the cave was meant to be the conclusion of the fight in the hall, and the final overthrow of the primary monster.

It is now agreed that the fight with the dragon did not originally belong to the Grendel story. Whether our poet joined the two together or whether they had been joined before, he shows a clear sense that the dragon story must not be made so important as the Grendel adventures. As he begins his whole poem with the genealogy of Hroþgar, so he rounds it off with the later history of his hero. He takes him home to his uncle, king Hygelac, relates very shortly how he eventually succeeded him, and then describes his death, of which the fight with the dragon is the cause. The essential theme of the second part of Beowulf is really an elegy on the death of a hero, to which has been given, as historical background or setting, episodes from the wars between the Swedes and the Geats.

A criticism frequently made against the Beowulf poem is that the poet has interrupted and somewhat obscured the central story by the many interpolations. When Beowulf is being received by Hroþgar, the poet stops to give us a long account of his earlier swimming contest with Breca. After the killing of Grendel there are naturally great rejoicings, and we are told that the scop entertained the warriors with the stories of Sigemund and Heremod and later with that of Finn. When Beowulf returns home to the land of the Geats, he is made to tell king Hygelac all the tragedy of Ingeld, and an allusion is introduced to the Anglian Offa and his virago queen Þryþ.

It must be allowed that this criticism is true to some extent. Nevertheless, the interpolations have their value. The story of Sigemund is short and does not interrupt much, moreover it comes in quite naturally. How could the scop pay a better compliment to Beowulf than by comparing him with Sigemund, who also killed a dragon and whose fame had, we know, spread far and wide into other countries than his own? Heremod is mentioned still more briefly and strictly in connection with the main story. He is introduced as an " awful example ", as a warning to Beowulf of a king who, at first popular, allowed himself to abuse his power and to degenerate into a tyrant. The story of Þryþ, again, is told quite shortly and is obviously only introduced to bring out by contrast the virtues of the gentle Hygd. It might be said that the fault is not so much in the insertion of these episodes as in the abruptness with which it is done. But they were well-known stories to the hearers for whom they were intended, and it is only to the modern reader that the aptness of their introduction is not so apparent.

To the interpolation of the Finn and Breca episodes, however, the criticism applies with more force. For the Breca story it may be said that it does give a more vivid idea of the daring and courageous generosity of the youthful Beowulf than any mere description would have done, and in that way it does serve a definite purpose, and if it had been shorter, its insertion would have been fully justified. The same cannot be said of the Finn episode. It has no bearing on the central story, as we have seen the others have. It is told in a manner very different from the rest of Beowulf, and in telling it, the poet has been carried away by the fineness of his theme and has forgotten, beyond the merest mention at the beginning and end that it is the song of the scop in Heorot, to subordinate it in any way to the main story. Indeed the very power of the tale tends to divert the attention of the reader from that main story. And yet we readily forgive the poet for, since the epic from which the episode is taken is lost, we would not willingly be without this glimpse into it which the Beowulf affords. The weak point in the Ingeld allusion is quite different. It is told shortly and does not delay the action much, and it serves to give us a picture of Hroþgar's court with its varied company, but, as generally interpreted, the poet is so carried away by his interest in his own characters that he makes Beowulf tell of events which had not happened yet. It is a good subject, a young prince torn between his love for his wife and his duty of avenging his father's death at the hands of her father. We may sympathize with the temptation to stray off to it, but nevertheless the story has no business there. On the whole, however, the poet may be said to be justified in these insertions; he has widened his theme by them and given us a better picture of the life he is describing, if at times he has allowed himself too long a digression.

The main interest of Beowulf is, of course, the story; the nature element is slight beside it, and generally as background only, but one passage stands out in strong relief. As in all genuine O.E. poetry, the aspects of nature described are stern or even gloomy and always in harmony with the action of the story. It remained for a later time for the poet of the M.H.G. Nibelungenlied of the thirteenth century to realize the effect of contrast and to heighten the pathos of the death of Siegfried by making him fall among the flowers. In Beowulf the fen in which Grendel and the hag live is reached across desolate moorlands. When Beowulf is killed it is again in dreary country near the sea and with forests close by in which his followers can hide themselves. It is true that when Beowulf sets sail for Hroþgar's court, the sea is calm, whereas in O.E. poetry as a rule only the sea in storm is dwelt upon at any length. But there is reason for this. The important thing was for Beowulf to get there quickly and the hearers were not to be distracted from the main theme by any stirring description of the sea. Here too, therefore, nature was in sympathy with the action, a suitable background for it. But as has already been said, there is one passage in Beowulf in which the poet enhances the effect of the action by a description of nature of extraordinary force and beauty. This is in telling of the mere in which Grendel and his mother dwelt. If[1] the poet has mixed up Danish and English scenery in his mere, and the " nikkers " and other monsters have no business in an English lake, they are most certainly there. The poet, vague as he generally is in his landscapes, has had sufficient imagination not only to see them for himself, but to convince his readers of their presence. The mere described is an inland lake, not an arm of the sea as has been suggested.[2] Every reader will be reminded of some bit of country which he knows and which with a little imagination could be taken as the original, so vivid is the presentation. It is not merely as background.

>If the poet of Beowulf has shown skill as a story-teller, he has proved his poetic quality no less in the richness of his vocabulary and in his brilliant use of the devices of the kenning and variation.

As in all O.E. poetry this richness of vocabulary appears chiefly in the terms for the lord, and for anything to do with the sea and warfare. Thus, for the idea of the lord we have not only terms like " cyning ", " dryhten ", " hlāford ", and so on, words which can mean nothing else, but we have picturesque kennings, such as " wine ", *friend* ; " eodor ", *hedge* ; " hlēo ", *refuge* ; and many others. Though, if it is agreed that

---

[1] Lawrence, Beowulf and Epic Tradition, p. 185.
[2] Sarrazin, Neue Beowulfstudien, Engl. Stud., XLII, p. 6.

the mere of the monsters is a lake, the actual sea only comes in as background, still the number of terms for it is surprising. We have " brim ", " flōd ", " geofon ", " sund ", and countless others. Terms for armour and fighting, of which the poem is full, are of course as numerous. A mere list would give no impression of their effect. The best way to realize the richness of the vocabulary for certain ideas is to try to turn a passage dealing with them into Modern English. The impossibility of finding a fresh word for each term in the original will appear at once and emphasize the enormous variety of expression which the O.E. poet had at his disposal, and the skill with which he has used it.

Further the poet of Beowulf makes full use of the ease with which compounds could be made. Doubtless many of those he employs were already established, but some give the impression of having been created for the moment. None are especially imaginative in themselves, " beadu-lēoma," *battle flash*, for sword is perhaps the best, but all serve to give the desired variety and colour without disturbing the general thought.

So again the poet gives picturesqueness and clearness to his description by his skilful use of variation. With a few master-strokes his picture is complete. The examples given in the introductory chapter were from Beowulf and it is unnecessary therefore to add others here. Similes are not wanted in a work full of kennings and compounds and only four are to be found in the whole poem. When a sword can be called a battle flash why stop to explain that it flashed like lightning ? The vocabulary of Beowulf shows also in a marked degree the virility mentioned in the introduction.[1] All inanimate objects are represented as conscious actors. When Beowulf and his followers are admitted to the presence of Hroþgar, we are told that their shields remained behind to await the issue of the words ; in the same way the ocean fights against the wind, when Beowulf plunged into the mere, his helmet was not only to guard his head, but it was to seek the tumult of the waves, his sword had to perform a deed of valour. Such expressions

[1] p. 17.

increase the impression of vigour made by the whole poem.

Three questions have arisen out of the study of Beowulf. First, can it be called an original poem or is it merely a sort of compilation of several independent lays ? Should the poet be looked upon rather as an editor than a creator ? Secondly, is it a genuinely O.E. poem or a translation from O.N., and thirdly does classical influence appear already in it ?

In considering the first of these questions it must strike every reader that there are very marked differences in style between the various episodes in the poem. Compare, for instance, the manner in which the three fights are described. That with Grendel is told with realistic vigour ; that with the hag is pictured in much more detail, while that with the dragon is shorter and given more as background for the account of the death of the hero than for its own sake. Then again the Finn episode is in a different manner from the rest of the poem. Further, certain contradictions occur in the course of the work, as when at v. 415 Beowulf tells Hroþgar that his people had urged him on to the adventure of cleansing Heorot because they knew his power, whereas in v. 2163 it is said that he was long despised by his countrymen who thought him slack. The views of the early scholars Müllenhoff [1] and ten Brink [2] need not be more than mentioned here, since they are no longer generally accepted. Both believed Beowulf to be a compilation, the contradictions being due, according to the first, to the number of authors working on it, which he believed to be seven ; according to the second, to its having been put together from older lays which offered variant versions. This compilation theory has been more recently supported by Schücking [3] but on other grounds, on those of syntax and diction. In spite, however, of the obvious contradictions and variety of treatment already pointed out and the subtler points adduced by Schücking, the whole story is

[1] Beowulf : Die Innere Geschichte des Beowulfs, Z.f.d.a., XIV, 193–244.
[2] Beowulf : Untersuchungen, pp. 242 ff.
[3] Beowulf's Rückkehr, 1905.

too well knit together to be the work of a mere compiler. The first part shows a definite plan which can only be the work of a single mind, and the connection between it and the second part is too close for any other theory. At the same time independent lays no doubt existed, dealing with the various episodes, indeed we have seen that in the case of another subject there must have been an epic on the story of Finn, as well as the fragment of a lay which has been preserved. These lays may well have varied in detail and character and the poet of Beowulf would have known them, and been influenced sometimes by one, sometimes by another. Hence the minor contradictions and variations of style to be noticed.

With regard to the second question, the nationality of the poem, it will be observed that all the principal characters and most of the others are Scandinavian, the Geats and Swedes living in the Scandinavian Peninsula, and the Danes belonging to the same northern division of the Germanic peoples. The scenery of the chief action is in the island of Zealand, that of Beowulf's death on Gautland, and resemblances have been found between the scenery described round Heorot and that round Leire. On these and other grounds a theory has been brought forward[1] that the English poem is a translation of a lost Norse original. But against this view it must be argued that, if such a poem existed, there is no trace of it, and there are many reasons besides those mentioned in speaking of "Wulf and Eadwacer", against Beowulf being a translation of such a poem. In the first place, all the proper names are in English and not Old Norse form and must have been long known in England, for they show all the sound changes which characterize Old English and are not found elsewhere. Hroþgar, for instance, had become Hroarr in Old Norse, and in a translation it would have been kept in that form. So with other classes of words found only or chiefly in Beowulf and O.N. works. These, when the forms in the two languages would have differed, always have the English form and cannot therefore have been introduced in a

[1] Sarrazin, PBB., xi, pp. 159 ff.

translation ; they must be descendants from a common original. But the great argument against the translation theory is the character of the poem. Beowulf shows all the typical features of O.E. poetry, its sombreness, its dignity, its gravity, the quality of its occasional humour, and this differentiates it from Old Norse with its greater liveliness, its fun, its interest in everyday life. Beowulf has for its subject matter foreign themes, but it can only have been written by an Englishman. If an O.N. epic existed, our poet must have the credit of having created a work entirely English in character out of his foreign material.

The third of these interesting questions which have arisen out of the closer study of Beowulf, is whether classical influence is to be traced in the poem and, if so, to what extent. Now Beowulf, though it seems to have been taken as a model for the general structure of later poems, stands in marked contrast to them in one particular. As has already been mentioned in speaking in Chapter I of classical influence on O.E. literature,[1] the Beowulf poet does not go to work in a straightforward manner in telling his story. He does not begin with the birth and the early years of his hero, but with all that led up to his first scene, that of Beowulf's reception in Heorot, and then he fills in his background as opportunity offers. Elsewhere, too, he uses what Professor Brandl has called the " nachholende Erzählungsweise " [2] which may be rendered here as the " harking back " method. This is in striking contrast to the way of the biblical poems, in which the story goes straight on from the beginning with no such " harkings back ", and, on the other hand, it is very much like the method of the Æneid.[3] That it is due to the influence of that poem cannot, however, be proved for we cannot tell that the feature was not shared by the other Germanic secular epics, the O.H.G. Hildebrandslied and the O.E. Waldere and Finn stories, since we have only one episode left of each of these.

---

[1] p. 12.
[2] Geschichte der alt-englischen Literatur, p. 1008, in Pauls Grdr.
[3] Klæber, Archiv., CXXVI, pp. 40 ff., and more recently, T. B. Haber, A comparative study of the Beowulf and the Æneid. The latter would leave the Beowulf poet little to his own credit.

That there are also very close resemblances in detail has been pointed out more than once, and this must be accepted by all ; but whether or how far the Old English writer has borrowed from the Latin poet it is impossible to say. There is plenty of evidence that Latin literature was well known in England about the date which we may accept for Beowulf, and a court poet may well have been familiar with the Æneid and other poems, and have been influenced by them both directly and indirectly. On the other hand, these resemblances may be explained, to quote Professor Chambers,[1] by the fact that " as nations pass through their ' Heroic Age ', similar social conditions will necessarily be reflected by many similarities in their poetry " ; for such similarities, as Professor Lawrence [2] says, are " such as might easily have arisen in classical antiquity and in the Heroic Age of Western Europe ". Moreover, without going so far as to deny that anyone imbued with Latin learning would have possessed either the inclination or the ability to compose such a poem as Beowulf,[3] it may perhaps be said that it is highly improbable that a poet, such as his work shows the author of Beowulf to have been, would, even in an age in which originality was of little account, have borrowed phraseology and vocabulary whole-sale from another writer, though he might well have been alive to the good effect of the Virgilian method and have accepted it for the general structure of his work, and have adopted a certain number of kennings which appealed to him.

The date at which this poet lived can be determined most exactly by the evidence afforded by the poem itself. It cannot have been composed earlier than the beginning of the seventh century, for the historical event on which it is based, the disastrous expedition of Hygelac, took place, as we have seen, about 520. If songs were composed very soon afterwards, yet some time would have elapsed before their hero would have become fused with the hero of the folk-tale, and before he would have been connected with

---

[1] Beowulf : An Introduction, p. 330.
[2] Beowulf and Epic Tradition, p. 285.
[3] Chadwick, The Heroic Age, p. 74, note 2.

the Danes and the building of Heorot, and the whole material have received epic treatment. The Danish dynasty to which Hroþgar belonged came to an end in 740 ; that of the Merovingians mentioned in one passage as if still reigning,[1] fell in 751. It is probable, therefore, that Beowulf was not written after 750, though a poet of that time cannot be expected to be too exact about his history. From this evidence, as far as it goes, we may place the poet somewhere between 600 and 750 and rather nearer the end than the beginning of that period.

The evidence of date afforded by the Christian element is equally indefinite, and has led to widely different conclusions. Müllenhoff and ten Brink avoided the difficulty by assuming that all Christian passages were later insertions, but they are too closely woven into the fabric of the poem in most instances for this view to be acceptable. Schücking [2] considers that the general tone of the poem points to a knowledge of Christian teaching so widely spread and well absorbed that the work cannot have been composed before the ninth century, and, elaborating a view earlier propounded by Earle, suggests that it was written for the instruction of a Danish prince, ruling in Northumbria or Mercia, by some Englishman living at his court. Professor Klæber,[3] while not accepting this late date, emphasizes the prominence of the Christian element still more. He believes the poem to be nothing less than an allegory, since Beowulf is represented as dying for the benefit of his people.

It is true that the whole tone of the poem is surprising in its gentleness, moderation, and generosity towards the foe. Beowulf is indeed drawn as " a verray parfit, gentil knyght ", but Christianity need not be entirely responsible. It is possible that some of this milder tone may be due to national temperament. All O.E. poetry suggests that the Anglo-Saxons were less fierce than the Scandinavians.

The actual Christian element is vague, and the Old Testament seems to have been better known than the New,

---

[1] Beow., v. 2920–1.
[2] PBB., XLII, pp. 347 ff.
[3] Beowulf: The Christian Coloring, pp. xlviii ff.

its stories doubtless appealing more to the people. We have
proof elsewhere of the popularity of its themes, especially
of those of the Creation and the Exodus. Thus, in Beowulf,
the poet is not sure whether God or Fate is the stronger.
In v. 572 we are told that Wyrd often saves the man not
doomed to die, in v. 455 we read that Fate goes ever as it
must, but in vv. 440 and 696 it is said that God decides
the fate in battle, overruling Wyrd. So, too, the ideas of
a future life and of heaven and hell are very general. The
term Demend applied to God seems to imply a definite
belief in the Last Judgment, but when we are told that the
object of the valiant warrior should be to leave a good name
behind him, " let him attain, who may, fame before death ;
that is best afterwards for the warrior when no longer living,"
there is no sign of the doctrine of future rewards or punishments, such as would have been taught then. Elsewhere,
too, the duty of avenging a friend is insisted upon. It is
better we are told than to mourn too greatly for him.

These considerations point to the early days of Christian
teaching when it was making its way in to a place among
the older beliefs, and before it had had time to sink very
deep into the general consciousness, as was the situation
during the sixth and seventh centuries, and the more
usually accepted view now is that the Beowulf must be
about 700.[1] This date is further indicated by syntactical
usage and the metre.[2]

What was the position of the poet ? From his knowledge
of the secular literature of his time and his skill in the use
of the native metre and metrical devices, he would seem
to have been a professional scop or minstrel, one to whom
the metrical rules and usages were a second nature. From
the style of his poem he doubtless had a place at court, and,

---

[1] See Chambers, Beowulf, an Introduction, p. 105, and Klæber, Beowulf,
p. cx, for a consideration of these tests.

[2] Several lines will not scan unless the later contracted forms be replaced
by the older fuller ones. Thus " hēan hūses " (116), *of the high house*,
must be read " hēahan hūses " ; " þēah þe he geong sy " (1831), *though
he be young*, must be taken " geong siē ", with two syllables in the last
word. These contractions are generally supposed to have taken place
about 700. Beowulf must have been composed before the old forms
had died out in the poetic tradition, even though they may have been
lost already in actual speech.

if a knowledge of Latin literature may be admitted as shown in the structure of his work and other details, and from his acquaintance with the Bible and biblical phraseology, he must have received his education in the school of one of the great monasteries of the day, such as Jarrow, Wearmouth, or Whitby. More than that it is impossible to say.

The poem of Beowulf exists in one MS. only, that in the British Museum, known as Vitellius A, in which it is somewhat buried amongst other matter. Vitellius A consists of two originally distinct MSS., which were already bound together when they appear in the possession of Sir Robert Cotton (+ 1631). Both are of about the year 1000. It is the second of these which contains Beowulf. This has been made by two scribes. In the first hand are the three things which come first in this second MS., the Legend of St. Christopher, the Wonders of the East, and the Letter of Alexander the Great to Aristotle, and then Beowulf up to v. 1939. Then with the word *moste* in that verse the second hand begins, finishes Beowulf, and goes on to copy Judith, which ends the MS.

The text of Beowulf shows a great mixture of dialects. While our MS. is mainly in W.S., Anglian and Kentish forms are common, especially in the part copied by the second scribe. Metrical and linguistic considerations [1] make it clear that the original was composed by an Anglian; whether he was of Northumbria or Mercia is disputed. Equally clear is it that the scribes who made our copy were West Saxons, not only because the bulk is W.S. but because the Judith which was copied by the second hand shows none of these dialectal features. They must have found the Anglian and Kentish forms in their original, and there must therefore have been an intermediate Kentish copy made at some time. Probably also there was an earlier copy of the whole poem made in W.S. The fact that so many copies can be traced, points to the popularity of the work before the Conquest.

Before coming into the possession of Sir Robert Cotton, this second MS. must have belonged to Lawrence Nowell,

---

[1] Especially uncontracted verbal forms such as weorðeð, W.S. wierþ, *becomes*.

Dean of Lichfield, since his name appears on the first page. In 1700 the now combined MS. was bought for the nation and lodged for a time in Ashburnham House, with the rest of the Cotton books. It was there when the serious fire broke out in 1731, and though it fortunately escaped destruction it was badly scorched, with the result that the edges of the leaves have since crumbled and words or letters been lost, while others have faded.

The first transcription made of Beowulf was by the Icelandic historian Thorkelin. His attention was attracted by Wanley's description of the work in his catalogue of A.S. MSS. as the story of the wars waged by the Danish king Beowulf against the kings of Sweden. Fortunately the MS. was then still fairly perfect, and though Thorkelin made some mistakes in copying owing to his imperfect knowledge of Old English, his copy is invaluable in helping to restore the original text in many cases in which it is now imperfect or obscure. In 1882 the E.E.T.S. published a facsimile with a transliteration and notes by the late Professor Zupitza.

Chapter VI

CÆDMON : ANDREAS

Allusion has already been made in the Introduction to the moderation shown by St. Augustine and his company of monks when they came in 597 to preach Christianity in England, and to the happy result of that moderation, as seen in their influence on English Literature. Realizing the great part played in the life of the people by their hero lays, they set to work to present the new teaching in similar form. They wrote poems in the native alliterative metre, in which they substituted Bible events and Bible or Christian characters for the old heroes and their doings, and sometimes, it must be confessed, a good deal of the old pagan element was allowed to creep into the treatment. That there was no general attempt to oust the old stories appears from the fact that it is to the copies written in the monasteries that we owe the few fragments of the old literature which we still possess. How deeply the native lays had permeated society and how peacefully they were allowed for a time to exist side by side with the new learning, may be inferred from Alcuin's rebuke to the monks at Lindisfarne, already mentioned,[1] " in the refectory the Bible should be read . . . patristic sermons, not pagan songs. For what has Ingeld to do with Christ ? "

The first writer of these religious poems whose name has come down to us is Cædmon.

While for the bulk of O.E. poetry we have poems whose authors are unknown, here we have a poet about whose works much uncertainty prevails, but something is known about the man himself, and that on no less authority than that of Bede. His account is well known.[2] He tells us that there was a cowherd employed at the monastery of Streoneshealh, the modern Whitby, who so mistrusted his

---

[1] Chap. I, p. 4. [2] Eccles. Hist., Bk. IV, Ch. 24.

own powers that, when at social gatherings he saw the harp approaching in order that he might take his turn in singing, he would get up and escape to the shippen to his cows. One night when he had done this, as he lay asleep, an angel appeared to him and bade him sing something. When Cædmon assured him that he could not sing and for that very reason had left the feast, the angel nevertheless insisted and gave him as a theme the Creation, whereupon Cædmon produced a verse of which Bede gives a Latin version, and which may be rendered thus :—

> Now we must praise the guardian of the heavens,
> the power of the Creator and the thoughts of His heart,
> the work of the glorious Father ; thus He of every marvel,
> eternal Lord, laid the foundation.
> He first created for the sons of earth,
> heaven for a roof, this holy Creator,
> the middle world, this guardian of mankind,
> the eternal Lord, assigned afterwards
> to the men of earth, the Almighty Ruler.

Bede then goes on to tell us that after this proof of Cædmon's poetic gift, the Abbess Hilda received him into the monastery and had him properly instructed, with the result that he afterwards composed other songs all in alliterative metre, whose subjects, speaking generally, covered the Old and New Testament stories. It is impossible to doubt a definite statement of an authority like Bede. He was almost a contemporary, having been born in 673, eight years only before Cædmon's death which is generally given as in 681, and Whitby, Cædmon's home, was not far from the monasteries of Jarrow and Wearmouth, where Bede passed his life. The story of Cædmon, therefore, would not have had far to wander to reach him and it would not have had time to become much modified. Moreover Bede was a trained scholar, accustomed to weigh evidence. Marvellous as it may appear, it must therefore be accepted that this cowherd, attached to the monastery of Whitby, did not realize the gift of song in his possession till he was at any rate well on into middle life, (of weakened age Bede says), and then only through a very strong influence, which

I

was naturally put down to a miraculous vision. On the other hand, it may be pointed out that it is the same sort of story as is told not only of certain classical poets, but also later of Cynewulf, and of the Old Saxon poet of the Heliand,[1] and need not be taken too literally.

It must then be accepted that Cædmon did write many poems on Old and New Testament stories, as well as the Hymn on the Creation. He would have been familiar with the general technique of the alliterative metre from hearing all the songs sung at the beer drinkings, such as the one from which he fled, but it must remain a matter of surprise that he could have been able in his later years to dictate as many poems as those for which Bede gives him credit.

A question which naturally arises at this point is, have we any of these poems now? Of his authorship of the Hymn we may be certain, for not only does Bede give us the upshot of its contents in Latin prose in his Ecclesiastical History, but in four MSS. of that work, versions in Northumbrian form have been added, and Ælfred has replaced Bede's outline by a W.S. verse rendering.[2] Beyond this, however, it is impossible to say that we have anything that is certainly Cædmon's. There is, however, in the Bodleian Library a MS., Junius XI, which is still often called the Cædmon MS., because it contains poems which were long thought to be his. These are, one on Genesis, a second on Exodus, a third on Daniel and three short passages on the Fall of the Angels, the Descent into Hell, and the Temptation, the last three being often classed together under the title, Christ and Satan. These poems are all in one MS., they treat of subjects with which we are told that Cædmon dealt; what is more natural than that they should at first sight have been assumed to be some of the poems indicated by Bede?

The earliest knowledge we possess of the MS. is that it belonged to Archbishop Usher (1581–1656), that he gave it to Franciscus Junius or Francis Dujon, librarian to the Earl of Arundel, and that Junius had it printed at Amsterdam

---

[1] Klæber, M.L.N., XLII, 390.
[2] Three Northumbrian Poems, A. H. Smith, Ph.D.

in 1655 and later bequeathed it with other MSS. to the Bodleian Library. It had been copied before, in the late sixteenth century, by the scholar William Somner. This MS. long continued to be accepted as containing Cædmon's work, but the increasing and more accurate scholarship of the last century caused doubts to arise. Thorpe,[1] already in 1832, seems to have expressed a doubt whether the three short pieces at the end were Cædmon's. Ettmüller [2] was the first to question whether all the rest could be his, and the result of more exact investigation has been to show, from linguistic and stylistic features, that at least seven authors must be allowed for. Genesis and Daniel are each compiled from at least two poems by different writers, and Exodus may be from two also. It is now generally considered that either part of Genesis or Exodus may be by Cædmon, and of these two it seems to the writer that part of Genesis is the more likely to be his. This is a long poem of 2,935 lines, which begins with a passage vividly recalling the Hymn :—

> It is very right that we, the King of Heaven,
> the glorious Lord of Hosts, in words should praise,
> love in our hearts.

This may have been, of course, a generally accepted form of introduction to a religious poem of the time, there is nothing individual about it, at the same time the resemblance to the Hymn is marked.

After the introduction the poet goes on to tell of the blissful state of the angels in heaven where they knew no sin, nor could work any wickedness until Satan and his followers sought to make themselves equal with God and were in consequence, as punishment, thrust down into a new " home ", filled with tortures, with fire and sudden cold, with smoke and red flame, and surrounded with perpetual night.

To fill their empty seats in heaven God went on with the work of Creation. First He created the heavens above and the earth below, but the grass was not yet green, the ocean

[1] Metrical Paraphrase of the parts of Holy Scripture in Anglo-Saxon.
[2] Handbuch der deutschen Litteratur Geschichte, S. 135 ff.

with its dark waves covered it far and wide till day was separated from night and, later, land divided from water. At this point a gap must be allowed for, for we are taken straight on to the creation of Eve, passing over that of Adam, and on to the happiness in Eden :—

> Fair shone
> that pleasant land, the running waters,
> the welcome springs. No cloud there yet
> brought rain upon the wide expanse,
> struggled against wind, and yet the land
> stood there adorned with fruits.

Then after mention of the four rivers of Eden, with verse 235 we are suddenly plunged into the middle of God's commands to Adam and Eve to avoid the fruits of the one tree, while enjoying freely that of all the others, and we have the story told over again of the rebellion of Satan and his followers. So far the poet has kept fairly closely to the Bible narrative, interpreting it as an Anglo-Saxon would, but from now on till v. 852 we get a far more independent work. Satan's strength and beauty are dwelt upon, his power and position as next to God Himself, and the way in which this led him to " overpride " and to his own destruction. The feelings which prompted him to rebel are given at length :—

> What shall I gain ? There is no need at all
> for me to have a master. I with my hands may work
> as many wonders. I have great power
> to prepare myself a goodlier throne,
> a loftier in the heavens. Why should I seek after His favour,
> bow before Him in such allegiance ? I may be God as well
>   as He,
> nor will I longer be His disciple.

Then was the Almighty angered and cast him down into hell, where he became a devil ; for three days and nights the rebel angels fell and were all changed into devils. Then after a description of hell, fuller than that already given, though essentially the same, we are brought back to the central figure of Satan, as we are told he is to be called henceforth, and we have a fine speech of his of nearly a hundred lines :—

> Alas ! had I control of my hands !
> and might I escape out for one hour,
> be outside one winter hour, then with this band . . .
> but iron bonds are round me,
> the binding chain " rides " me. I am without a realm.
>
> .   .   .
>
> There lie around me
> great bars forged with heat,
> of hard iron, with which God has
> chained me by the neck. Thus I know that He had learnt
>   my thought,
> and that the Lord of Hosts knew also
> that mischief would grow up between us, between Adam and
>   me,
> about the kingdom of heaven, if I had the use of my hands.
> But now we endure tortures in hell, which are darkness and
>   heat
> grim and bottomless. God Himself hath
> swept us into these dark mists.
>   While He may not impute any sin to us,
> that we have wrought evil against Him in the land, He hath
>   yet banished us from the light,
> cast us into the cruellest of all tortures, nor may we take
>   vengeance for this,
> repay Him with aught of evil, because that He hath thus
>   banished us from the light.

Then he went on to plan vengeance :—

> He hath now marked out a middle world, where He hath
>   created man,
> in His likeness, with whom He will again people
> the kingdom of heaven with pure souls. Let us think eagerly
> how we upon Adam, if ever we may,
> and in his children likewise, may appease our wrath.
> . . . Nor may we ever attain so much,
> as that we should weaken the purpose of God. Let us then
>   snatch away
> from the sons of men this heavenly kingdom.
>
> .   .   .
>
> If I to any thane in days of yore,
> gave princely jewels while we in that blest kingdom,

lived happy and had possession of our thrones,
then he to me in a more welcome time could ne'er
repay my gifts . . .
than if he up from hence might come,
from out this prison and had himself the power
that he with wings might fly,
wind through the welkin to where on earth
created stand Adam and Eve,
with wealth encompassed, while we are cast out hither
into these deep dales.

One of the fallen angels, accordingly, with helmet firmly
secured on head, flew up to earth to where he found Adam
and Eve.   Near them stood two trees laden with fruit,
that of the one, the tree of life, was pleasant, beautiful,
bright, and desirable ; that of the other, of the tree of death,
was altogether black and dull looking. He who ate the one
would live for ever in happiness, whereas he who ate the
other should, indeed, know both good and evil, but should
live by toil and should be cut off by old age from deeds
of valour and from joy, and should die. The evil spirit,
having taken the form of a serpent, gathered some of the
fruit of the tree of death and went up to Adam with lying
words. " I am God's messenger," he said, " come from afar.
Not long ago was it that I sat beside Him and He bade me
go on this journey, bade that thou shouldst eat this fruit,
so that thy strength and courage should become greater
and thy form more beauteous :—

Broad in the world
are its green plains and God sitteth
in the highest kingdom of the heavens,
the Allruler, above. He would not Himself
bear the toil of faring on this journey,
the Lord of all mankind, but He hath sent His servant
for speech with thee.

Obey thou readily
His message, take this fruit into thy hand,
bite it and swallow it. Greater shall be thy heart,
more beauteous thy form. The Lord God,
thy Master, hath sent thee help from heaven.

Adam, however, refused to accept him as a messsenger from God without any token, he was not like any angel whom he had ever seen, and offered no pledge ; he knew what God Himself had commanded him and trusted Him, for He could send benefits without any messenger.

Then the tempter turned to Eve and threatened her with God's anger when he should record the ill-success of his errand ; if, on the other hand, she would eat the fruit she would be able to see over the whole world and even the throne of God Himself. If she would persuade Adam, he would not repeat the latter's abusive words. Eve yielded to persuasion and Adam at last also consented. Eve spoke thus :—

> Adam my lord ! this fruit is so sweet,
> so pleasant to the taste and this messenger so beauteous,
> the holy angel of God. I can see from his raiment,
> that he is the messenger of our lord.
>
> He may intercede for us with the Allruler,
> heaven's King. I can see from here
> to where He Himself sits (that is in the south and east),
> surrounded by riches, He who created the world.
> . . . Who could give me such understanding,
> if he had not come certainly from God,
> heaven's Ruler ? . . . I can hear
> the celestial joy in heaven.

All this had been since she ate of the fruit, some of which she had with her, and which Adam at last accepted from her. At this the evil spirit laughed and danced and went back to tell Satan that their punishment was now compensated for by this act of Adam. Adam and Eve realized their sin and Adam bitterly reproached Eve. "Now may I rue it that I prayed the Lord of Heaven, the holy Ruler, to create thee for me from my body, now that thou hast led me astray into the anger of my Lord— now may I rue it always that ever my eyes looked on thee."

Eve answered meekly : "Thou mayest reproach me, my beloved Adam, with thy words. It cannot worse grieve thee in thy thoughts than it does me in my heart." Then

with the coming down of God to seek them the poem returns
to its earlier manner and may be given more shortly.   It
tells simply the story of the expulsion from Eden, beginning
with God's words to Eve :—

> Lo, daughter ! didst thou not enjoy good things enough,
> the newly created things of Paradise,
> increasing gifts, that thou thus greedily
> didst seize upon the tree, didst take the fruit
> and give to Adam ?

After the expulsion from Paradise follow the account of
the birth of Cain and Abel and the story of the death of
Abel, with Cain's despair at his punishment :—

> Nor dare I hope for any mercy
> in the kingdom of the world, for I have forfeited,
> O lofty King of Heaven ! Thy goodwill,
> Thy love, and Thy protection.   Therefore must I,
> expecting misery, wander o'er distant tracts,
> lest one should meet me, the guilty one,
> who far or near should call to mind the feud,
> the murder of a brother, for I have shed his blood,
> his gore upon the earth. . . . I accursed must,
> O Lord ! from sight of Thee now turn away.

For the descendants of Cain and Seth the poet follows
the Bible very closely, merely adding that the city which
Enos built was the first " weallfæsten " ever set up under
the heavens.   Jabal and Jubal are confused, it is Jabal
who is mentioned, but he is made the inventor of the harp.
Over the account of the Flood the poet allows himself to
expand somewhat but he seems to have been a landsman
himself, for he has let the opportunity go for a fine sea picture.
He says merely :—

> The Lord sent
> rain from heaven and let wide founts
> of water gush forth upon the world
> from every stream, dark currents
> of water roar ; seas mounted up
> above the barriers of their shores.

Then he goes on to describe how the waters gradually
covered the mountain tops and floated the ark, and how

when, after one hundred and fifty nights they began to subside, and the ark rested on the mountains of Armenia, Noah sent out first the raven and then the dove, and finally he and his family went out, Noah, his three sons, Sem, Cham, and Jafeð with their four wives, Percoba, Olla, Olliva, and Ollivani. These names of the women are from Irish tradition and Cædmon, if he is the author of Genesis, would have known them from Irish missionaries at Whitby. His name shows that he himself was of Celtic origin.

The descendants of Sem and Cham are then enumerated. From Eber, son of Sem, they were called Ebrei (Hebrews), while a descendant of Cham was the first prince of Babylon.

The Ebrei spread over the field of Sennar and in their pride began to build the tower of Babel :—

> But from this folly
> the stern-hearted king restrained them,
> when he, angry in heart, appointed
> for the dwellers on the earth, diversity of speech.

The battle of the kings is told in Germanic fashion :—

> Then met together (javelins were loud)
> the angry murderous hosts, the dark bird sang
> among the spear shafts, dewy-feathered,
> in hopes of carrion . . .
> there was cruel play,
> the exchange of spears, a mighty shout of battle,
> loud sound of fighting. With their hands
> the heroes snatched from scabbards ring-graved swords,
> doughty of edge.

After an account of the meeting of Abraham and Melchisedek reminiscent of the native poetry, the poet goes on to tell of God's promise to Abraham, the birth of Ishmael and Sarah's jealousy of Hagar, the separation of Abraham and Lot, and the destruction of Sodom and Gomorrah :—

> When first the sun,
> protecting candle of the nations, rose,
> sent, I have heard, the Ruler of the sky
> brimstone from heaven and swart flames of fire,
> in punishment to men, a raging fire,
> because that they in days of yore had angered God.
> . . . High terror seized

the heathen race ; in the cities rose a cry,
the clamour of the wicked, at the point of death,
of all that noble race. Flame destroyed all
that it within the city found of green,
so likewise round about, no little part
of the wide world was overspread
with burning and with terror.

Meanwhile Abraham had journeyed to Abimelech and
deceived him, declaring Sarah to be his sister. Having learnt
the deception in a dream, Abimelech remonstrated in dignified
words, emphasizing the breach of hospitality, a crime
which would appeal especially to the Germanic warrior :—

How have I deserved this (he asks)
that thou shouldest prepare a snare for me ? . . .
We entertained thee and, in friendly fashion,
assigned thee a dwelling in the nation,
and land for thy pleasure. Thou dost now reward us
and thank us for this kindness in unfriendly wise.

When the birth of Isaac and the sending away of Ishmael
have been told, the sacrifice of Isaac is narrated with telling
simplicity, with but slight expansion of the Bible story :—

Then he (Abraham) began to build the pyre, to rouse the
    flame,
and firmly bound the feet and hands
of his son, and lifted on the fire
the boy Isaac, and then quickly seized
his sword by its hilt : he would slay his son
with his own hand, drench the fire
with the blood of his child. Then the servant of the Lord,
an angel from above, to Abraham loudly
called with his voice. . . .
        Slay not the child,
but snatch thy son still living from the fire,
thine heir.

With this episode the poem comes to an end.

The beginning and end of this work, passages 1–234 and
852 to end, known as Genesis A, are told on the whole in
a pleasant style, if sometimes it is rather cumbersome.
They keep close to the Bible version and, for the Fall of the
Angels, follow the tradition of Gregory, but the poet never

attains to any great height. These parts might have been written by a man who had not much education beyond such as he would get by having the books of the Bible translated to him and such as he would imbibe from the constant hearing of the old lays, and who had poetic feeling but no great poetic gift. Or they might have been by more than one author, since such continuity as they possess could have been supplied by the Bible narrative.

The middle passage, however, vv. 235–851, Genesis B or the Later Genesis, is in a very different style. The author has not followed the Bible so closely as the first writer, but has used as well the works of Bishop Avitus of Vienne, and, as will have been obvious, he has been altogether freer in his treatment of his subject than has the author of the beginning and end. The passage is written with great vigour and from a different point of view from that of Genesis A. In it, it is Satan who is the hero, and the poet is interested, not so much in his rebellion as in his character and motives, in the causes which led him to that rebellion, and with his regrets and plans for vengeance. So vivid is the writing, indeed, that one wonders whether the poet had not some historical personage in his mind, possibly some prince or chieftain who had resisted Charlemagne. Moreover the metre is different. The passage is full of long lines with three feet in each half, such as were common in O.S. poetry. The vocabulary, too, contains words not found elsewhere in O.E., or not till after the date of this poem, but usual in Old Saxon. Various explanations have been offered for the presence of this passage with its O.S. element. It is obviously an interpolation and might have been inserted by an English monk living in a Saxon monastery, whose native speech had thus acquired this foreign tinge [1] ; or it might have been the doing of a Saxon monk living in England—it might even have been the work of the John of Athelney whom Ælfred brought over, and the Saxon element be thus accounted for.[2] Again it might have been

---

[1] Stopford Brooke, History of Early English Literature, Vol. II, pp. 97–8.
[2] ten Brink, Early English Literature, translated by H. M. Kennedy, pp. 83, 377.

a translation from a lost O.S. poem,[1] a view which was supported by an existing tradition that the author of the O.S. Heliand or Saviour, writing somewhere between 822 and 840, had composed Old Testament poems, too, of which this might, therefore, be one.

In 1894 the question was decided and the third theory, that of Professor Sievers, proved to be right by the discovery in the Vatican Library by Professor Zangemeister, the late Librarian of Heidelberg University, of an O.S. MS. containing four fragments of verse. One was from the Heliand, the three others from an Old Testament poem and of these one is clearly the source of this O.E. passage. While slight differences in style and character make it improbable that the Old Testament passages are from a work by the author of the Heliand himself,[2] the general resemblance between the two poems makes it likely that the writers were of the same school and date, and renders improbable a more recent identification of the author of the fragments with a Saxon cleric who, about the year 1000, wrote a life of St. Dunstan.[3] Genesis B, therefore, though treated here for convenience' sake, represents O.E. poetry of a much later date than Genesis A.

Readers of the poem will be struck by the likeness between the hell depicted in it and in Paradise Lost, a likeness which extends even to some details, as in the mention of fire which gives heat but no light. Junius printed the MS. ten years before Milton completed Paradise Lost, and it is therefore possible that the latter knew the work, for the study of Old English was gaining ground during the seventeenth century at the Universities. But there is no evidence to support this conjecture. On the other hand, it is equally possible that the hell described with such vividness and force by the O.E. poet became the traditional one and that Milton borrowed certain details in his picture from such popular tradition.

Next in the MS. comes the Exodus, a short poem of

[1] Sievers, Der Heliand und die ags. Genesis, 1875.
[2] Braune, P.B.B., XXXII, pp. i ff.
[3] Gerould, The Transmission and Date of Genesis B, M.L.N., XXVI, pp. 129 ff.

591 lines, which is in an entirely different style from either Genesis A or B. It treats chiefly of the events narrated in chapters 13, 14, and 15 of the Book of Exodus. The poet's imagination has been fired by one episode, the crossing of the Red Sea, and he has treated his theme as he would have done a native story of the kind, telling it with great wealth of detail and vigour of description, and giving us pictures full of life and movement. He is a powerful rather than a finished story-teller, but he carries his reader with him by sheer force in spite of crudities and technical shortcomings. The first lines recall the beginning of Beowulf rather than that of the Genesis, but soon some influence from Cædmon's Hymn can be detected :—

Lo ! we have heard told far and near,
over the world, the decrees of Moses,
the glorious law, pronounced for all generations of men,
(promising) in heaven above, for each of the blessed,
the reward of life after this span of evil,
long lasting blessings for each of the living.
Let him hear who will.
Him, in the wilderness, the Lord of Hosts,
the righteous king, honoured
with power like to his own, gave him the gift
of (working) many miracles, the Eternal Ruler.

Having thus introduced his hero, the poet goes on to do the same by his subject, telling us briefly how Moses triumphed over Pharaoh, and the Lord of Victories granted him the lives of his kinsmen, and to them, the sons of Abraham, a land of their own in which to dwell. The first time that God approached Moses He taught him about the Creation and many wondrous truths and named His own name, which men had not known before. He endowed Moses with true power to effect the escape of the Israelites when the greatest of the hosts of Pharaoh was drowned, overcome in death. Then the poem goes on to tell how the cruel foe, the slayer, the injurer of the people, had at midnight slain many of the firstborn, and the land lay covered with corpses when the valiant band of Israelites went forth; the makers of laughter were silenced, but the people allowed to enter on their journey.

The day was glorious on which the multitude of the Israelites went forth, wandering through narrow defiles, along unknown tracks, until they, in their armour, reached the mist-covered land of the Guþmyrce. Then, on the second night, Moses bade his followers surround the city of Ethan in full force, necessity had forced them on to a northerly track, for they knew the land of the sun-dwellers to be to the south. For them a canopy of mist overshadowed the burning heavens, dividing earth from sky, drinking up the fiery rays, moving through the clouds in the path of the sun, and every evening a sign arose, a fiery pillar appeared with its bright light, dispersing the dark shadows of the night, but threatening destruction to the Israelites if they would not obey Moses. It was the third encampment of the people, at the end of the next day's march, when God came down to seek them out. The fourth day brought them to the Red Sea. Arrived there, wearily they flung them down, while the bold attendants went round with food and they renewed their strength. When the trumpets rang out, the sailors spread their tents along the slopes, at this fourth encampment, the resting place of warriors, beside the Red Sea.

But a new fear came upon them, the terror of pursuit from those who had so long held them in captivity. The Egyptians had broken the pledges made to Joseph, when a new king arose and sought to repay with treachery the gift of life received from him, a deed for which they paid with their blood. The Israelites were filled with despair when they saw the hosts of Pharaoh approaching from the South, in battle array, with banners waving and trumpets sounding. "Birds of battle screamed, eager for fight, dewy-feathered; wolves barked their dire song in expectation of a feast, awaiting, untroubled, in the track of the foe, the fall of the band." The Israelites were hemmed in between the sea and the hostile army.

Next, leaving them thus encamped, we are taken to the Egyptian army and shown the king at the head of his men,

in front of the banner, exhorting them. Around him were
two thousand kings and kinsmen of kings, chosen from among
the most famous of the people, each of whom led with him
every warrior whom he had been able to find in the time.

Then was terror in the Hebrew camp, the sound of
weeping, a dire evening song, when the terrible tidings
spread. The pursuers were resolute in their shining armour
till a mighty angel transformed the proud foes so that they
could no longer see each other. The expedition was stopped.
Thus, though they could go no farther, the fugitives had the
respite of a night and Moses at dawn bade the heralds arise,
summon the people with their brazen trumpets, and call
the band nearer to the shore. The men, scattered along the
slopes, snatched up their tents in haste. Then they counted
against the foe twelve companies, each of which contained
fifty cohorts chosen from the valiant of the people. In each
cohort were ten hundred famous warriors, not counting the
old and feeble, or those too young to wear armour. Having
thus collected his followers, Moses addressed them, urging
them to courage and promising that God would give their
enemies into their hands :—

> Lo ! ye now shall see with your own eyes,
> O most beloved of nations ! a certain wonder.
> How I now strike with this right hand,
> with this green twig, the depths of ocean,
> The waves rise up and quickly turn
> the waters into ramparts. The paths are dry,
> grey battle roads, the sea is cleared away,
> the old foundations bared, which I ne'er knew before,
> in all the world, the feet of men to tread,
> once fields of foam, which up till now
> from all eternity the waves have covered,
> the salt sea depths. . . .
> The sheltering walls rise fair and steep,
> a wondrous path of waves up to the vault of heaven.

Then follows the actual crossing of the sea. Judah goes
first :—

> The song of the beloved one approached nearer,
> the sound increased, the volume of the song,
> when the fourth tribe went on in front,

strode into the waves, the warriors in a band,
passing over the green plain.

After that band come the sailors, the sons of Reuben,
whose birthright his brother had snatched from him,
but nevertheless he was bold.   Then followed Simeon, with
banners waving above the spear-armed host ;   in warlike
formation his tribe pressed onwards, dew on their spears.
The sounds of dawn awoke over the ocean. God's " beacon "
in morning brightness, in power came forth as the tribes
marched on one after the other, led by one who was greatest
in mighty power.

And now the poet apparently leaves the tribes to take
their way while he entertains his readers with the story
of Noah who in former days had saved his family and every
living creature from the danger of the waters. This leads him
on to the story of Abraham's sacrifice of Isaac, and he
tells how he took him to Mount Sion, on which afterwards
the wise son of David built his glorious temple.   There he
kindled the fire and would have slain his son, the child so
long hoped for, as an offering, had not God prevented him.

Having thus allowed time for the Israelites to pass
through the Red Sea, the poet comes back to his main
theme, giving a wonderful picture of the confusion and
panic at the return of the waters. A page has been lost,
and we now find the Egyptians in the midst of the water,
apparently after a battle. The army was terrified ;   panic
seized their despairing souls. The slopes of the cliffs were
wet with blood, the sea spat out gore, there was clamour
in the waves, the water full of weapons—a deadly mist
arose.   The Egyptians turned back, terrified they would
seek their homes, their boasting was humbled. But down
upon them fell the dire surge of the waves, nor did anyone
escape from the army to his home, but fate held them close
in the waters. Where before had been paths, the sea now
raged ;   the force was drowned, the currents returned again
to their place, the storm rose high to the heavens, the
mightiest of battle clamours.   The ramparts (of water)
were broken down, the army imprisoned in the deep, the
sands awaited the return of the wandering waves,

the blue air was mingled with blood,
the floods foamed, the doomed fell,
the walls of water swept back to the ground, the air was
  stirred,
the watery ramparts gave way, the billows broke,
the towers of water melted, when the Almighty slew
the proud nation.

Not one returned to announce to the wives within the cities this greatest of evil tidings, the fall of the heroes.

The poem ends with the exhortation of Moses to the Israelites to keep God's laws, their song of thanksgiving and their division of the spoils of the Egyptians thrown up on the shore.

It will be seen at once that this poem cannot be by the author of either Genesis A or Genesis B.

The poet must have been a churchman, for he has been able to make use of the " De Transitu Maris " of Avitus, the fifth century Bishop of Vienne, besides drawing from popular tradition, but his Christianity does not seem to have greatly influenced his outlook. The tone of this poem is entirely free from it. The love of fighting is as prominent as in the Waldere or in the actual fights in Beowulf, his description of the eagle and wolf following the army are entirely from the native poetry. While in Beowulf we have old native material in an atmosphere largely due to Christianity, here we have a Bible story in an atmosphere essentially pre-Christian. The poet can never get away from the native poetry in phraseology or in details. While he gives an effective picture of the walls of water towering up on either side, and the crests tumbling over on to the Egyptians, he cannot resist a final touch of horror, taken from the usual battle scenery, when he describes the waves as filled with blood as well as weapons. The resemblance in phraseology between this poem and Beowulf is very noticeable and emphasizes the connection of the Exodus with the native poetry generally.

Exodus must have been composed some three hundred years before the MS. which we possess was copied, and in that time many miswritings have crept in which may well be due merely to careless copying. Moreover the sequence of events in our version is not right. At v. 93 the pillar of fire and the pillar of cloud are alluded to as though both had been described already, whereas only that of cloud has been mentioned, and later when the pillar of fire is spoken of it is as of something quite new. This can be explained if we allow for two sheets having been wrongly folded in an earlier MS. and the proper sequence thus thrown out.[1]

Much has been written about the insertion of the stories of Noah and Abraham. There is no great difference in style or date to suggest that they are interpolations from some other poem as in the case of Genesis B. At the same time their presence requires some justification since they certainly interrupt the story.

While the account of the Flood might be taken as an instance of the O.E. poet's tendency to digress, or as an insertion from some contemporary poem by a scribe, led to it by the connection of ideas between the two stories of saving from drowning, both of which explanations have been suggested, no such reason can be brought forward for the insertion of the story of the Sacrifice of Isaac. It merely interrupts.

It has been pointed out that all three stories occur in the Liturgical Service for the baptism of catechumens on the Saturday before Easter,[2] and it is possible that the poet was influenced by his familiarity with this, but on the other hand it is not easy to picture one who was so stirred by the theme of the escape of the Israelites from bondage, and especially by their safe passage through the perils of the sea, as suddenly remembering the other stories to be found in one of his sources and interrupting his narrative at the exciting moment to bring them in.

An outstanding feature of the Exodus is the masterly handling of crowds. It is the whole band of Israelites whom we follow as they escape from Egypt, and whom we are made to see in their nightly encampments, especially in that by the Red Sea. A whole army spreads its tents, next morning

[1] Napier, M.L.R., Vol. VI, No. 2, p. 165 ff.
[2] Bright, M.L.N., XXVII, p. 97.

a whole army strikes them. In this the poet is the forerunner
of the author of Judith, who has the same gift, and also
of the later Langland. Further the poet of Exodus has an
eye for colour not often found elsewhere in the writings
of the time, and he gives us a clearer picture of how things
looked than do other poets. They describe action, but he
shows us, for instance, the walls of water with the dry sea
bottom between, and he mentions the blue sky. This is
a characteristic which the Exodus shares with the little
poem the Ruin,[1] already treated, indeed there the colour
details are more definite. But in both poems, the writer
describes a scene which he has actually seen or pictured
to himself, not giving, as in the later Phoenix, the traditional
description merely, and rather an absurd one.

Though, as has been shown, the poet must have been a
churchman from his choice of theme and its source, certain
intricacies of metre in which he indulges, such as phrases
like " flōd blōd gewōd ", *blood entered the flood*, with even
three rhyming words in the half line, as well as the tone of
his poem, suggest that he was originally a professional
minstrel. He certainly delights in what may be called
metrical conceits, and he wrote for the enjoyment of his
subject ; his principal object cannot have been didactic.
Further his sea pictures are his own and unsurpassed of
their kind in all O.E. literature. Churchman or minstrel,
he knew the sea well enough to visualize and depict it in
other than the traditional scenes.

The third poem deals in 764 lines with episodes from the
earlier chapters of the Book of Daniel. The episodes treated
are Nebuchadnezzar's first dream and its interpretation ;
the ordeal of the three Hebrews in the fiery furnace ; the
interpretation and fulfilment of Nebuchadnezzar's second
dream and Belshazzar's feast ; and these are treated with
some degree of independence. The poet can hardly have
been the author of the Exodus, because, though he shows
the same feeling for a fine situation, he falls far short of the
latter in his power of developing it. But he seems to have
known it or some other poem on the same subject, for he

[1] See Chap. I, p. 17.

prefixes to his stories from Daniel a considerable introduction joining the events on to those narrated in Exodus, and explaining how the Babylonish Captivity was a punishment for neglect of the Covenant made with Abraham. He begins :—

> I have heard how the Hebrews lived in prosperity,
> in Jerusalem, dealing out treasures of gold,
> holding the kingdom which was theirs by right
> since, through the might of the Creator,
> success in war was given into the hand of Moses,
> and the multitudes departed forth out of Egypt in a
>   mighty band.
>
> .   .   .   .
>
>   Prosperity was theirs
> as long as they would keep the covenant made by
>   Abraham,
> till that the desire for the things of earth
> led them away from the divine precepts.

Then God became angered against those to whom He had given prosperity, and who had been dearest of all mankind to Him.

With this preamble begins the series of stories. The first, that of Nebuchadnezzar, is told very shortly. Having collected from North and South a fierce band, he marched westwards to the lofty city, where the chieftains of Israel had lived in happiness as long as it was permitted to them. There he ravaged the " wine city " of men, plundering the temple of Solomon of its red gold and its treasures, and carrying off everything to Babylon, together with the race of the Israelites who were there enslaved. Then his chieftains were set to seek out among this " sorry remnant " of Israel any of the young men who might be taught the wisdom of the Chaldeans, and in this way two noble youths were found. These were Ananias and Azarias with a third, named Misael, chosen of God. They were brought to the prince and orders were given that they should not be allowed to suffer any lack of food or clothing. While the lord of Babylon, famous over the world, was thus living in every kind of arrogance, there came upon him as he slept the terror of a dream. He dreamt how the course of the world changed from age to age and how a terrible end must come for every human joy in every kingdom. Then he awoke, troubled with the horror of the dream, and yet he could not remember the substance of it. Those who were most skilled in divination were summoned and, though the king knew neither word nor gist of the dream, he bade them explain it. Sadly these prophets of the devil asked how they could see the secrets of his soul, or interpret the decrees of fate, if he could not even tell them the beginning. Nebuchadnezzar retorted in his anger that if they could not obey him, they were not so much above other men as they had declared themselves, and that they should die unless he learnt the true meaning of the dream which was troubling his soul. But all were unable to tell him till Daniel came in, the chosen of the Lord, wise, and steadfast, and the head of the sad band which had to obey the heathens. An angel had told him what the dream was, and he had come therefore at dawn to interpret it to the king. In consequence he had great glory in Babylon among the learned. He could not, however, bring the king to believe in the might of the Lord, and he continued to work evil on the plains of Dura.

The second story, that of the fiery furnace, is told at some length. Nebuchadnezzar, having set up a golden image, there was a hush among men when the sound came with the note of the trumpet to all the dwellers in the city, as they knelt, bowing down to the image, honouring the idol, knowing no nobler course.

But there were three men of Israel in the royal city who would not accept the decree of the king ; they were faithful, the sons of Abraham, and they made it known that they would not have a piece of gold for a god, but the King above, the protector of souls, who had given them grace. The king's servants, having reported to their master that these wretched captives were of this mind and would not honour the idol, Nebuchadnezzar declared in great anger that they should suffer great distress, the terrible burning of fire, unless they would seek peace by worshipping the golden image.

When they refused to do this, the furnace was heated as fiercely as it could be and the men thrust in. The surging of the restless flames could not however injure them, but when the king had caused fresh fuel to be piled on, the fire turned from the holy ones against their heathen foes. The youths were glad at heart, the flames turned back to the destruction of the evil ones, while the king looked on. The roaring (of the flames) was no grief to them ; it was to them as when the sun shines in summer and the dewdrops in the day become scattered in the wind.

Here follows the Song of Azarias and later that of the Three Hebrews. The Song of Azarias contains a simile as beautiful as the one just given and very like it. " Then when the angel came, it was in the furnace breezy and pleasant, most like the weather when in summertime the falling raindrops are sent during the day, the warm shower from the clouds." The astonishment of Nebuchadnezzar and his nobles at the miracle is next related with the conversion of the former and his arbitrary pronouncement that anyone who denied the Hebrew god should be declared guilty of death.

The next story is that of Nebuchadnezzar's dream of the tree, which by itself supplied food for all birds and beasts, but which was ordered to be cut down, bound in chains, and thrown into torments, with its roots, however, left in the ground. Again the chieftains were summoned to interpret, not that the king believed that they could answer, but that he wished to know what they would say. Again Daniel came to the rescue. He explained the meaning of the dream to be that the king should be cut off from his kingdom, " thou shalt have no memory of human joy, nor understanding of anything but the habits of the wild beasts. Living long, gambolling like the hart, shalt thou dwell in the woods, with no food but the grass of the moor, nor any resting place ; the rain shower shall rouse thee and drive thee forth as it does the beasts." And thus seven winters passed until the comrade of wild beasts looked up and remembered the high king of heaven and returned to mankind, a wondrous exile, humbler in mind than when he ruled in pride. The kingdom had been waiting for him and he ruled it till death took him. Afterwards his descendants distributed wealth, twisted gold, mighty treasures in the lofty city.

To the third generation of these descendants belonged Belshazzar, whose story follows next. His rule saw the last day in which the Chaldeans held the kingdom. After them God for a little while bestowed the rule on the Medes and Persians and let the glory of Babylon decline. It had been the greatest and most famous of fortified places until Belshazzar tempted God. As he sat at the feast on that last day he bade the treasures of the Israelites, the holy vessels of the temple, be brought in, those which had been carried away from Jerusalem.

Then the angel of the Lord let his hand be seen in the hall and wrote on the wall mysterious words in crimson letters before the men. Belshazzar was terrified and many crowded to see the wonder and question what the writing might mean. The magicians could not interpret till Daniel came, wise and truthful. He refused all reward. " I do not carry the decrees of the Lord among the people for payment, nor know I any good news for thee, but without bargaining will I declare fate, the mystery of the words, which thou mayest not turn aside. Ye devils have set out to drink from the holy vessels, which the Israelites used for religious ceremonies, till pride led them astray." Then he went on to point out that even Nebuchadnezzar had never attempted such sacrilege as to use them, because of his reverence for God, the Ruler of Creation, who had given him his fame and glory. Belshazzar, however, had denied Him, who ruled over devils by his own power.

Here the poem ends.

In Daniel as in Genesis and perhaps in Exodus, we must allow for two poets. The passage from v. 280 to v. 408 containing the Song of Azarias and that of the Three Holy Children, must be an interpolation, and it does not fit well. The appearance of the angel in the furnace has already been mentioned, but in v. 335 he is represented as coming again in response to the song. The resemblance between the two similes which come so near together is also suggestive in this connection. There is in the Exeter Book a poem known as Azarias, which deals with the same episode and corresponds almost word for word with our passage for seventy-five lines. After that the resemblance is less close. It is possible that the poet of the Daniel knew this poem and filled in a gap with it, writing it down from memory and not noticing that it introduced slight discrepancies and repetitions, and that after seventy-five lines his memory began to be less exact. More probably the poet, or still more likely the scribe, drew independently from the same source as the author of the Azarias of the Exeter Book to fill in his gap.

Although the writer of the Daniel has shown some independence in selecting and arranging his material, in condensing and expanding it, he is never very far from the Bible story. His phraseology is that of the native poetry and has little as a rule to distinguish it. His forte is in the selection of his themes and in his feeling for nature in the charming and suggestive, if badly expressed, similes of the rain falling in the summer or the dewdrops being blown about by the breeze. Celtic influence may perhaps be seen here.

The three remaining poems, the Fall of the Angels, the Descent into Hell, and the Temptation, are all short, not exceeding 728 lines together, and are of little importance. All are later (of the ninth century) than the poems already discussed and the first may have originated in Kent, while the other two are Northumbrian.

Thus the Junius MS. (Junius XI) consists of :—

I. Genesis A, vv. 1–234 and vv. 582 to the end of the whole work, a poem dating from the late seventh or early eighth century.

Metrical considerations show that this was written in Northumbria.

II. Genesis B, the intervening passage, containing vv. 235–581, a translation from an O.S. poem which cannot be dated before the second half of the ninth century and in which alliteration shows Kentish features. It must have been made by a Kentish scribe, probably at Canterbury.

III. A poem on Exodus, of the late seventh or early eighth century. Metrical considerations are not quite conclusive as to its place of origin. Two lines show in their alliteration a feature distinctive of Kentish, but both are susceptible of emendation, and may be due to a scribe only. Other linguistic tests, such as uncontracted verbal endings and the frequent omission of a final " n ", point to Northumbria.

IV. A passage in Exodus telling of the Flood and sacrifice of Isaac which may be from another poem, but is of the same date and also probably from Northumbria.

V. A poem of the early eighth century containing stories from the Book of Daniel, also written in Northumbria, but with Kenticisms, due to an intermediate Kentish copy.

VI. A passage inserted into the Daniel containing the Song of Azarias and that of the " Three Holy Children " from the same source as the similar poem in the Exeter Book and of the same date and dialect as the rest of the poem. These are all in one handwriting, in a W.S. copy of the early eleventh century.

VII. Three short poems in another hand in a copy of the same date. Our MS. is therefore a compilation by two W.S. scribes of several poems, most of which are of undoubted Northumbrian origin, and some of which have undergone interpolation or revision in Kent. The present binding is of the fifteenth century, and in this binding, or some earlier one, some of the pages appear to have been misplaced or wrongly folded.

It is difficult to determine the relative dates of the three longer poems, the evidence from language, metre, and syntax being inconclusive. On the whole it may be said that Genesis and Exodus appear to be slightly older than Daniel.[1]

Because Exodus shows some marked points of resemblance with Beowulf in phraseology, it has been assumed that the writer borrowed from that poem and was writing later [2]; on the other hand, Exodus, despite its subject, shows

---

[1] Among other tests their early date may be proved by the presence of the form " tiber ", *sacrifice*, with " b " written between vowels for voiced " f ", modern " v ". Later the form would have been " tifer ", had it been recorded. The absence of such a form in Daniel may, of course, be merely chance, but in other respects that poem appears to be a little later.

[2] Sarrazin, Von Kædmon bis Kynewulf, pp. 45–6.

less of the influence of the new teaching ; it is altogether more primitive in character and it is possible that it was the poet of Beowulf who did the borrowing.[1]

This MS. is almost unique is being furnished with a number of very interesting illustrations.   These are usually brown in colour, but with an occasional effective use of black, red, and green, especially in the later pictures.   They are by two artists, the one illustrating up to the middle of the story of the Flood, and the last picture of the ark being by the second artist.   The illustrations continue up to Abraham's journey into Egypt ; after that blanks have been left for the pictures but not filled in.

Artists and scribes appear to have worked together, the illustrations pointing to the same date as the handwriting. While all are of great interest, some of the pictures show considerable skill in composition and many of the figures are very graceful.

Next in date to the poems of the Cædmon School comes almost certainly the Andreas.   This is a poem of 1,722 lines dealing with legendary episodes in the life of St. Andrew which is in the Vercelli MS. in the Library of Vercelli near Milan.   It occupies a position midway between the works of the Schools of Cædmon and Cynewulf, but it is included in this, rather than in the following chapter, because the poet, while, like the writers of the later school, choosing the life of an individual saint for his theme, has treated it, even more than they, in the manner of the native epic, having clearly taken Beowulf for his model in structure and having borrowed from that poem for vocabulary and phraseology.   Thus the poem begins in the style of Beowulf if not quite in the same words :—

> Lo ! we have learnt in days of yore,
> of twelve glorious heroes beneath the stars,
> servants of the Lord.   Nor did their valour fail
> in councils of war when banners clashed,
> after they had separated, as the Lord himself,
> high King of heaven, assigned to each his lot.

Then corresponding to the description of the sufferings

---

[1] Klæber, Beowulf, CXIV.

of Hroþgar at the hands of Grendel comes one of the persecution of St. Matthew by the Mermedonians. Matthew was
one of those whom God sent out. He was sent to an island,
where no stranger might enjoy a home or even life. All that
region was filled with deeds of violence, for in place of
bread and water the inhabitants devoured blood and the
flesh of men, come from afar. Such was their custom that
they took for their food, when needing sustenance, every
stranger who sought the island, and they put out their
eyes, the jewels of their heads, with the point of the spear.
Then the magicians blended with cunning skill a horrible
draught, which changed the understanding, the thoughts
of the men within their breasts, so that they recked no
longer of human joys, but ate hay and grass when needing
food. Accordingly as soon as Matthew had come to this
island of Mermedonia he was seized and bound, his eyes
were put out and he was given the terrible draught of poison.
But this did not seem to have the usual effect, for through
everything he continued to praise the Lord of Heaven, so
firmly was the love of Christ rooted in his heart. As he thus
prayed a light appeared, bright as the sun, and the voice
of God was heard, promising him final victory, but bidding
him endure for a time the violence of the people. Soon
Andrew should be sent to his help and comfort against the
enmity of the nation. After twenty-seven nights he should
be freed triumphantly from captivity. Then was Matthew
inspired anew. The shades of night fled away and the light
of dawn came in their wake. At this point a few days must
be allowed to have elapsed before the poem goes on. The
Mermedonians came crowding up, armour clashing, spears
screaming, to see whether any remained alive in the prison ;
and which of them in that case they might first slay for their
food, according to the allotted time, for they had the order
of the men written down in letters and figures, in which
they should become food for the hungry ones. There they
found Matthew, the battle-bold, awaiting his fate. The
time was past according to their reckoning, all but three
nights, for (they seem to have been very systematic) they
sat in council every thirty days, arranging the order in

which they should devour with bloodstained jaws the flesh of men for food.

Like Beowulf, St. Andrew goes to the rescue, but in his case reluctantly. God remembered Matthew and called to Andrew who was teaching the people of Achaia the way of life. He must go at once to Mermedonia to where his glorious brother was cast in bonds and would have to die in three days unless Andrew could arrive first. Andrew expostulated :—

> How may I, O Lord, over the deep paths,
> achieve this journey, along distant ways,
> so quickly, O Creator of the Heavens ?
> Thine angel may easily do it from out of Heaven,
> he knows the expanse of the sea,
> the salt streams and the swan's paths,
> the tumult of the surf and the terrible waters,
> the ways over wide countries. I have no friends,
> the men are strangers there, nor know I
> the nature of the men, nor are the cruel paths
> over the cold waves familiar to me.

God, however, reproaching him for his reluctance, bade him at once with the dawn of the very morrow enter his boat at the edge of the sea and make his way over the ocean. He should have God's blessing wherever he went.

The description of the voyage which follows recalls the epic. Andrew's disciples are his thanes, their code of morals is that of thanes :—

> Then Andrew departed, with the break of day,
> over the sand slopes to the sea strand,
> bold in heart, and his thanes with him,
> passing over the ground. The sea resounded,
> the currents beat upon the shore. The man was filled with hope,
> as soon as he found a broad ship on the strand.

> . . . .

> Then bright as morning
> came the fairest of beacons, hastening over the waves,
> holy from out the darkness, the candle of the heavens,
> over the flood of the waters.

Sitting in the ship, St. Andrew found three men, mighty thanes and bold, as if they had just come across the sea.

They were God Himself and two angels, in the garb of sailors. Andrew greeted them in much the same terms as those in which the coastguard accosted Beowulf. "Whence come ye," he asked, "travelling in your keel, mighty men in your boat, the wave-beater? Whence has the ocean brought you over the rolling of the billows?" He is answered, "We are of the tribe of Mermedonia, having come from afar, till tossed about we sought this land, so has the wind driven us astray."

Hearing that they were from Mermedonia, Andrew begged the leader to take him and his companions in their "beaked" ship to that country, "though I have few rings, adornments of value, thy reward shall be with God." He was answered, however, that no stranger or traveller might dwell in that region, but all suffered death in the city who had come from afar. Undeterred by this danger, Andrew still begged to be allowed to go, and the master of the boat at last consented to take him whither he wished as soon as he had paid his fare. But Andrew had nothing with which to pay. "I have neither plated gold nor treasure," he said, "wealth nor food, twisted wire nor land, nor interlinked rings with which to excite thy desire, thy pleasure, as thou hast asked." Whereupon he received the natural answer: "How didst thou come to seek the sea cliffs without treasure? Thou hast no bread for food, nor clear water to drink for thy comfort and benefit. It is a stern manner of life for those who long explore the paths of the sea!" Andrew replied that he had been sent out before by God with the command to take on the journey neither silver nor gold, and the master of the boat having at last consented, the bold ones, St. Andrew and his followers, entered the ship, each rejoicing in heart.

They started, but a storm soon arose :—

Then was troubled,
disturbed the sea of the whales, fish swam around,
glided through the water, and the grey mew
circled, eager for carrion. The sun grew dark,
the wind increased, the waves roared,
stirred up the currents, the rigging creaked,

wetted by the waves. Panic arose at the might of the threats,
the thanes were terrified.

But when the master of the boat suggested that they should
be landed to await the return of St. Andrew, they refused
with indignation :—

> Whither shall we turn without a lord (they asked)
> sad of heart, destitute of good,
> stained with sin, if we fail thee ?
> We shall be hated in every land,
> despised among the nations, wherever the sons of men,
> bold in courage, shall sit in council (deliberating)
> which of them has best followed
> his lord in battle, when hand and shield,
> on the plain of battle slashed by swords,
> in fierce strife endured hardship.

At this the master of the boat bade Andrew calm the fears
of his followers and beguile the long journey with stories from
the teaching of Christ, whereupon he related that of the
stilling of the tempest, assuring his frightened disciples
that they would be saved in like manner. Thus reassured
they fell asleep. This gives the poet an opportunity for
another fine description of a storm at sea, with the waves
beating over the boat. Andrew was astonished at the skill
with which the ship was managed. Though he had been
sixteen times in a boat amid raging seas, he had never
seen another so skilfully steered. Though at full sail
and with the foam dashing too over the prow, yet most
like a bird it was gliding smoothly along over the ocean.
It was just as if it were resting still on land where no storm
might reach it, and yet it was hastening swiftly under
sail. And the steersman was still young ! Finally after
other stories of miracles Andrew himself was overpowered
by sleep, and when he awoke it was to find himself lying
near a city with brightly tiled roofs and towers and with
steep cliffs before its gates, by which he knew that he was
in Mermedonia. Beside him lay his followers, who told
him the vision they had seen in heaven, whither the angels
had borne their souls while they slept. And now Andrew
understood that it was God who had been in the boat,

and he was filled with consternation at the freedom with which he had talked with Him. Being commanded to go forth at once to the rescue of Matthew, he found seven jailers standing before the gate of the prison. All were, however, struck with death at once, the prison doors fell open at a touch of the Holy Ghost, and the hero, bold in battle, entered. Matthew was found sitting alone and sad in the prison, but as soon as one saint saw the other, joy was renewed and each embraced and kissed the other. Here the MS. is defective for a few lines but it soon goes on to tell how Andrew freed two hundred and forty men, leaving none in the prison, and also of women fifty all but one. They did not stop for reprisals but Matthew led the multitude away, in God's protection under the cover of the clouds, before their old foes could come to stop them with their arrows.

After encouraging each other, the two saints parted and Andrew went into the city and sat down to wait beside a column of brass. Meanwhile crowds of the people had collected (the poet even calls them armies), and gone with the chieftains to the prison. There they found the keepers lying lifeless before the open doors, and turning back they announced to the citizens that they had found no single stranger alive within and the jailers lying dead outside. Fearful of hunger, since their intended victims had escaped, the leaders sent for the divining rod that it might indicate which of the natives should first give up his life as food for the rest, casting lots by devilish devices. The rod turned towards an old comrade who was a wise man and a leader in the army. Quickly was he seized and bound, but " bold in heart " he cried out that he would give them his own young son for their satisfaction in his stead. The people were so filled with the desire for food, so cruelly were they threatened with hunger, so fiercely did its pangs assail them, that many sought the death of the youth in spite of his prayers for mercy. Andrew, however, was filled with pity for him and, when the people hastened to slaughter the youth with their spears, their weapons all melted like wax. Thus the victim was saved and other means had to be considered.

While they were taking council together a devil appeared and pointed out Andrew as one who had come from afar and who had also emptied the prison, urging them to kill him. After the two, the devil and the saint, had had some argument and God had encouraged Andrew, promising that he should not be slain, though he should suffer cruel blows, he was seized, bound, and dragged along over hills and rocks as far as ways were to be found among the cities, over roads paved with stones. This went on till evening till the bright sun glided to its place, after which he was taken back to prison for the night. For four days the saint was tortured, the narrative being gruesome in its details and the chief variety in the accounts being found in the descriptions of the nights. On the first night the sufferings of the saint were increased by the cold, the description being taken, of course, from the poet's own experience :—

> Snow bound the earth with wintry storms,
> the air was cold with hard hailstones ;
> rime and frost, hoary, stalking foes,
> locked the houses of men, the seats of the people.
> The land was covered with chill icicles,
> the mighty waters frozen in the streams.
> ice bridged them over, making a pale path over the floods.

During the second night the devil came into his cell to tempt him. When on his way back on the third day, he cried to God for His promised protection, he was bidden look back to the bloodstained track which he had left behind him and Lo! wherever his blood had fallen, trees now were standing in full bloom. Finally, at the end of the fourth day, God appeared again and told him that his sufferings were now at an end. With this the poet finishes the first adventure of St. Andrew and explains that someone wiser than he must tell of his further sufferings, he will only relate a little more. It is an old story that he endured many hardships in that city.

Then suddenly he begins again without any preamble. Andrew saw two columns of stone, great and weather-beaten, standing beside the wall and apparently within the prison.

At his prayer the stone yawned at once and a stream gushed out, flowing over the ground, foaming waves covered the earth at dawn, the flood increased, panic arose, the armed warriors cast off sleep, the troubled waters swallowed up the ground, the doomed died. Then (with a touch of irony) the cupbearers delayed not, the servants, for each one was drink enough prepared after daybreak. The men lamented, they had a mind to flee the pale stream, they would fain save their lives and seek some way of escape among the hill caves. But an angel withstood them, he covered all the city with a pale flame, with fatal billows. One, however, was found to point out that fate was punishing them for keeping Andrew chained in prison and to advise them to set him free and ask his help. When the saint perceived that the pride of the bold ones was humbled, he bade the water, which by this time was up to the shoulders of the men, be still. As, bold, he stepped forth from his dungeon, a road was straightway cleared for him through the waters, ever was the earth dry where his foot passed. The citizens were glad of heart, joy had come out of sorrow, the sea went down at the bidding of the holy one. Then the hill opened, showing a terrible earth cavern and let therein the flood, the pale waves, be swallowed up together with the most wicked also of the men; of the hostile evildoers, fourteen departed in the waters, hastening to their fate beneath the earth.

Then all were terrified and cried out with one accord that it was the true God, King of all, who had sent His messenger to their help, and that they must hear Him willingly. The saint bade them be of good cheer, and upon his intercession the young men who had been drowned rose again uninjured from the dead and received baptism. St. Andrew bade a church be built upon the spot and appointed a bishop, Platan, to succeed him, being desirous, himself, to leave the gold city and its treasures and to seek his boat on the strand. God, however, commanded him to remain yet seven nights, and he, therefore, returned teaching many, and, to the grief of Satan, driving out the heathen priests and destroying those perverted in faith; then at the appointed time he prepared himself to return to Achaia, where we are told he was to suffer death.

The Mermedonians accompanied him to the shore and stood there weeping as long as they could see his boat on the water. The poem ends with this hymn :—

> One eternal God is there of all creation,
> His power and His rule over the world
> are widely spread, and His glory shines,
> above all in the splendour of the heavens,
> His beauteous glory for ever and ever,
> eternally among the angels. That is a noble king.

Two versions of this legend exist in Old English, one in prose of which we have two MSS., and this one in verse. Though the ultimate source must be Greek, Professor Krapp [1] has shown that our author probably used a Latin version chiefly, a translation from the Greek. Fragments of such a Latin text were discovered a few years ago, from which the poet may have drawn, though he may also have consulted the Greek. His version is, anyhow, by no means a mere translation. He has taken his subject and treated it independently in his own way. His work marks a definite stage in the history of O.E. religious poetry. While the older writers of the Cædmon School took books or episodes of Bible history for their subjects, later poets chose individual saints, treating their lives as far as possible on the lines of the old hero stories and this is to be seen more markedly in Andreas than in later works. Thus St. Andrew is represented as a chieftain, whose thanes follow him wherever he goes. Their ideal is perfect loyalty. When the saint declares that he has nothing with which to pay his fare, he mentions interlinked rings, such as the Germanic king or chief would break off from his chain in order to reward a follower. The thanes talk of the times when men should sit in council, deliberating who had best helped his lord in the strife, a picture which suggests a similar passage in the Battle of Maldon : " Think of the speeches which we oft uttered at the mead-drinking, when we upon the bench raised our boasts, we men in the hall, about hard fighting." Such

---

[1] Andreas and the Fates of the Apostles, p. xxi.

resemblances to the native epic might be multiplied, but these are enough.

The structure, too, of the native epic has been adopted if we may take Beowulf as the model.

As Beowulf goes across the sea to the scene of his exploits, so does St. Andrew ; as Beowulf first saves Heorot from Grendel, so the saint first incurs danger in rescuing St. Matthew ; as Beowulf goes on to finish his work with the destruction of the hag, so does St. Andrew through his own suffering gain his further object, the conversion of the Mermedonians. Finally, as Beowulf returns home afterwards, regretted by the Danes, so the saint goes back to Achaia amid the tears of the Mermedonians, when his work is completed. Perhaps, too, a recollection of the break between the accounts of the deeds of Beowulf in his youth and in his old age, has led the poet of Andreas to emphasize the pause between St. Andrew's rescue of St. Matthew and his own sufferings. The hymn at the end certainly recalls the eulogy of the fallen king which his retainers sang round his funeral pyre. Vocabulary and phraseology are also strikingly alike in Beowulf and the Andreas, but whereas in the first parallelisms are used with skill to develop the idea, in Andreas we seem to have a poet who loved words for their sounds, and the parallel phrase for its metrical effect in his line rather, sometimes, than for its value in working out his thought. The description of the cold, given above, will illustrate this.

The great merit of the Andreas poet is in his scene painting. The bargaining on the beach, the stormy crossing, the using of the divining rod, the picture of the column with the water gushing out and rising higher and higher, are all excellently drawn. Like the other O.E. poets, he has gained his effects by keeping to what he has seen and known himself or can imagine from his own experience, and can therefore describe convincingly ; he has made no attempt at local colour. The cold from which St. Andrew suffered is that of the English climate, which the poet himself had endured.

The connecting narrative, however, between these admirable pictures lacks the clear and certain touch of the

Beowulf poet. If the latter obtrudes his own personality too frequently, the author of Andreas allows his didactic element too much prominence. In short it is clear that the Andreas was written primarily for edification and that the poet had not the art to conceal that object.

He must have been a scholar, who could use his Latin and perhaps his Greek sources for himself, but who also knew and could enjoy the native literature. The best parts of his work are those which are most under native influence, such as his descriptions of the sea.

The poem must from linguistic tests have been written by an Anglian who lived rather later than Cædmon. Who he was is unknown. Scholars as late as ten Brink identified him with Cynewulf, assuming that a short passage on the Fates of the Apostles which follows in the MS. and a few lines which again follow that and which contain the name of Cynewulf in runic characters, are both part of Andreas, forming a conclusion to the whole work. This is not now generally allowed.

It has been mentioned that the MS. is at Vercelli near Milan. How it got there is a matter of conjecture still. We have no facts to go upon.[1] It is, however, a noteworthy point that the Church at Vercelli is dedicated to St. Andrew, and is English in the character of its architecture, in striking contrast to the usual Italian style. An English-looking church and an O.E. MS. in an Italian town suggest some connection between the two. Now the church was built by Cardinal Guala who was much in England and played a considerable part in English politics under John and Henry III, being rewarded by the gift, among other things, of the Priory of St. Andrew at Chesterton, near Cambridge. He was also a great collector of books which he bequeathed at his death in 1227 to his church at Vercelli. Two of these at any rate were written in English and of them the Vercelli MS. may have been one. This seems the most probable solution of the mystery yet offered. It is more satisfactory than that of Professor Wülker,[2] who

---

[1] Krapp, Andreas and the Fates of the Apostles, p. x ff.

[2] Grundriss zur Geschichte der Angelsächsischen Litteratur, III, § 194.

suggested that the MS. might have been left at Vercelli by some English pilgrim, bound for Rome, since, according to tradition, there was originally a hospice there for English pilgrims, and a library may have been formed for their use.

CHAPTER VII

CYNEWULF

From the earlier School of Cædmon we pass on through the Andreas poem to Cynewulf and his School, and here we are less fortunate in the matter of external information than in treating of Cædmon. An immense amount has been written on him and his literary activity, but all that we know for certain of him is his name, and that he wrote four poems, because he has introduced that name in runic symbols into as many works. We can also tell fairly closely from the form of his name when he lived. This cannot have been before the early ninth century if he was a Northumbrian, or rather earlier if he was a Mercian.[1] Many poems have been ascribed to him from time to time besides the four with the runes but, as he had apparently a habit of signing his works, it may perhaps be assumed that no complete work is his unless the runes are there. The poems which he certainly wrote are the following : first, one on the martyrdom of St. Juliana ; secondly, a hymn to Christ, and, thirdly, a poem on the finding of the Cross by St. Helena, or Elene, as the name appears in it, and that is probably the order in which he wrote them. At some time he must also have composed another poem, which may have been on the Fates of the Apostles, but all that we can be sure of as his are a few lines which contain the runes.[2]

Beyond his name and the date at which he lived a certain amount may also be gathered about Cynewulf from his poems. He must have been a scholar since all his works have Latin sources. The Martyrdom of St Juliana is based on the Acta St. Julianæ in the Acta Sanctorum for

---

[1] Cynewulf must represent an older Cuniwulf, since " y " is the mutated form of an original " u " ; and, since the poet spells his name Cynewulf, or Cynwulf, not Cyniwulf, he must have lived after the unaccented " i " causing the mutation had become " e " and could be elided in a medial position. These considerations bring us to the approximate date given.

[2] See Chap. VI, p. 148.

16th February; the middle part of Crist, the part which contains the runes, is from a sermon of Pope Gregory the Great on the Ascension ; and the Elene is taken probably from another version of the story found in the Acta Sanctorum for 4th March. Further, from the subjects which he chose, it is likely that Cynewulf was an ecclesiastic, possibly a monk. At the end of the Elene there is an epilogue which is thought by many scholars to be autobiographical. If this is the case he must have occupied a position of some importance, since he speaks of the rich gifts (appled gold and steeds) which he had received from his lord. Such gifts might have been for achievements on the battlefield, or, as would be more likely in this case, for valuable services as councillor. Rewards of such value would hardly have been given to a mere wandering minstrel for his songs. Moreover, in spite of his literary achievements, he does not seem to have been a professional singer ; his didactic purpose is always too prominent and he does not appear to have been initiated into all the secrets of the profession. If this epilogue is autobiographical, Cynewulf lived in the world in his earlier days and took orders later. It tells us that the bow and the bison were the joys of his youth, and that the sight of the galloping steeds raised regrets in his breast for the pleasures of past days. It hints at some occurrence which altered the course of his life and led him to enter the Church, and says that it was after that that he discovered his gift of song. "Till God," it says, "bestowed wisdom on me, a comfort to the old man, a peerless gift . . . opened out the power of song," but this statement recalls so clearly the story of Cædmon, which, we have seen, was a sort of commonplace about poets, that it raises a doubt whether the Epilogue, if accepted at all as autobiographical, is to be interpreted too strictly.

Cynewulf was certainly an Anglian. This is clear from metrical points and rhymes.[1] Whether he was a Northum-

---

[1] In verse 1242 of Elene we find the rhyme written miht—þeaht, which is only possible if we accept the Anglian forms mæht—þæht. See Kenneth Sisam, Cynewulf and his Poetry, Proceedings of the British Academy, Vol. XVIII.

brian or Mercian is more difficult to determine. Metrical points do not help us here, and any dialect form may have been introduced by a scribe. In favour of a Northumbrian origin for him it may be argued that Northumbria preserved its prestige as the centre of learning for Western Europe during the eighth century and into the ninth. Egbert, Archbishop of York (732–766), and his successor, Æthelbert (766–782), were both well known for their encouragement of learning. The famous scholar Alcuin (732(?)–804) was a pupil in the School at York; the library there was celebrated, and still flourishing in 850. It may well have been in it that Cynewulf found the books in which he tells us he searched for the story of the Cross. Finally it was in Northumbria that the veneration of the Cross began in the eighth century to play a prominent part in the services of the Church, a practice which may have inspired the Elene and the Dream of the Rood. On the other hand the incursions of the Danes were beginning at the end of the century; in 793 they attacked Lindisfarne, though it was not abandoned by the monks till nearly a century later; the following years saw the continuance of their ravages, and gradually the temporal supremacy passed to Mercia. Further, could it be proved that Cynewulf was the author of the life of the Mercian Saint, Guthlac, that fact would give some support to the theory of his Mercian origin. This cannot, however, be proved and since we know of no very celebrated monasteries or libraries in the more southerly kingdom, it seems probable on the whole that Cynewulf was a Northumbrian rather than a Mercian.

Several attempts have been made to identify him but without success. It has been sought to find him in the Cenwulf or Kenulphus, abbot of Peterborough,[1] who died in 1014; in the Cenwulf or Cynwulf of Mercia,[2] a contemporary of Aldhelm, and more recently and with more general support in the Bishop Cynewulf of Lindisfarne,[3]

---

[1] Kemble, Archaeologia, xxviii, p. 363, but the date is much too late.
[2] Grimm, Andreas and Elene, pp. li–lii, but this date is too early.
[3] Dietrich, De cruce Ruthw.; Grein, Kurzgefasste ags. Gram., S. 14; Trautmann, Kynewulf, pp. 93 ff.; Carleton Brown, Eng. Stud., 33, pp. 225 ff. The chief reason for this connection is the similarity of name. But

who died about 782, and of whom Simon of Durham tells us that he was imprisoned for a long time at Bamborough by Eadberht of Mercia, and, though set free later, resigned his see in 780, worn out by old age and troubles. Yet another identification has been with a Cynulf who attended a synod at Clovesho in 803 [1] and signed his name to a document there. But nothing can be said to be proved.

At one time many poems were attributed to Cynewulf on very slight grounds, and it is still a matter of uncertainty whether we have anything of his besides the four works which bear his signature. We may pass lightly over the views of early scholars who divided all the O.E. poetry we possess between the two names which were known to them, those of Cædmon and Cynewulf, and of most of those who were inclined to ascribe all the poems in the Exeter and Vercelli Codices, at any rate, to Cynewulf. That of Grein [2] may, however, be mentioned at greater length because, though his view is no longer accepted, by it he founded what may be called the Cynewulf Saga and exercised a great influence on later criticism. He gave the poet, besides the signed works, the Riddles, the Dream of the Rood, Andreas, Guþlac, the Phoenix, the Physiologus, the Ruin, the Rhyming Song and other short poems of minor importance, and from these, elaborating the Epilogue to Elene, he constructed a biography for the poet, as follows : " Born of a noble and wealthy family at the beginning of the eighth century, Cynewulf would seem as a boy to have conformed to the custom of his time and to have attended one of the monastic schools. The gay time of his youth and the first years of his adult manhood he describes in the first part of the Rhyming Song, and to this period doubtless belong his Riddles. But as youth passed Cynewulf entered the priesthood (why we are not told)

---

had the bishop been the author of such poems as Cynewulf's it is hardly possible that no allusion to the fact should be found in any mention of him. Moreover there is nothing in the Epilogue to Elene, granting it to be autobiographical, to suggest that Cynewulf held a high position in the Church, and the date is rather early for the signature Cynwulf.

[1] A. S. Cook, The Christ of Cynewulf, pp lxxiii ff. This date would suit, but it makes the poet a Mercian.

[2] Kurzgefasste ags. Gram., S. 13.

and from henceforth devoted himself to sacred poems. But after he had been made Bishop of Lindisfarne in 740, his high office seems to have brought him nothing but trouble and anxiety in those disturbed times. For a while he was kept a prisoner at Bamborough and his poetic activity may have been a great consolation to him during that time. In 780, bowed with age and worn out by his troublous life, he resigned his see and withdrew into obscurity, dying three or four years later." But it is now realized that all this story is without foundation, though it seems to have been a starting point for later investigations. More recently even Dr. Sweet,[1] with all his linguistic acumen and literary flair, allowed Cynewulf to be the author of several works besides the signed poems. As for instance the Riddles, Andreas, Guþlac, and the Dream of the Rood. The authorship of these has either been already discussed, or will be considered in the right place. It is enough to say here that though the Riddles were long accepted as certainly Cynewulf's, that view is now definitely given up,[2] and that the two poems without signature most generally attributed to him at present are the second part of Guþlac and the Dream of the Rood. The end of the first has been lost and may have contained the runes. His authorship cannot therefore be disproved and, if not by him himself, it is certainly by some member of his School and the author must have been much under his influence. The chief reason for ascribing the Dream of the Rood to him is the interest in the same subject shown in it and the Elene and, more especially, in the likeness in the description of the Cross in the two poems. It does not, however, contain the runes, and the description of the Cross in both is doubtless the conventional one. It again is more likely to have been of the School of Cynewulf than his own work, to have been written by a contemporary, stirred by the same theme, but possessing very different poetic gifts. Thus the only certain works of Cynewulf are the four mentioned above, Juliana, the middle part of Crist, Elene, and the

[1] Sketch of the History of Anglo-Saxon Poetry (Warton's History of English Poetry), Vol. II, pp. 16–19.
[2] pp. 205–6.

fragment following the Fates of the Apostles, which are all signed with his name. It is to them that we must look for our knowledge and appreciation of the poet.

The first of these is probably the story of the Martyrdom of St. Juliana, in the Codex Exoniensis or Exeter Book in the Library of Exeter Cathedral. This may be taken shortly, for as a whole it has little literary merit, though it contains some interesting passages. In 751 lines the poet has told the story of the sufferings and death of the saint at Nicomedia in the reign of Maximinian.

He begins in the orthodox way :—

> Lo! we have heard men ponder,
> the bold in deed relate, that which happened
> in the days of Maximinian, who throughout the world,
> a ruthless king, spread persecution,
> killed Christian men, felled churches,
> poured out upon the earth, this heathen warrior,
> the blood of the saints, of those praising God,
> of workers of righteousness. His kingdom was broad,
> widespread and excellent among the nations,
> extending almost over all the world.

After this introduction the poet goes on to tell how the maiden Juliana was betrothed by her father to a powerful and wealthy reeve, Heliseus (Lat. Eleusius), dwelling at that time in Commedia. She, however, rejected his addresses, expressing herself in no uncertain terms. If he would believe in the true God, she told him, she was ready without wavering, but, she went on, " if thou dost purpose sacrificing to a lesser god, thou shalt not have me for thy bride." No torture should turn her.

When Heliseus, naturally angered, complained to her father, the latter declared that, if his words were true, he would not defend her, but would give her up to Heliseus to punish as he wished. At first he remonstrated with Juliana gently enough though Cynewulf calls him angry. He began, " Thou art my dearest daughter, sweetest to my heart, the light of mine eyes," before going on to reproach her for refusing a rich and noble bridegroom whom it would be good to have as a friend. But when Juliana

continued to resist, saying that Heliseus might look elsewhere for his bride if he remained a heathen, Affricanus,
as we are now told he was named, became really angry and
finding her continue obdurate in spite of threats and beatings,
gave her up to Heliseus.

When brought before the reeve, all marvelled at her
beauty. He, like her father, at first tried persuasion. " My
sweetest sunbeam, Juliana," he began, " lo ! thou hast
radiance, a wondrous gift, the glory of youth." But when
she still resisted, he ordered her to be stripped and scourged,
and, when this did not move her, hung by her hair to a tree,
where she endured blows for six hours, after which she was
taken down and thrown into prison.

There a devil in the form of an angel came to tempt her.
He had been sent from God, he told her, to advise her to
sacrifice to the gods of Heliseus that she might escape the
terrible tortures prepared for her. But when Juliana,
suspicious of such advice, made him confess who he really
was, he admitted that it was he who had instigated the
soldier to pierce the side of Christ, Herod to behead John
the Baptist, and many others to cruel deeds. Satan was his
father ; he sent devils out in this way and, if they did not
succeed in doing some harm, they were bound and scourged
in the fire on their return. After this he went on to tell
her at considerable length in a noteworthy passage how he
set to work with his temptings. " Soon I am ready," he said,
" so that I can see through the whole man, and find out how
the heart is secured within, how the resistance is prepared.
I open the gate in the rampart through suffering ; when the
tower is pierced, an entrance opened out, then I first send
in a flight of arrows, bitter thoughts into the heart, till at
last it seems to the man better to fulfil the lusts of the flesh
than to praise God. . . . I could not relate, though I should
stay the summerlong day," he went on, " all the hardships
which I have brought upon men out of wickedness, since
first the sky was raised, the course of the stars fixed, and
the earth made firm." Never had he met anyone before
to resist him as she had done, he would have no cause to
laugh over this journey when he should have to pay the

penalty for his failure in his gloomy home. Not before
Juliana is summoned before Heliseus next morning, did she
set the devil free to seek the darkness of hell.

At this point, a considerable part of the MS. must have
got lost, if one may judge by the Latin version. We skip
the account of further tortures, of how the saint was bound
to a wheel set with sharp swords, and was also thrown into
fire, where an angel, however, put out the flames, and how
her executioners were converted and put to death. Here we
are told next how Heliseus caused a vessel to be made of
clay, filled with lead, and heated with piles of wood heaped
up round it and set on fire. Into this the saint was thrown,
but while the boiling lead spurted out, killing seventy-five of
the heathen, she remained in unblemished beauty. No
fringe nor garment of hers, neither hair nor skin, body
nor limb, was marked by the fire.

Finally the reeve, gnashing his teeth and raging like a
wild beast at Juliana's continued resistance and abusing
his gods, commanded her to be beheaded. As the saint,
rejoicing at being at the end of her sufferings, was led forth,
the same devil appeared and called upon the people to
avenge him for the night of suffering he had endured at
her hands. As soon, however, as she turned and looked at
him, he fled, crying, "Woe is me! Now I am undone."

Juliana, having been brought to the place where she was
to be put to death, exhorted the people :—

> I will teach you
> how ye should make your house secure, lest with sudden
>   blasts
> winds overthrow it. The walls must be the stronger
> to withstand the stormy showers,
> the thoughts of evil. With kindly love,
> clear faith, shall ye, strong of heart,
> make the foundations firm in the living rock.
> . . . Peace be with you,
> true love for ever.

Then her soul was borne away from the body into eternal
joy by the blow of a sword. Later, Heliseus having set out
on a voyage with his thanes was drowned with them and all

went down to hell, where his followers had no cause to expect treasures from the prince, those who before had received appled gold in the wine-hall on the beer benches. The poem ends with the passage containing the runes.

It is from its character that Juliana may be assumed to be the earliest of Cynewulf's works which we possess. Though he has shown some independence in the handling of his material, the style is bald and there is no attempt at shaping the story. But before considering the poem in further detail, it will be well to pass on to the Crist and Elene and to take the three together as illustrating the development of Cynewulf's literary power, its strength, and its weakness.

The next of Cynewulf's works is probably the Crist. Folios 8a–32b of the Exeter Book contain what was at first looked upon as a collection of hymns, arranged in three groups, five having as their subject the birth of Christ (vv. 1–339) ; five dealing with the Ascension (vv. 340–866) ; and seven with the Day of Judgment (vv. 867–end).

Later, however, these lines were considered to form a single poem treating of the three comings of Christ, the coming to earth at His birth, the coming to glory at the Ascension, and His last coming at the Day of Judgment, the three being closely connected.[1] Opinion has now, however, reverted generally to the earlier view in modified form, and it is now believed that we have to do with three distinct poems rather than with three groups of poems, which may all possibly be by Cynewulf, but are more probably by different authors. Either the second or the third may conceivably be his, because the runes stand between the two, but most probably they belong to Part II, since the verses in which they occur (797–810) are based on the same sermon on the Ascension by Pope Gregory the Great as is the rest of Part II, whereas Part III is from a different source.[2]

[1] Dietrich, Haupts Ztschr., 9, pp. 193–214.
[2] Further reasons are that in Juliana and Elene Cynewulf has introduced his runes near the end of the work, signing it as it approached completion, and, on the analogy of these poems it is likely that the runic passage would belong to what goes before rather than to what follows. Further in the MS. a space for two lines has been left between vv. 339–340,

Here therefore it is assumed that Part II only is Cynewulf's, and it only will be considered.[1] Parts I and III will be kept till treating of the writings of Cynewulf's School.[2]

The Ascension is very different in character from the Juliana. Besides being from its theme more lyrical, it shows a great advance in poetic thought and expression. It begins on a note of triumph with a slight reference to the birth of Christ, pointing out that angels did not appear in white garments then as they did at the Ascension. It then goes on to tell how the disciples hastened to follow their Lord to Bethany, where He revealed to them many wonders and gave them His last commands. " Rejoice ye in your hearts, never will I depart from you. Go forth now over the whole vast world, along its wide paths ; preach the glorious faith, and sow peace in the souls of men. I will be with you." After these words the only-begotten Son, the Co-eternal, ascended to His Father.

> Then was straightway heard a sound
> loud in the air, a troop of Heaven's angels,
> a beauteous shining throng ; the messengers of glory
> came in a company. Our king had passed
> through the temple's roof, while they looked on,
> who yet remained behind the loved one
> upon that meeting place, his chosen thanes.
> They saw their Lord ascend into the Heavens,
> the Son of God from earth. Sad were their souls,
> burning their hearts, their minds were filled with mourning
> because they might no longer see beneath the sky
> the one so loved. Then raised their song
> the heavenly messengers, they praised the Prince,
> extolled the Lord of Life, rejoicing in the light
> which shone upon them from the Savour's head.

Then the disciples saw about the glorious king two angels in shining robes, who cried out to them :

that is between the first and second parts, and between vv. 866–7, that is after the runic passage, as though the scribe meant some division at those places, whereas no such space occurs between vv. 796–7, just before the runes. Lastly, v. 867 begins with a capital, as if for a new poem.

[1] For full discussion of this question see A. S. Cook, The Christ of Cynewulf, xvi.

[2] See pp. 159 ff.

Why tarry ye, ye men of Galilee ?
We with this band will bear the Lord
in through the gates of heaven,
to the bright city, with this joyous troop—
of all the sons of victory the best
and noblest—which ye here gaze upon,
and see in happiness with riches shine.

Then bold in heart, but sad of mood, the disciples turned
to go to Jerusalem, into the Holy City and all awaited there
for yet ten nights the promise of the Lord as He had bidden
them, before He, the owner of the sky, the Ruler of all,
ascended up into the keeping of the heavens. It was right
that angels, brightly clad, should come to meet Him in
multitudes in the sky. That was the greatest of festivals
in glory, when the angels saw the Lord of Heaven welcome
on His high seat the Saviour of the nations. Here follows
the hymn of the angels in heaven :—

Now has the Holy One plundered Hell
of all the tribute which she in days of yore,
in strife unjustly swallowed up.
Now are o'ercome, in living torment,
abased and chained, and in Hell's depths
cut off from blessings, the warriors of the devil.
Nor might the adversaries succeed in war,
in weapon clashes. . . .
. . . Open ye, ye gates !
The Lord of all will enter in,
the King into His city with no mean company,
the Creator of the works of old shall lead the people
into the joy of joys, whom He from Satan's power
hath saved through victory.

Then the poet resumes :
Since the Saviour through His coming has given to every
man living the choice between the misery of hell and the
glory of heaven, bright light and hideous night, joy with the
Lord or clamour among devils, it is meet that the peoples
should give thanks to the Lord who has given us all wealth
and prosperity over wide lands and even pleasant weather
beneath the sky. Sun and moon are for all. The sentence is
reversed which said :

I created thee of earth, on it thou shalt live in sorrow,
inhabit with toil and endure misery,
thou shalt return again to that same earth, the prey of worms,
whence thou shalt seek thy fiery punishment.

Many talents has Christ scattered among men ; to one
wise speech ; to another noble understanding ; a third
may touch the harpstrings, and so on, with a long list
of gifts, among which comes the curious one of being able
to climb the steep high tree.

Thus has God honoured His own work.

Then comes a sort of application.

As the moon sends its light over the world, so does the
Church of God shine clearly in its unity of truth and right,
since the Ascension of the Son of God. The Church has
endured the persecution of law-breakers under the rule
of heathen guardians, when foes paid no heed to the truth.
But the glory of God's servants has come forth through the
grace of the spirit of that same Ascension.

After a passage dealing with the prophecy of Solomon,
when he said that the king of angels " shall ascend the
mountains, leaping over the high hills ", and a warning
that the Judgment is near, follow the lines with the runes
mentioned above, and the poet ends with an admonition
to all to prepare for the last day :—

When the Lord of might shall come to the council place
with the greatest of companies, a wide spread terror
and a loud, shall be heard, with clamour from heaven,
the cry of those lamenting. Sadly shall they weep,
before the face of the eternal judge,
who to their deeds can little trust.

Now it is as if we on the ocean flood
o'er the cold water wander in our keels,
over the wide sea on our ocean steeds,
fare in our wooden ships. Fierce is the current,
countless the waves on which we here are tossed
throughout this changeful world, wind-driven the seas,
over deep tracks. Stern was the way of life
ere we to land had sailed
over the raging surface. Then came help to us,

M

and us to a safe harbour bore
God's Son divine and gave us grace,
that we might see over the vessel's side,
where we could make secure our ocean steeds,
the old wave-coursers now make fast at anchor.

Leaving any detailed consideration of this work as of Juliana, till later, the great advance in poetic feeling and skill in Crist may be pointed out in passing. The theme may have been more inspiring, certainly the poet has gained in sureness of touch, in power of expression, and in grace of language.

The Elene, to which we now come, is generally considered to be Cynewulf's masterpiece. It must be his last work, for the Epilogue, already mentioned, whether it be taken as strictly autobiographical or not, must imply that the poet was an old man when he wrote it. In this poem of 1,321 lines, which like the Andreas is in the Vercelli MS., the poet tells the story of the finding of the Cross by St. Helena, the mother of Constantine the Great. The development of Cynewulf's powers can be seen by comparison of this poem with his earlier account of the martyrdom of St. Juliana. Both show the same influence of the warlike spirit of the native poetry in the figures of the saints. St. Helena is as uncompromising in her treatment of the Jews as is St. Juliana before Affricanus and Heliseus, but the Elene shows this influence also more directly in the account of the battle and voyage with which it begins. In Juliana Cynewulf concentrates upon his one theme, and shows only a general influence from the native poetry in the whole tone of his work ; in Elene he has become more sure of himself, the years have widened his outlook, and he has deliberately allowed himself to introduce themes which belong to that poetry, dwelling upon them with evident enjoyment.

He begins straight away with his story. Two hundred and thirty years had passed since Almighty God had been born, and the sixth year had come of Constantine's rule as emperor. . . . He was a just king whom God supported. But hostility threatened him, the tumult of war. Huns and Hrethgoths, Franks and Hugas collected their forces against him. Spears glittered and linked coats of mail. Amid shouts and the clashing of shields they raised their banners, and as soon as the bold warriors were collected the army marched forward. The wolf uttered his battle cry in the forest, did not conceal the secret of the strife ; dewy-feathered, the eagle raised his note, following the foe. Quickly this mightiest of forces, such as the king of the Huns had been able to summon from his neighbours on any side, hastened onwards, infantry supporting cavalry, till they encamped on the bank of the Danube with all the clamour of an army. They would take by force the kingdom of the Romans, plunder it with their troops. Then Constantine, aware of their coming, summoned by the sending of an arrow his warriors at once to battle. The Romans were soon ready, but they had a smaller band than that of the king of the Huns. The ravens screamed above them, black and eager for carrion, the trumpeters galloped forth, the heralds shouted. But the king was terrified as soon as he looked on the forces of the foreigners. He had small hopes of keeping his kingdom for want of men ; he had too few comrades against that overwhelming force of tried warriors.

But as he slept that night among his host, covered with his banner, a vision came to the emperor. A man beauteous, bright, and shining, appeared to him, and as he started from sleep, quickly spoke to him, naming him by name, while the shades of night slipped away. " Constantine ! the king of the angels," he said, " the controller of fates, hath bidden me offer thee a covenant. Fear thou not, though strangers threaten thee with fierce fight. Look up to the heavens to the Lord of Glory, there shalt thou find protection, the emblem of victory." Then with an open mind the king at once looked up as the friendly messenger of peace had bidden him and saw, above the roof of the clouds, the beauteous tree of glory, bright with ornaments :—

> adorned with gold, gems glittered,
> on the bright tree was written in letters
> shining and clear, " In this sign shalt thou,
> in this thy fearful peril, overpower the foe,
> and stay the hostile band."

As soon as he had seen the sign, Constantine bade men make a cross, the symbol of Christ. Then with the dawn he had his warriors roused, his banner raised for the fight and the holy tree carried before him into the multitude of the enemy, the divine symbol of God. Here follows a description of the battle in true Germanic style :—

Trumpets sounded
loudly before the armies, the raven rejoiced in the work,
the dewy coated eagle watched their course,
the warfare of the fierce. The wolf raised his cry,
the comrade of the woods. The terror of battle arose,

.   .   .   .

some of the foe battle destroyed,
some with difficulty saved their lives,
in that expedition ; some half dead
fled to security, and hid themselves
among the rocky cliffs, clung to the shores
around the Danube ; some drowning carried off
in the watery torrents at the end of their lives.
Then were the forces of the bold one full of joy.
They pursued the foreigners till evening time
from break of day ; their spears they hurled,
the snakes of battle.

.   .   .   .

The host was cut to pieces,
the shield-armed band of foes. Few escaped
of the army of the Huns back to their homes from thence.

Then it was seen that the Almighty king had given to Constantine fame in that day's work through the Rood tree.

Having returned home, he summoned his wisest councillors to a synod and demanded whether there were any in the wide throng, old or young, who could tell him truly what God it was whose emblem had appeared to him.

At first none could answer, but at last the wisest declared that it was without doubt the emblem of the King of Heaven. When the few who had been baptized heard, they rejoiced that they had now opportunity to expound the grace of God before the emperor. He received baptism and with joy in his heart devoted himself to the service of God.

Then he learnt in the Scriptures where the Lord of

Heaven had been hanged through malice on the Rood-tree,
and he charged his mother to set out over the floodways
with a band of men to seek carefully where the glorious tree
was hidden beneath the earth.

Nothing loath Elene was soon ready and with a multitude
of followers set out for the sea :—

        The ocean steeds
along the strand stood ready,
sea steeds at anchor, resting on the waves.
Then was well known the woman's enterprise
when with a band she sought the surging flood.
There many a proud one by the curving coast
stood on the shore. At times they hastened onwards,
over the march's paths, one force after the other
and then they laded with their battle coats,
their shields and spears, with warriors corslet-clad,
with men and women, the coursers of the waves.
These sent they hastening o'er the monsters' deep,
these lofty threshers of the waves. Side oft received,
above the eddying deep, the billows' blows,
the sea gave forth its voice.
There might he see, who on that journey looked,
the wooden ships breaking their way across the waves,
hastening under the swelling sails, the sea steeds tossing,
the wave floaters moving onwards. The warriors were glad,
the bold at heart, the queen rejoiced in her journey,
as soon as to the haven the ring-bound prows
over the fastness of the sea had glided onwards,
into the land of the Greeks. Their keels they left
on the seashore, lashed by the waves,
their old sea homes, secure at anchor,
to await upon the water the business of the men,
till that the warlike queen, among her band of followers,
should seek them once again across the eastern roads.

They landed, bearing aloft their banner, that precious
woven treasure, the gift of the king. All those Jews were
summoned to come to council, who were best versed in
the mysteries of God and could expound the law aright.
Three thousand were chosen for this purpose, and these the
" gracious " queen addressed in words which were, however,
anything but gracious. She had learnt through the words of

the prophet that they had been dear in days of yore to God, but they had doomed Him to death who Himself had awakened many from death in the earlier life of the race. They must go at once and choose men who had the law deepest rooted in their hearts, who could answer truly each question which she should put to them. This time a thousand were found who knew well all the earlier traditions of the Jews, and these hastened to where the queen awaited them in pomp upon her throne. She addressed these in much the same way as the others. They had received the teaching of the Apostles and prophets, but had wearied of it and followed false doctrine. They were to go at once and find those who could answer her out of the greatness of their knowledge. This time five hundred were selected, and these, when summoned before the queen and upbraided in the same fashion, answered with one accord that they had indeed learnt the Hebrew law, but did not know at all what offence towards her they had committed. However, they also were sent away to find out those who possessed the most wisdom and intelligence and who would boldly and directly answer her.

Then one, named Judas, came forward and explained to his fellows that the queen was asking about the tree of victory, on which God's own Son had suffered, whom their fathers had hanged, though guiltless, on the high tree. They must be careful not to say where the cross was hidden, for his grandfather Sachius had told his father Symon : " If ever thou shouldest hear wise men ask about the holy tree and disputations arise thereover, make it known at once ere death take thee. Nor shall after that the Hebrew rulers keep the kingdom, but the glory and dominion shall live for ever of those who worship and love the crucified king." The plots against Christ had not succeeded, he added, for after three days the Ruler of the skies, the Light of Lights, had risen again and appeared to his disciples. The other Jews declared that they had heard nothing of all this before. Judas must do as he thought best if he were questioned. The man would need wisdom and wariness of speech who should answer the noble queen before this company

in the meeting place. While still pondering and disputing
they were summoned with ceremony to the council chamber.
But here they were stiff, harder than any stone, and would
not give any answer about the mystery and where the Lord
had suffered. Elene, now really angry, threatened them
with death if they persisted longer in their falseness, and
nevertheless they would not be able to avert fate and conceal
the mighty secret. Terrified now for their lives, they pointed
out Judas as of noble race, wise in word-craft, and the son
of a prophet, bold in the council hall. He would make known
words of wisdom to her through his great skill.

After this all were sent home except Judas who was given
his choice of life or death, according to whether he would
reveal where the cross was buried or not. He answered :—

> How could it be with one who in the desert,
> weary and foodless, treads the moorlands,
> in hunger's grip, if bread and stone
> together both should come into his sight,
> the hard and soft, that he should take the stone
> as shield from hunger and neglect the bread,
> turn him to poverty and refuse the food,
> should scorn the better when he may have both ?

Judas was, however, still torn between the fear of losing
heaven for himself or this present kingdom for the Jews,
and tried to temporize. How could he find out what happened
so long ago ? More than two hundred years had passed since
then and, when Elene pointed out that the siege of Troy
had been earlier still and yet men knew all about it, he
answered that those events had been written down of
necessity, whereas no one had heard of this happening till
now. Finally, when, after threats and abuse from the
queen, he still refused to speak, he was bound in chains
and thrown into a dry pit, where he was left to suffer the
pangs of hunger for seven nights. At the end of that time,
however, he could hold out no longer. " I implore thee,"
he cried, " by the God of Heaven, to let me out of this
torment, miserable from hunger's pangs. I will willingly
reveal the holy tree, now that I can no longer conceal it
because of hunger. This captivity has been too strong,

the affliction too severe, and the suffering too hard during these days. I cannot endure more nor conceal longer the truth concerning the cross."

As soon as he had been released, all set out for the hill of the crucifixion, though Judas did not yet know exactly where the cross had been buried. After a hymn of praise to God, he prayed that a sign might be given him as one had been given to Moses to show him the tomb and bones of Joseph. Immediately a vapour arose and, after giving thanks, Judas began, resolute and glad, to dig at once beneath the earth, till at last twenty feet down he found the crosses buried together. Joyously he seized one in his hands and raised it from the tomb, and the nobles returned into the city and set down the three before the queen. Being unable to tell Elene on which the Son of the Almighty God had been crucified, for they had heard that two others had suffered with him, Judas bade all be set up in the middle of the town to await some sign from the Almighty King. Triumphantly they sat there singing and discussing until the ninth hour ; then came a multitude bringing with them a dead man on a bier, young and lifeless. Judas bade them lay the corpse on the ground and raised up two of the crosses over the lifeless body. It remained dead, the limbs growing cold. But as soon as the third cross was raised up, the dead man arose at once, soul and body together again, and all gave praise to God, the Father and the Son, calling to mind the miracles which the Lord of Hosts had worked for the benefit of men. Then an enemy, the devil from hell, rose flying into the air and crying, " What man is this who destroys my followers, plunders my possessions ? Sinful souls may no longer dwell in my keeping, now that a stranger has come . . . and has robbed me of all my treasures. Much harm hath he done me who was brought up in Nazareth, since he grew out of childhood. . . . Through one Judas I rejoiced formerly . . . through another I am put to shame, outlawed and friendless."

The news of the finding of the cross, which had so long been buried, spread far and wide throughout the country, the greatest of griefs to the Jews. The queen sent messengers to Rome to tell the emperor the wondrous tidings. It was for him the greatest of consolations when the warriors brought him the news. He commanded them to hasten back to the holy city to greet the triumphant Elene and bid her build a temple to God, to the glory of Christ, on Calvary, where the cross had been found. Those most gifted with skill in stonework were sought out to prepare the church ; the cross was adorned with gold and cunningly set with all kinds of precious stones and enclosed in a silver box. Here it remained ever after, a refuge for the sick in every kind of suffering, adversity, or sorrow.

After a while Judas, having received baptism, would have chosen the "better part", but fate prescribed that he, so full of faith and dear to God, should remain in the world, and Elene, by the advice of men in conference, bade Eusebius, the wise bishop of Rome, be fetched that he might consecrate him as bishop in Jerusalem and name him afresh Cyriacus. But still Elene was not satisfied. She remembered the nails with which the Saviour's feet and hands had been pierced, and prayed Cyriacus to find where they still remained hidden in the earth as he had found the crosses. Prostrating himself to the ground therefore, on Calvary, he prayed that the mystery might be revealed to him, and a sign shone forth at once where they were gazing, a dancing flame brighter than the sun. The people saw the nails shining from beneath the earth like stars or golden gems glittering brightly. Great rejoicings followed. Many believed, having seen the token of victory, the true wonder for themselves. With tears of joy Cyriacus took the nails and brought them to the queen and, when she asked what would be best to do with them, bade her have them put into a bridle for Constantine, the noblest earthly king. With them he would overpower every foe. He who had them in his bridle would have victory in fight everywhere. As the prophet had sung :—

That shall be known that the bit of the king's steed
shall be honoured, the ring of the bridle. That emblem
shall be called holy and he blessed with triumph,
honoured with victory, whom the charger bears.

The bridle was made and sent over the sea to the emperor.

Lame, palsied, halt, wounded, lepers, blind, despised, and sad, all came from afar to Cyriacus and ever found healing with him.

When, at last, she was ready to depart, Elene called all the noblest of the Jews to her in the holy city and exhorted them, giving gifts of treasure to Cyriacus. By that time spring was passed and it was within six days of the coming of summer. Finally after a prayer for the welfare of all who honour the true cross the poem ends and the Epilogue follows. Because of its importance it is given here in its entirety :—

Thus I old and ready to depart by reason of the mortal flesh,
wove with skill in words and collected wondrously,
pondered from time to time and sifted my thoughts
closely of a night. I did not know fully
the truth of the cross till a larger view
through His glorious might, in the thoughts of my heart,
wisdom revealed. I was stained by my deeds,
chained by my sins, tormented with cares,
cruelly bound, oppressed with trouble,
till He bestowed wisdom on me through the holy orders,
as a comfort to the old man ; a peerless gift
the mighty King meted out to me and poured into my mind,
revealed the bright light, increased it from time to time,
set free my body, unlocked my heart,
opened out the power of song, which I have used joyously,
and willingly in the world. I had thought
about the tree of glory, not once but often
before I revealed the marvels
of the bright tree, as I found them in the books,
in the course of events, set forth in writing,
concerning the emblem of victory. Ever was the man till
    then
buffeted by waves of care, a drooping torch,
though he had in the mead hall received treasures,
appled gold. The comrade in distress
mourned for his bow, endured the clutch of sorrow
in self-communings, when before him the steed
paced the mile-paths, boldly galloped,
adorned with ornaments of wire. Hope is lessened,
joy, in consequence of years, youth has passed away,

the old pomp. The bison was in days of yore
the pride of his youth. Now are his days
according to the allotted span passed hence,
his joy in life departed, as the waters glide away,
the hastening streams. For each are riches
but passing beneath the sky ; the beauties of the land
vanish under the clouds, just like the wind
when it arises loud, before men's eyes,
chases through the clouds, fares raging
and again straightway grows silent,
closely penned in prison cells,
cruelly suppressed.

The whole work is brought to a conclusion by a short
passage on the Doomsday with the usual division of people
into three groups. The soothfast shall be above in the fire,
the band of the blessed, so that they can endure, bear the
flames easily, without hardship. The sinful, those tainted
with evil, shall be afflicted in the middle, men sad of heart,
in the hot flames, smothered in smoke. The third part,
the accursed evildoers, shall be at the bottom of the fire,
because of their earlier deeds, the company of the wicked
in the grip of the flames. They shall be wiped out from the
mind of God in that dwelling of death. Those who are washed
like pure gold, cleansed in the burning from every spot, shall
see God.

Cynewulf must also have written a fourth work, for, as
has already been mentioned in speaking of the authorship
of the Andreas,[1] the runes spelling his name occur in some
lines in the Vercelli MS., which were discovered there by
Professor Napier in 1888. These lines are not complete in
themselves and have been assumed by some to belong to
a short poem on the Fates of the Apostles, which comes
just before, in which case the Fates must be, of course, by
Cynewulf. Others have gone farther and taken the Fates
as a continuation of Andreas. They consider it a sort of
epilogue in which the poet finishes up his full story of one
apostle by a general survey of the fates of the others, and
they therefore ascribe the whole to Cynewulf. There seems,
however, little beyond proximity to support these views.

[1] Chap. VI, p. 148.

No common features of style or diction are to be observed between any two, and both the runic passage and the Fates are very inferior to Andreas. While too much must not be made of that argument, for great inequalities of style and treatment are to be found in all works of any length, and the use of an accepted poetic diction tended to produce a certain superficial similarity in all works, still it may be questioned whether a poet who had dealt with so much power and fulness with the life of one saint would be likely to content himself with merely summing up the fates of the others. Moreover Andreas is too early to be Cynewulf's. It is safer to assume with Sievers [1] that the rune passage is a survival from a quite distinct poem, but it is too short to give us much idea of the character of this fourth work of Cynewulf's. [2] He must therefore be judged as a poet on the merits of the three works, Juliana, the middle part of Crist, and Elene. There is no proof that we have anything else, beyond the fragment, by him, nor have we any information about his personality beyond what may be gleaned from those works.

In Juliana Cynewulf has followed his original very closely on the whole, though allowing himself some liberty in drawing his heroine. In the Latin as in the Middle English version she tries to temporize with Heliseus. First she refuses him till he shall have attained a certain rank. Then, when he has attained that and again comes forward, then and then only, does she declare she will never marry a heathen. Among the Anglo-Saxons straightforwardness was a much esteemed virtue, if we may judge by such passages as that in which Beowulf rejoices in looking back over his past life, because he has not sworn false oaths. Cynewulf, to make his subject more acceptable to his public, and no doubt to satisfy his own sense of fitness, has made Juliana declare from the beginning that she will never marry Heliseus unless he will accept Christianity. And, though he has made her quite as unbending and uncom-

[1] Anglia, XIII, pp. 21 ff.
[2] For a discussion of the whole question see Andreas and the Fates of the Apostles, ed. by G. P. Krapp.

promising as any Germanic warrior could have been, there is nothing vindictive in her speeches. Cynewulf has pursued the policy of the Church of the time for the spread of Christianity by producing a poem as near as possible in character and form to the native poetry, but with a saint in the place of the native heroes. In Elene he has allowed himself much more freedom. He has taken his story and added greatly to it, thereby increasing its appeal to his public. He begins with the preparations of the Huns and other nations against Constantine, gives the dream as in duty bound, and then indulges in a full description of the battle and of St. Helena's journey, in perfect Germanic style, with the conventional figures of wolf, eagle, and raven and all the regular terms for ships and waves. All the way through he expands his original to some extent and finally he adds an Epilogue of his own and a short passage on the Day of Judgment, a favourite theme of the time.

Unfortunately, however, he has marred the quality of his work by his treatment of it in other ways. He set out to be a didactic poet ; his aim was to instruct, and he has allowed that aim to be too prominent. The speeches in Juliana and Elene are too long and often dull. In both works it will be seen that Cynewulf's gift was not for story-telling. In neither has he been able to maintain the interest by differentiating his episodes. In Juliana, if no name were mentioned, it would be difficult to say in any particular scene whether the saint was confronting her father or her suitor. In the same way in Elene, unless the number of the Jews present were given, it would be hard to say in any particular passage whether they were being summoned before the queen for the first or the second time. The third occasion, on which the Jews are made to answer back, is more distinct. In this respect Cynewulf's stories may be contrasted with Beowulf and Andreas. In both these works each episode, the three fights in the one and the various adventures of St. Andrew in the other, stands out absolutely distinct.

Again Cynewulf is behind the poets of Beowulf and Andreas in character drawing. In both of these one can understand the motives and follow the doings of the actors, though in Beowulf some of these are admittedly monsters. It is true that at the first glance the poet's psychology seems at fault in Andreas; it is at the moment at which the old senator is offering his son to be slain in his place that he chooses to give him the epithet brave. But it is clearly only a stereotyped term, possibly used ironically; the people round as well as the poet himself are obviously alive to his cowardice. In Beowulf and Andreas the delineation of character is elementary certainly, but it is there.

But stereotyped, however, as Cynewulf's personages are, occasional human touches appear, as when, for example, the devil is made to come and taunt Juliana on her way to execution, but flees at a glance from her; and in the description of Judas in his prison, with all power of further resistance destroyed by starvation; and there is some attempt at development of character in the account of the rising anger of Affricanus and Heliseus at Juliana's persistent opposition; but the crudity of wooing by torture has not struck the poet, nor the want of tact, to say the least of it, shown in Elene's addresses to the Jews. Though elsewhere he has not hesitated to alter his original, as in making Juliana straightforward in her dealings with her suitor, here he has been content to accept the facts as he found them, without attempting to give any connection between motive and action.

It is in his pictures, in his scene painting, that Cynewulf excels and, to a less extent, in his lyrical passages. Even in Juliana there is some indication of this power in the figure of the saint before her judges and when led to execution. In the Crist, though there is less opportunity for such descriptions, the picture of the Ascension with which it begins is finely drawn. But, naturally, it is in Elene that we get this power best illustrated. Each scene between Elene and the Jews, taken by itself, gives a good picture; in them we see the queen seated on her throne, and we hear the trumpets sounding to summon the Jews. But it is in those in the style of the native poetry that we get the finest effects, in the account of the battle at the beginning, with the figure of the Cross shining out from the sky. Only less good is that of the voyage. From this it is clear that Cynewulf was at his best when he allowed himself to turn to the native literature. His battles and sea descriptions are traditional, he had probably been neither a soldier nor a sailor ; he had not been in a battle himself nor made a difficult voyage, but he had entered sufficiently into the descriptions of others to be able to reproduce such scenes in a telling fashion.

The Crist does not show the force of emotion or passion of the Dream of the Rood, the Wanderer, or the Lament of the Wife, but it betrays a sincere feeling for beauty of thought and form, and it is written with a certain grace and pathos ; at times it rises to something more. Cynewulf must have held himself severely in check over Juliana if he could turn from a work of its stern tone to one of the emotional fervour of the Crist, in which the lyrical quality is further enhanced by the thought being made to end with the line instead of in the middle of the verse, as in the case of the epic.

In Elene, Cynewulf has revealed himself at the height of his powers. He has gone back to his earlier style in his choice of a theme and of narrative form, but he has allowed himself much greater freedom of treatment. Advancing years have widened his sympathies and his outlook. While the lighter touch developed in his more lyrical poem, the Crist, has relieved the plainness of his style, as seen in Juliana, he has no longer thought it necessary to turn his back on the secular literature of the period but has interwoven its material and spirit with those of his religious theme, to the great enrichment of his work. By this method he has achieved what is certainly his masterpiece.

If, as has been suggested, he was originally a professional minstrel in his youth, it would explain his ease in his battle and sea pictures but, in other respects, it seems doubtful. His kennings individually are often good, and his use of variation pleases the ear ; he has a large vocabulary and he is evidently sensitive to the sound of his line ; in short he is an artist in words. At the same time he has not made

the same use of his kennings as has the poet of Beowulf.
They are often mere synonyms, giving variety of sound
only, each adding nothing more to the thought. Thus within ten lines in the description of Elene's voyage, the ships
are called strandhorses (fearoþhengestas) ; seahorses
(sǣmearas) ; wave horses (wǣȝhengestas), all of which mean
precisely the same thing and are merely variants to the ear.
It is true that later on the terms threshers of the deep
(brimþissan) and seahomes (ȳþhofu) are used, which do
add to the idea, but in the others Cynewulf has missed his
opportunity by which a fine picture might have been made
still richer.

Cynewulf's feeling for pictorial effect shown in his scene-
painting is seen also in his similes, in that when in Juliana
the devil describes his attacks on the human soul under
the figure of the taking of a city [1] or when the heart is compared to a house which must be guarded with care,[2] or
still more when, in Crist, life on earth is compared to a
voyage with its dangers.[3] Here also may be mentioned
Judas's comparison of his perplexities with those of a traveller
in a desert, who is offered his choice between bread and
a stone.[4]

Finally a word must be added on Cynewulf's use of the
end rhyme which was gradually making its way in beside
the alliteration. This is seen most strikingly in the Epilogue
to Elene which he begins with a passage of fifteen lines
in which with one exception, (probably therefore corrupt),
the two halves of each long line rhyme together. Thus
he begins :—

Þus ic frōd ond fūs þurh þæt fǣge hūs.

Thus I old and ready to depart through this mortal house
(*of the flesh*), and so on through the passage, with alliteration
and end rhyme together.

[1] Jul., vv. 398, ic bēo ff.   [2] Ibid., vv. 647 ff.
[3] Cr. II, 410, or 850 of whole.   [4] El. vv. 609 ff.

Chapter VIII

POEMS FORMERLY ASCRIBED TO CYNEWULF

As has been said elsewhere [1] many poems have been attributed to Cynewulf by one scholar or another of which his authorship cannot be proved because the runes are absent. Of these the one perhaps most generally given to him is the Dream of the Rood. It is in the Vercelli MS., where it is divided from the Elene by four sermons. In it the Cross is represented as appearing to the poet in a dream, and giving an account of the Crucifixion in which it had played an unwilling part. Like Langland in later times, the poet has by his use of the Dream convention secured to himself freedom in the handling of his matter and, in his personification of his subject, has been able to give an extraordinarily living and vigorous picture of the scene.

The poem opens, like the secular lyrics, with an introductory passage, in which the poet describes the situation before beginning his actual story :—

Lo ! I will relate the most glorious of visions,
the dream which came to me at midnight
after the owners of speech were lying at rest.
It seemed to me that I saw a wondrous tree
borne into the air, surrounded with light,
the brightest of trees. All that emblem was
flooded with gold, gems lay
fair about its foot, in like fashion were five
above at the span of the arms. Angels of the Lord watched,
beauteous through all eternity. That was indeed no Cross
    of a malefactor,
but holy spirits gazed upon it there,
men throughout the world and all this glorious creation.
Peerless was that tree of victory and I stained with sin,
wounded with evil.

[1] Chap. VII, p. 153.

Then the poet goes on to say that though the tree was worthily covered with " weeds ", gold and jewels, yet he could perceive through the gold the earlier struggle of the wretched, since it was at times wet with the flow of blood, as well as at times adorned with treasure. At last, after lying long in contemplation, he heard the tree begin to speak :—

It was in days of yore (I remember it still),
that I was hewn down at the edge of the wood,
severed from my roots. Mighty foes took me thence,
set me up for a spectacle, bade me raise their outlaws.
Men bore me on their shoulders till they set me up on a hill,
foes enough made me fast. I saw the Lord of mankind
hasten with great valour, that He might mount upon me.

But the Cross durst neither bend nor break against the command of the Lord, when it saw the earth tremble, though it might have felled all its foes :—

I trembled when the warrior clasped me, nor durst I bow to
the earth.
As a cross I was set up, and I lifted up the mighty king,
the Lord of Heaven, nor durst I bow in allegiance.

When the foes pierced it with dark nails it did not dare to injure them :—

They reviled us both together ; I was all streaming with the
blood
shed from out the side of the man after He had given up the
ghost.
. . . Darkness had
veiled with clouds the body of the Allruler.
Shadows drove out the bright gleams
black under the clouds. All Creation wept,
lamented the fall of the King. Christ was on the Cross.
However there came eagerly from afar
nobles to the one in His solitude. All this I beheld.

The Cross then goes on to relate how, while it was left neglected and pierced with arrows, Christ was lifted from that grievous torment and laid down, weary of limb, while He rested for a while, worn out after great strife ; how a tomb was hewn out of bright stone in full view of the murderer (the Cross) and how His disciples sang, sadly, a song of sorrow in that evening hour, when they had to depart, leaving their glorious Lord to rest there " with no great company ".

> The voice of the warriors rose up ; the corpse,
> fair house of life, grew cold.

Finally it tells how it and the other crosses were thrown down and buried deep in the earth until the servants of God learnt of this and (here is a gap) . . . adorned it with gold and silver. Moral reflections follow on the veneration shown to the Cross now as contrasted with the contempt which it had formerly endured.

It is not certain where the poem ends. After this fine picture follow many lines in the MS. of very inferior quality, but with no indication by punctuation or capital that another poem has been begun. It is, of course, possible that a poet who could rise to such sublime heights in description was unable to attain anything of the same level in other directions, or these lines may be an addition made by the scribe from another poem because of the similarity of subject matter. Such a proceeding is suspected in other cases. Anyhow, whether the poem in the Vercelli MS. is by Cynewulf or not, it is not original, but a working up of an older one from which three short passages almost identical with lines here, are found on the Ruthwell Cross already described.[1] These are in the Northumbrian dialect and of an early date.[2]

The question of Cynewulf's authorship of the later version has been much disputed. The general resemblance in subject matter in the Dream and Elene is obvious. Not only is the Cross the central theme in both, but there is a definite similarity in the description of it in the two poems. Moreover certain kennings are common to both, such as, for instance, the terms " Wuldres trēow ", *tree of glory* ;

---

[1] See Chap. I, p. 18.
[2] This is shown by the retention of the " i " of unaccented syllables in its original form and possibly by the word " heafdum ", *head*, v. 63, which has been explained by some as a survival of an old instrumental singular, used as a dative and found occasionally elsewhere. See Streitberg, Urgermanische Grammatik, § 171.

" sigebēam ", *tree of victory*, for the Rood ; and in the Epilogue Cynewulf speaks of himself as having been occupied before with the thought of the Cross. But against these arguments it may be urged that the description of the Cross was probably the conventional one which would have been used by anyone treating the subject ; that the kennings common to both poems are either such as are obviously appropriate to the theme, or may be found elsewhere, and that Cynewulf's statement of his earlier interest in the Cross need not be taken to mean that he had treated it before. Moreover the one absolute proof of his authorship, the presence of the runes, is wanting and the poem is complete. Further it must be allowed that the two poems differ greatly in character and style. In the Elene it is in the accounts of the battle and the voyage that Cynewulf has shown his greatest power, nowhere in it has he given any indication of such lyrical gifts, such emotional quality, and power of sustained passion. If we are to look for qualities in Cynewulf's proved works which at all suggest his authorship of the Rood, it is to the Crist that we must turn. There we do find something of the same emotional fervour, but no indication of such sustained power of vivid representation. It is, of course, possible that a poet who had already treated his theme in lyric form was moved to go on with it and extend it into a narrative, or that a poet having treated the subject in narrative form was inspired by the central theme to work it up alone as a lyric, though this would be against the implication of the Epilogue. But it is at least equally probable that such a theme would have appealed to more than one man, especially at that time.

The veneration of the Cross had been a regular part in the services of the Church since the sixth century, and in the seventh was gaining further prominence. Bede tells us the story of the piece of the Cross which had been brought to Constantinople at the beginning of the fifth century, and of the discovery of a similar piece in St. Peter's by means of a vision, which appeared to Pope Sergius I in 701.[1] Abbot Ceolfriþ of Wearmouth was in Rome that year and

---

[1] De sex ætatibus seculi, for 701.

may well have brought back the news to Northumbria. In any case it would have been known and would have been likely to inspire more than one poet to take the Cross as his subject, whether for a narrative or for a lyric. Whoever the author of this exquisite little poem may have been, it is well worthy of study. A poet of those days made no attempt to give local colour to his story, and our author, whether or no he had any idea that the setting of the Crucifixion was different from anything that he himself had seen, has, in telling his story, visualized the scene for himself and presented a telling picture to his audience, in a form and terms which would be understood.

Thus, though the term " Rood " for the Cross is retained sometimes, as the one used in the Bible story, that of " gallows ", the native instrument of death, occurs as frequently. So Christ is represented as a native chieftain, the disciples are his thanes. The description of the burial is very similar to that of Beowulf.[1] The disciples sang their song of sorrow in the eventide, just as Beowulf's followers, sons of princes, valiant in battle, lamented their care, bemourned the King, related tales, and spoke about the man.

As in all O.E. poetry, nature is in sympathy with the tragedy enacted, it forms a harmonious background ; the darkening of the heavens is, of course, taken from the Bible narrative, but in giving the final touch to his scene the poet has not been afraid to draw from heathen poetry. " All creation wept, lamented the fall of the King," is an echo of the description of the death of Baldor, the sun god, for whose untimely end all nature lamented, and whose death forms the subject of a most telling story in the old mythology.

But, in spite of this feeling for harmony, the poet was fully alive to the value of contrast in getting his effects. This comes out very clearly in the description of the Cross, at times covered with blood, at others shining with jewels, and it is equally striking in the poet's choice of terms. He is careful to use the expressions " God of hosts, Ruler and

[1] Beowulf, vv. 3169 ff.

King " at the very moment of telling of the ignominious death on the gallows. The force of contrast is conveyed, too, in the picture of the nobles coming to the one left solitary. Still more clearly is it emphasized in the passage comparing the dishonoured burying of the Cross with its later decoration with gold and silver. Admirable as is this use of contrast, yet more admirable is the poet's restraint when he reaches his climax. After describing the sufferings of the victim, the sorrow of nature, while all creation wept, the actual climax, the Crucifixion, is given in one simple half-line : " Christ was on the Cross." It is as though the tragedy itself were cut off from all else by a wall of silence round it.

Here one must pause for a moment for a word about the metre. Without attempting to go into the whole subject of O.E. metre, it may be pointed out that the poet has allowed himself to use freely the longer line of three feet to the half-line whenever he has felt that it, with the accompanying greater number of unaccented syllables and correspondingly greater freedom of movement, was more suited to the emotional character of his theme. This longer line occurs in the fragments on the Ruthwell Cross and cannot therefore, as in the case of Genesis B, where it also occurs, be attributed to O.S. influence. It is found also, though not so frequently, in some of the secular lyrics, which suggests its use in England in early times before it gave way, perhaps before the increasing prominence of narrative poetry, to the short line.

Of great interest for the history of our early literature is the representation of the Cross as half tree, half man. This mystic element must have been in the original poem, since it is to be seen in the lines on the Ruthwell Cross, it must therefore be a very early instance of indirect Greek-Oriental influence, the direct inspiration for the poem having been from Rome.

Another poem often ascribed to Cynewulf is Guþlac, the story of the temptation and death of the hermit Guþlac of Croyland. It comes directly after the Crist in the Exeter Book, and follows on so simply that editors differ as to where the one poem ends and the other begins. There is

nothing in the MS. to give any indication.* Here Guþlac is
taken to begin with the sentence : " Many orders of men
there are who rise up into the number of the saints," as
an obviously good introduction to the life of one particular
saint.

Under this one title are included two distinct poems,
written at different dates. In the first part, which extends
up to v. 790, Guþlac A, the poet represents himself as
writing from oral tradition. He says " as we have lately
heard", and he tells us later that Guþlac was tempted
within the memory of living men. This part is concerned
chiefly with the saint in his hermitage, persecuted by evil
spirits. The second part from v. 791 must be independent
and rather later, because the poet speaks of books which
tell of Guþlac's sufferings as his source. Moreover the story
of the Fall with which it begins, reads like the introduction
to a new work. This part deals chiefly with the saint's
death. It may be Cynewulf's, the date of the language
would allow it, and the end, which is missing, may have
contained the runes. His authorship cannot be disproved.

Guþlac A begins with reflections on the present evil
state of the world. The love of Christ is growing cold,
the predictions of the messengers of God in former days
are coming true. All the fruits of the earth are losing their
virtue, and no one need hope for improvement until the end
of the world shall come. There are some who like to bear
the name of priest, but who will not act like priests, some
there are, however, who do obey God's laws, give alms
and comfort the friendless, and some of these dwell in
lonely places, waiting for their heavenly home. After this
general introduction the poet goes on to tell of Guþlac,
one of these hermits, how in his youth he loved bold

* The last twenty-eight lines of the Crist, as usually given,[1] do not fit on
well with either what goes before or what follows. Though most editors
take them as the end of the Crist, Gollancz [2] has therefore assumed them to
be the beginning of Guþlac. Cosijn [3] has gone further and denied
them to either poem, believing them to be a fragment of an independent
work.

[1] As in Grein-Wulker, Bibliothek der angelsächsishen Poesie, Bd. III
Hälfte 1.

[2] Cynewulf's Christ, p. 191.

[3] Anglosaxonica, IV, PBB. 23, pp. 114-15.

adventures, till the time came that God sent an angel to him and his sinful desires weakened.

Two angels fought for his soul, the one praising the everlasting riches of heaven, the other urging him on to seek by night the meetings of evil doers, and to act with daring, like those who shrink not from taking the life of a man, if thereby they can obtain plunder. Finally the good angel triumphed and remained with Guþlac, instructing him, till the desire came to him to inhabit a solitary dwelling on a hill.

But there a fearful and strange terror came upon him. Evil spirits, who had before taken up their abode there, attacked him and their attacks are told with a good deal of monotony. These evil spirits had been accustomed to use the wilderness as an abiding place after their sufferings, they rested there for a space, enjoying peace, when they came back weary from their wanderings. Now they had no longer any region upon earth, nor could the air cradle their limbs, but shelterless they must forgo a home, lamenting and waiting for death. They were naturally moved to anger against Guþlac and attacked him in various ways. First they threatened him with burning, fire should swallow up his body, and his sufferings be a cause of sorrow to all his friends, unless he would give up his solitary life and go back to his fellow men. Next they warned him that, though he might have the land, no one would bring him food there ; he would find hunger and thirst cruel foes. Such an undertaking as to go out from his own country and live like a wild beast was nought. If he stayed they would trample his dwelling under foot, tear him in pieces, and stamp upon him. After this they carried him up into the air and let him see all the doings in the monasteries, how many passed their lives in pleasure and arrogance, surrounded by useless possessions and clad in boastful garments, as is the way of the young who are not guided by reverence for age. Finally as a supreme temptation, finding that all others had failed, the evil spirits led Guþlac to the gates of hell and tried to reduce him to spiritual despair, but again they had no success.

The O.E. delight in fighting comes out in the way in which Guþlac opposed his persecutors, carrying the war indeed into their country. Undismayed by threats of fire or death, he said to them : " Go ye, ye accursed and weary-hearted, from this place, in which ye stand ; flee ye hence ; here shall be my earthly home and yours no longer."

When they warned him that none would bring him food, he retaliated that the Lord had already been sending him every day what was needful by the hand of a man. When they twitted him with bearing with the loose rule and undisciplined lives of the younger men in the monasteries, he read them a lecture. God, he told them, created youth and human joy, and the fruits of age are not to be looked for in youth :—

> The young rejoice
> in worldly pleasures, until that a share of winters
> has passed into their youth, so that the spirit loves
> the sight and presence of an older nature.
> Many men
> show wisdom, lose their arrogance,
> as soon as the foolish spirit of youth departs.

After the last temptation St. Bartholomew was sent to Guþlac's help. He bade the devils see that there was not a broken bone, bloody wound or blemish of body, or aught of hurt upon him :—

> Set ye him down unharmed whence ye took him,
> he shall for this possess the plain, nor may ye withhold it
> from him.

Guþlac is accordingly taken with great care and triumph to his home, where the birds make known his return. Oft had he fed them when hungry they flew round his hand,—

> greedily eager, rejoicing in his help.
> Pleasant was the plain of victory, new the dwelling,
> fair the note of the birds, the earth in blossom,
> the cuckoo proclaimed the (time of) year.

On this note of victory the first poem ends after some moral reflections. " Lo ! " the poet says, " we are witnesses of these wonders, all this came to pass in our time."

In the second poem, after the reference to the Fall already mentioned, the writer passes on somewhat abruptly to tell how the fame of Guþlac's wondrous doings had spread throughout Britain, after which we hear again of the attacks of the evil spirits :—

Sometimes raging like wild beasts
they shouted in a band, sometimes they returned,
these evil doers, in human shape
with the mightiest of clamours ; sometimes they changed,
these accursed warlocks, into serpent form,
these wretched demons, spewing poison.

A pleasanter picture follows :—

But at times to his hand, oppressed with hunger,
flew the race of birds to where they found
the appointed food and honoured him
with solemn voices, sometimes human
messengers humbly sought him out.
. . . None indeed were there
who despairing, journeyed back
hopeless and miserable, but the holy man
healed through his noble power each one
who, tormented, sought him in his need.

But the last day of his earthly struggle was near at hand after fifteen years spent in the wilderness.

His sufferings and the fortitude and submission with which he bore them are told at some length and with a good deal of repetition. One disciple alone remained with him, apparently the one who had brought him his daily food. Going into the temple one morning, he found his master lying ill there. Guþlac, hardly able to draw his breath, warned him that he had but seven days to live ; then perceiving the young man's grief, he went on to comfort him. The devil could impute no sin to him, he (the devil) and his companions should lament, bewail their exile, drowned in waves of sorrow, in the dwelling of death, deprived of every joy and delight, but he (Guþlac) knew his reward, an everlasting one and a holy, to be on high whither his spirit was minded to go.

On the Sunday the saint arose as best he might for his

great weakness, and did service to God in His temple and taught his follower, who had never heard the divine mysteries so profoundly explained before. It seemed to him rather as though it were an angel speaking from above than any man upon the earth. On the seventh day at the sixth hour, knowing himself to be at the point of death, Guþlac gave his disciple his last instructions. As soon as he should be dead, he was to go to his sister and explain to her why he had refused to see her in this life. It was in order that their next meeting should be in the glory of the skies. He was also to bid her have his body buried on the hill. And now the young man ventured to ask whose was the voice that he had heard in talk with the saint every evening and also at dawn? Guþlac answered that it was that of an angel sent from God to comfort him, who had taught him wisdom more various than men might know. In consequence of it no man who came into his presence could conceal from him his secret thoughts. Never had he told anyone before and now he told it only in return for the love and companionship of his disciple. Thereupon he turned to the wall, covering his head, and from his mouth issued a scent, sweet as when, in summertime, flowers blossoming and honey-laden give out their fragrance over the plain. When the sun set and mist overshadowed the world, a bright light, and a holy, shone from heaven over the dwelling. It shone throughout the night till the shadows melted away. From evening gloom it shone till the sounds of dawn came from the east, the hot sun arose, and Guþlac bade his follower go forth on his errand. Then strengthened with the holy Eucharist and raising his hands and looking up to heaven, he sent his spirit, made beauteous by works, into the joy of the realms of glory. Angels bore his soul into eternal joy, and a heavenly light enveloped his dwelling, as if a tower of fire were rising to the sky, brighter than the sun or the glory of the stars. The place was filled with sweet fragrance and holy song, divine melody. The disciple, weeping and terrified, took his boat and hastened away. Having arrived where the sister dwelt, he told her with some preamble of the death of his master, " thy brother, the best between the two

seas whom we have known born as man among the English,"
and so the second poem comes to an end.

The Life of St. Guþlac in the Acta Sanctorum for 7th
April was written by Felix of Croyland between 747 and
749, at the end of the reign of Æthelbald of Mercia. The
saint died in 715. The author of Guþlac A, though certainly
a contemporary, may have lived on long enough to have
known the Life as well as the legends. It is impossible to
say. Guþlac B cannot have been written till the second half
of the eighth century and may have been later.

For the modern reader the length of the description and
the repetitions must take off from the value of Guþlac A
as a whole, but it must be remembered that an audience
of those days was less difficult to please. The same criticism
doubtless applies also to Guþlac B to some extent, but here
it is made up for by the strength and pathos of the treatment.

This poem occupies an interesting position in O.E.
literature. It marks a new stage, for it is not concerned
with the life of kings and courts, or even with that of
warriors ; its hero plays no part in life on a large scale as
does St. Andrew, he is a hermit, living his solitary life
among his birds and poorer neighbours with his own special
temptations, an early St. Francis. We get a glimpse of humble
life not to be found elsewhere except perhaps in the Riddles.
Further, emotion is no longer to be unduly repressed by
those anxious for glory, as in Beowulf. While much of
Guþlac is, it must be allowed, dull, the work as a whole
gives us a delightfully human picture of the saint, whose own
excesses in his youth have given him understanding of the
frailties and temptations of the young ; whose wide
sympathies, described as a direct angelic gift, enable him
to see into men's hearts and make him rouse himself,
though ill and suffering, to comfort his grieving disciple.
Touching, too, is the bond between brother and sister, who
consent to live apart in this world for the greater joy in
the reunion of the future.

In Guþlac we have, too, a subtler note of character study
than usual, in the final attempt of the evil spirits, when all
others have failed, to reduce the saint to spiritual despair.

In speaking of Cynewulf's certain works it has been mentioned [1] that his Crist comes in the Exeter Book between two other poems, which have been held by some to belong to it. The preceding poem consists of a set of hymns, based on Antiphons of the Breviary to be sung before Christmas with the Magnificat at Vespers. They are to be distinguished from the Crist proper, as taken in this book, by this difference of source, and by difference of style, for they are more lyrical in character and without the descriptive power of some passages of that work, as well as by the concluding verses which seem to be meant for an ending : " Where he (the good man) shall dwell in bliss for ever and ever, world without end.   Amen." The hymns treat of subjects connected generally with the Nativity ;   they are, for instance, to the Virgin :—

> Hail thou famous one in all the world,
> thou purest of women upon earth,
> of all who have ever lived throughout the ages.
> Now thou, rightly, all with gift of speech,
> call upon and declare, all men throughout the earth,
> with joyful heart, to be the spouse
> of the holiest Ruler of the skies.

or to Jerusalem :—

> Hail thou vision of peace ! holy Jerusalem !
> noblest of royal thrones ! the city of Christ,
> the dwelling place of angels ! ; in thee alone
> the souls of the faithful rest for ever,
> triumphant in their glory.

or to Christ Himself :—

> Hail to Thee, Messenger, brightest of Angels !
> sent unto men, throughout the world,
> the soothfast light of the sun,
> shining bright above the stars.   Thou at every time
> from Thine own self dost give forth light.

The third poem, that on the Coming to Judgment or the Doomsday, as it is usually called, may be taken to begin with v. 867 of the whole set of poems.

[1] Chap. VII, p. 158.

> When suddenly upon the dwellers on the earth,
> shall come that great day, with the power
> of the almighty Lord, at midnight.

It is a fine work of 797 lines telling of the coming of Christ
to judge the world and of the fates of mankind at that
judgment. Though the effect of the whole is somewhat
marred by long didactic passages, the picture of the Judge
coming in the midst of a host of attendant angels, with
fire before Him, the sun and moon falling and the devastation
on the earth, is painted in vivid colours. The description
of the terrors of that last day gave the Anglo-Saxon poet
scope for the exercise of his particular gifts and he has made
full use of it. Less easy to find in O.E. literature are passages
with such pathos as that of Christ's speech of reproach
to the wicked when condemning them to hell. The poet
may have had his material, but the elaboration is his own.

After a few lines telling how the last day shall come like
a thief in the night, the poem goes on :—

> Then from the four corners of the world,
> from the farthest (plains) of the kingdom of earth,
> angels all bright shall blow at even
> their trumpets in a blast ; the middle world shall tremble,
> the ground beneath men's feet. They shall sound together,
> powerful and clear, along the paths of the stars
> they shall sing out and resound from south and north,
> from east and west over all created things.
>
> .   .   .   .
>
> Then shall come the wondrous vision of Christ,
> the glory of the noble king, from the eastern skies,
> sweet to the souls of His people,
> but bitter to the evil ; of wondrous form,
> for blessed and accursed, of unlike form.

The righteous man need not fear when he sees the Lord
come and on each side of Him a troop of heaven's angels
faring about Him, a company of shining ones, armies of
saints, in multitudes enough :—

> The deep creation echoes and before Him goes
> the greatest of raging fires, over the wide ground,
> the hot flame roars, the heavens give way,

mighty and glorious the stars shall fall.
Then shall the sun be turned to darkness,
with the hue of blood, that which brightly shone
through former ages o'er the sons of men.
The moon in like wise, which before for mankind
illumined nights, shall fall to earth,
and the stars also shall scatter from the heavens
driven by the storm with power through the air.

A picture of the destruction of the earth follows, telling
how the ruined city walls shall fall, the hills, the high cliffs
melt, those which before held the earth fast against the
floods; death in the flames, that raging warrior, shall
overtake each beast and bird. All treasures of the craftsman's
art, all riches shall be burnt up.

After this background of noise and confusion, the poet
goes on to fill in his scene.

Then quickly, the rest in the earth at an end, the race of
Adam shall assume its flesh again, each man shall arise,
alive, with limbs and body renewed, soul and body together
again, and with his soul laden with all the good or evil
deeds, which he has done during his lifetime. Not in mercy
to them shall the sinful see before them the Cross, brightest of
emblems but now moistened with the blood of the heavenly
king. " They see for their harm what should have been for
their help, if they would have received it to their gain."
The dumb creation, the green earth, and the sky saw and,
terrified, felt the sufferings of the Saviour, and the sun
was darkened, cruelly beclouded.

When all have arisen from their graves, then shall be
collected the " pure " folk on the right hand and Christ shall
bid the band of evildoers depart to His left. Three " tokens "
shall distinguish the blessed. First they shall shine brightly
before mankind, in glory and splendour, above the city
dwellings. Secondly, they shall possess unalloyed joy, in
bliss among the angels. Thirdly, we get a touch which,
though it does not appeal to modern ideas, is found elsewhere
in poems of this date :—

> The blessed band sees the evil ones
> enduring pain, in punishment for sin,

the raging fire and the bite of worms,
with cruel jaws. . . .
From that arises for them a joyful happiness,
when they see the others enduring ill.

The wicked, in the same way, suffer from three causes.

One is that they know much misery, hellfire ready for
their punishment. The second is that all, not only God
but the angel hosts and the sons of men, can see through
their flesh the sins in their souls, as one can look through
clear glass. Thirdly, they behold the blessed rejoicing because
of those good deeds, which they (the accursed) despised
doing.

Then after a passage of moral reflections the poem returns
to the scene of the Judgment. The righteous are bidden
take possession of the joys of Heaven which they earned
when they received the needy, fed the hungry, and did
other good deeds, but the Judge turns to the wicked with
a long speech full of dignity and feeling :—

Lo! I created thee with my hands
in the beginning, and gave thee understanding,
from clay I made thee limbs, I gave thee a living soul,
honoured thee above all creatures, bestowed on thee a form,
a beauty like to my own, I gave thee abundance of power,
wealth in every land. Nought didst thou know of sorrow,
of darkness that thou shouldst endure it. But thou gavest
  Me no thanks for this.

    .   .   .   .

Then I set thee in a fair world,
to enjoy of Paradise,
in bright profusion, the shining hues,
But thou wouldest not obey the word of life.

    .   .   .

Then it repented me that my handiwork
into the power of enemies should pass.
. . . And I myself came down
born of a mother, though her maidenhood
was still inviolate.
Little seemed I to the sons of men. I lay on the hard stone,
an infant in the manger, because I would take death from
  thee.

For love of man my head
bore cruel blows.
For me they blended bitterly together
an unsweet drink of vinegar and gall.
. . . I that pain for thee
all in humility endured,
insult and cruel speech.

And so on through all the sufferings of the Crucifixion :—

I received thy pain that thou mightest in bliss
and happiness enjoy my native realm.

Why didst thou forsake that beauteous life
which I for thee, with mine own body,
a comfort to the wretched, bought in mercy ?
I was poor on earth that thou mightest be rich in heaven.
I was poor in thy house that thou mightest have wealth in
   mine.

After this fine passage the poet adds a sermon of his own
and ends on lines which recall the Phoenix :—

There (in heaven) is neither hunger nor thirst,
sleep nor heavy sickness, nor burning of the sun,
nor cold nor care ; but there the grace of the King,
the company of the blessed enjoys for ever,
the most beauteous of bands, glory with the Lord.

The Doomsday is based principally on a Latin hymn
which the poet may have got from Bede,[1] who quotes it,
but other sources have also been used. A striking feature
of this poem is the frequent occurrence of the long line, either
with three feet in each half, or with an unusual number of
unaccented syllables, such as we have seen in Genesis B,[2]
and which have shown themselves admirable in a work
in which action is subordinated to descriptions of thought
and feeling. Partly for this reason and partly from the
vocabulary, Binz [3] has suggested that the poem is, like
Genesis B, a translation from an Old Saxon original, since
the long line and large number of unaccented syllables are
characteristic of O.S. work.

---

[1] De Arte Metrica, Chap. 2.   [2] Chap. VI, p. 123.
[3] Untersuchungen zum A. E. Sogenannten Crist, but see also Grüter,
Bonner Beit., Heft 17, S. 1–50.

More definite proof of this origin than that of metre is afforded by the vocabulary. Words occur in Doomsday which are not found elsewhere in O.E. literature, but are not uncommon in O.S., and, more convincing still than such negative evidence, words have their O.S. meaning and not that in O.E., in cases in which they differ in the two languages.

If an O.S. origin be accepted on these grounds, the interest shown in motive rather than in action may be taken as corroborative, for in this respect also Doomsday shows something of the same character as Genesis B.

Another work, earlier thought to be by Cynewulf, is the Phoenix. This is a very free translation of a Latin work of the fourth century, usually attributed to Lactantius, in which the O.E. poet has made 380 verses out of the 170 hexameters of the Latin poem, thus more than doubling the length. He has also added 297 more as an allegorical interpretation, following for this the teaching of St. Ambrose and, to some extent, that of Bede. He begins in the regular manner of the O.E. poet :—

> I have heard that there is far hence
> in eastern parts, the noblest of lands
> known among men. That region of the world
> is not accessible to many owners of the earth
> in all the world, but it has been put far off
> through the might of the Creator from evildoers.
> Beauteous is all the plain, joyously blest
> with the fairest scents of earth,
> peerless the island, noble the Creator,
> bold, rich in might, who established the world.
> There are the doors of heaven ever open before the blessed,
> there is revealed the joy of melody.

Then the poet goes on to describe in detail this happy land in which there is neither rain nor snow, fire nor hail ; neither heat nor cold is too great and no storms do injury to aught. There are also no hills, mountains, or slopes of any kind, or anything uneven. The whole plain is twelve fathoms higher than any of the mountains which here tower aloft under the stars.

There fruits never fail
nor bright blossoms,[1] but the trees stand
ever green as God has commanded them,
in winter and in summer alike the wood
is decked with flowers, never do the leaves
decay in the air, nor shall fire injure
them for ever and ever, till the change (destruction)
of the world shall come.

When the flood covered all the rest of the world, this happy land was saved, and thus it shall remain blossoming till the coming of the Judgment, when the graves of men shall be opened. There, too, is neither old age nor sickness, neither poverty nor death, neither sorrow nor sleep,[2] but there the streams :—

wondrously beautiful, the rivers gush out,
from their fair springs they water the earth,
these joyous floods from the middle of the wood.
It is the command of the Lord
that twelve times a year the happy waterfloods
shall play over that glorious land.

The wood is inhabited by a bird wondrous fair, which is called the Phoenix. He watches the course of the sun, as that noblest of stars, which has been hidden under the waves in the West, concealed in the twilight, reappears gliding from the East. Before its coming the glorious one bathes twelve times in the stream near which he lives, and drinks as many times from its waters. Then he sets himself proudly on a high tree to watch, and as soon as the sun is high above the salt streams he departs and flies singing towards the sky. The song is more beautiful than any son of man has heard since the creation. No trumpet, horn, harp, or human voice can compare with it. Neither can the melody of the wings of the swan. So he sings and makes music till the sun is approaching towards the South : then he is silent and listens, inclining his head three times, and three times shaking his feathers, keen for flight. It is decreed that the Phoenix shall enjoy on the plain life and happiness

---

[1] Or fruits.
[2] A mistranslation of " curæ insomnes ".

for a thousand winters, but after that, when he has become old and grey, he flees the green earth, and seeks a kingdom in the world where no man lives. There he, mighty, receives the lordship over the race of birds and among them inhabits for a while the wilderness, till, troubled with age, though still strong in flight, he turns westwards. Birds fly around their noble prince, each desirous to serve his noble lord, and so he seeks the land of the Syrians in a great company. Then he hastens away till he comes to a desolate spot in the shade of a grove, in which he dwells concealed from man. The lofty tree which he inhabits is called Phoenix, too, after the bird. It is the brightest in blossom of all flowering trees, and will remain unharmed as long as the world lasts. When the wind has fallen and the weather is fair, then the Phoenix begins to prepare a nest among the boughs. So he collects from far and near the sweetest roots and woodland fruits, every noble fragrance, every pleasant plant which the Father of mankind has created in the world for the benefit of men. These he carries to the tree, builds his nest, and settles himself in that upper chamber, surrounded by these holy scents, and the finest flowers of every earthly plant. Then the hot sun shining on his arbour kindles the house, the herbs grow warm, the dwelling steams with a sweet vapour and the bird burns with his nest.

However new life comes to him in due time, when the ashes begin after the violence of the flames to join together again, pressed into a ball. Then a thing most like an apple is found among the ashes, out of which comes a worm wondrous fair, just as if it had come from an egg, bright of shell. Next it becomes in appearance like the young of an eagle, and so it goes on growing joyfully till it is like the full-grown bird, and after that it becomes as it was in the beginning, gay of plumage. It is as when in summer, at the time of reaping, the fruits of the earth are carried home to be harvested before the winter come, lest the rain destroy them under the clouds. There they find safety when frost and snow in violence cover the earth in its winter raiment. From those fruits shall the wealth of the world again come forth, from seed sown clean, when the summer gleam, the token of life in spring, awakes the treasures of the earth so that the fruits are born again after their own kind. In the same way the bird which was old in years, becomes young again, enfolded anew in the flesh.

No food does it take but a portion of the honey dew which falls at midnight. By it the bold one supports his life until he seeks again his own home, the old dwelling-place.

When he has thus grown up he collects the bones charred by the fire and, wrapping them in the herbs, carries the whole back to his own country and buries it there. As the Phoenix thus flies homewards, men and women come out in crowds to see the bird, whom the Creator has made fair above all others. They marvel and make known in their writings and in marble the day which showed him to them. The birds, too, come in crowds from all parts, praising and extolling the Phoenix in song with loud voices, and lead the noble one towards his home till he, desirous of solitude and swift of wing, flies away to where the troop of rejoicing followers cannot come. Thus he seeks his old home and the birds turn aside, sad of heart, returning to their own countries.

God alone knows what his nature is, whether he be male or female. When the Phoenix has thus lived on for another thousand years, he again builds his pyre and again wakes to a new life. Therefore he fears no death, knowing that life will ever be renewed to him. He is his own son and his own father and also heir to their inheritance.

Here the Latin poem ends and our poet goes on to expound his parable. First he takes the Phoenix as symbolical of humanity in general and then of Christ and His Resurrection. For the first he supports himself on the authority of Job, who has said, " Though my body shall decay in the tomb, . . . nevertheless the God of Hosts shall redeem my soul after death and awaken it in glory." After this comes an account of the joys of heaven with the Song of the Blessed, and the poet ends with his second interpretation of the Phoenix, as symbolical of Christ and His Resurrection, and a short epilogue half in Latin.

Hafaþ ūs alȳfed lucis auctor,
þæt we mōton hēr meritare
gōddǣdum begietan, gaudia in celo.

The poet, whoever he may have been, has allowed himself great freedom in his translation. Not only, as has been said, does he expand his original, but he changes it whenever it suits his didactic purpose. This is most noticeable in his treatment of allusions to the classical mythology, as when he substitutes the story of the Flood [1] for that of Deucalion, or translates the grove sacred to Phoebus [2] merely as the sunny grove. Such changes are perhaps not surprising. What is remarkable is his choice of a theme. The nature he depicts in the happy land is a plain with no mountains or even hills to be climbed, with no storms but perpetual sunshine, a land watered by streams at regular intervals, with trees ever laden with fruit and flowers. If he wanted the Phoenix for its obvious allegorical value, he had of course to accept its habitat with it, but he has not merely accepted it, he delights in it, it is largely these nature descriptions which he has expanded so greatly. An Anglo-Saxon poet must have travelled far before he could entirely give up his native stormy seas and mist-clad mountains and choose a sunny plain as subject, even though he has treated the new ideas in the style of the older poetry, using the old poetic terms.

Foreign influence is to be seen in metre as well as subject— in the use of rhyme. Like Cynewulf in the Epilogue to Elene, the poet of the Phoenix has given us sets of lines in which the two halves of each are joined by end-rhyme as well as by alliteration. Thus we get lines such as

ne forstes hryre, ne hrīmes dryre,
ne sunnan hǣtu, ne sincealdu.

(no fall of frost or rime, neither heat of the sun, nor great cold.)

The subject afforded ample opportunity for the use of variation, and the poet has availed himself of it fully in his descriptions.

Hitherto Latin influence, coming in through the monastic

---

[1] v. 41.   [2] v. 33.

schools, had not done much more than give the O.E. poets new heroes and heroines and suggest a modification of form. In the Phoenix it has introduced a new world to be described ; we have reached another stage in the history of pre-Conquest literature in this appreciation of Nature in her milder aspects. We may also be said to have reached a new stage in the detail of the descriptions. Hitherto, very few definite colours have been mentioned. It is the general effect that is given. Now, however, we get many more enumerated as is to be seen in the wondrous plumage of the bird, and we are told with great precision where each one is to be found. We read that the bird is fair to look upon, bright with varied colours about its breast in front, its head is green behind, curiously variegated, blent with scarlet, its tail is in part brown, in part purple studded cunningly with red spots ; the wings are white at the tips and the neck green. In fact, we have a catalogue of colours, rather than a picture.

Following the Phoenix in the Exeter Book, and akin to it in subject, are three short poems, also at one time attributed to Cynewulf, of which the first is on the Panther, the second on the Whale, and the third, a fragment merely, is generally accepted as having to do with the Partridge. These form what is known as the O.E. Bestiary or Physiologus. In them, as in the Phoenix, the appearance and habits of the creature are first described according to the knowledge of natural history of the times, and then an allegorical interpretation is added to each.

These poems are of importance, not for their own value, but because, like the Riddles, they represent a very early and widespread form of literature. Professor Cook [1] gives the date of the compilation of the first Physiologus as before 140 B.C., and places it at Alexandria. Its Egyptian origin is to be inferred from some of the animals mentioned in it, such as the phoenix and the crocodile. The first version must, he thinks, have been in Greek, but later other versions, more or less complete, appear in most European languages. There is one in Middle as well as in Old English, which must,

---

[1] The Old English Elene, Phoenix, and Physiologus, pp. lviii.

however, have been drawn independently from Latin or French sources, for not only does it contain many more animals, but the descriptions of those found in the two versions differ a good deal in detail.

When the O.E. Physiologus with its three creatures is compared with the much fuller ones in other languages, the question naturally arises : Can this be the whole or was there originally much more ? Certainly the beginning of the Partridge has been lost, for all that we have is the allegorical interpretation and, with it, it is impossible to say how much more has gone. The Panther seems to have been intended to begin the set, for it opens with what reads like a general introduction. The writer tells us that there are many and various races in the world, whose nature we cannot rightly describe nor tell their numbers, and many multitudes of birds and beasts also scattered over the earth within the encircling water. Of these we have heard tell of the glorious nature of one, called the panther.

The Partridge must have been intended to close the series, for the author has written " finit " after it, which he has not done after either the Panther or the Whale. When one considers how much O.E. literature must have perished, one is inclined to the view that our Physiologus originally contained many animals, like those of other countries, for there does not seem to have been any reason why the O.E. writer should have selected just these three creatures for treatment and no others.

After the introduction the writer goes on to say of the Panther that it is the friend of every form of life, except the serpent alone ; its coat, in the brightness and variety of its hues, is to be compared with that of Joseph. After a meal it goes to sleep for three days in a secret place among the hill caves, and, when it rouses itself on the third day, the most musical cry comes from its mouth and the sweetest fragrance, which attracts to it men and beasts alike.

Then follows the allegorical interpretation. The panther represents Christ.

The legendary character of the Whale is as extraordinary. The description of its rocklike appearance suggests that it

is really the giant tortoise or shield turtle that is meant.
It is the symbol of deceit, of the cunning of the devil. We
are told that it lies on the surface of the sea, looking so like
an island that seafarers fasten their "sea-steeds" to it
and land ; but as soon as they light a fire the cunning one
feels it and dives down, seeks the bottom of the sea and
thus destroys ship and sailors together. Further, when
it is hungry it opens its jaws wide and sends out such a
sweet breath that all kinds of fish are attracted and crowd
in unsuspectingly. Then it shuts its jaws !

Of the Partridge only the allegorical part has been
preserved.[1] Thus in the Physiologus we see England,
already the leader in the native literature of the Germanic
nations, since the Old Norse Sagas were not written down
till some time later, beginning to take her part in her own
tongue in the literary activities of Europe, and not only
borrowing learned works for translation, but copying popular
forms and subjects also.

From the Phoenix and Physiologus one passes on naturally
to the Riddles. First because, like the Phoenix, they were
long attributed to Cynewulf, and, secondly, because, like
the Physiologus, they are the O.E. representatives of a
widely spread class of literature ; in them England took
her share in what may be called an almost universal form
of literary activity.

In the Exeter Book are two collections of Riddles in
poetic form. The first is now considered to contain fifty-
nine ; how many there are in the second it is more difficult
to decide. The MS. has been much injured from various
causes and, in some cases in which a beginning or an ending
has got lost, it is not easy to say whether the fragments we
have left belong to one poem or two. Thus Tupper [2] allows
for thirty-four, Grein [3] for twenty-eight. Besides these two
sets two riddles are found in a separate place in the MS. Of
these the first is merely a second version of one in the first set,
while the other offers another of the many problems which

---

[1] For a discussion of the origin of these legends, see A. S. Cook, The Old
English Elene, Phœnix, and Physiologus, pp. lvii ff.

[2] Riddles of the Exeter Book.

[3] Bibl. der ags. Poesie, III, pp. 183–238.

complicate the whole of this subject. While some scholars, Miss Kershaw among them, deny it to be a riddle and look on it as the first part of the poem " the Message of the Husband ", others believe it to be a riddle with the answer " a reed ".[1]

A great number of subjects are treated in these little poems. In common with all O.E. poetry they deal with armour and weapons, but even more frequently their themes are birds or beasts, and these are not so much the wolf, the eagle, and the raven, figures familiar in the epic, as those associated with everyday life, the hawk, the sparrow, the starling, the bullock, the sow, and the badger. Gnats and oysters even appear among the subjects. Other riddles have for themes the beer and mead which figure so largely in the social life of the Anglo-Saxons. Plants such as the onion, the leek, barley, and corn are also treated. Others again form a source of information about the musical instruments known at the time, for they describe the organ, the flute, the bagpipe, the fiddle, and the shawm as well as the harp and the horn, familiar in other poems. Useful objects of everyday life give the answers to some, as, for instance, the chopping-block, the broom, the plough, dough. On the other hand, more poetical themes are by no means wanting. A storm, an earthquake, clouds and wind, night, time, the sun and moon, fire, are all subjects which have been productive of poems of real literary beauty.

In all the subjects are personified, the personifications varying in their completeness, and, as in all O.E. poetry, the inanimate object is made the doer of the action or its activities the subject of the description.

While all show some skill in versification and nearly all must be classed among the literary, rather than popular, riddles, the quality of the verse varies as greatly as do the themes. Some give us magnificent descriptions of nature, unsurpassed elsewhere in O.E. poetry ; others show a delicacy of fancy or a richness of imagination which entitles them to be ranked as true literature. But some are merely quaint or even commonplace, and a few are coarse. In the

[1] See Chap. III, p. 55 and Note, for a fuller discussion.

third (Tupper, 4) we have a wonderful picture of the storm force first imprisoned beneath the earth and producing the earthquake :—

At times my lord confines me closely,
sends me beneath the fertile plains'
broad breast and bids me wait,
holds me in darkness, me, this power
by force, in prison. There heavy rests
the earth upon my back, nor know I any way
from out that torment ; but I make heave
the native homes of men. Then shake the gabled halls,
the dwellings of mankind. Then tremble walls
towering above the homesteads. Still appears
the air over the land, the sea keeps silence,
until from out my cell I upwards press,
just as He guides me, Who in chains
in the beginning laid me first,
in bonds and fetters, so that I may not twist me
from out His power, Who points me out my ways.

Next the storm force is depicted as let loose over the sea :—

At times I from above must lash the waves,
stir up the currents, drive upon the strand,
the flint-grey flood. Foaming strive
the waters 'gainst the cliffs, gloomy rolls up
a watery mass over the deep, and dark behind it,
in swirling tumult, comes another
so that they meet together near the shore,
two lofty towering crests. There the wooden ship is loud,
there is clamour of the ocean guests. Silently await
the steep and rocky cliffs the fighting waves,
the tumult in the bay.

In the following riddle [1] the eternal alternation of sun and moon is represented as a constant strife in which the sun triumphs over the moon. In this the personification is complete :—

I saw a being in wondrous wise
between her horns bear hence her booty—
a bright " air vessel " skilfully adorned—
her booty to her home from off her raids.

[1] Riddle XXX.

She would within the city set up a bower,
build it with skill, if thus she might.
Then came a wondrous being o'er the ramparts' top
who is known to all dwellers upon earth,
rescued the booty and homewards drove
the outlaw 'gainst her will ; turned her westwards thence
faring in anger, hastened onwards.
The scent of earth rose up ; dew fell upon the ground,
night came forth. No man afterwards
might know whither that being went.

It must be noted that the poet has become confused
between the Latin and Germanic genders, for he has made
the moon feminine as in Latin, and the sun feminine as in
Germanic. Perhaps he knew a Latin riddle on the subject.

The ingenuity of some of the riddles is seen in the following,[1]
to which the answer " fire " has been given. This is personified
as a warrior, but the personification is not carried out so
completely as in the riddle just given. In this one we are
nearer to the modern idea. There is something of the modern
puzzle :—

A warrior there is on earth of wondrous birth,
useful to men ; by a dumb pair,
glorious, engendered, when to his hurt there moves
one foe against another. Him this mighty one,
often a woman chains. If men and women
attend upon him to a right degree,
and feed him fittingly, he obeys them well,
docile, he serves them, with his benefits he gives them
the joys of life. Fiercely he repays
those who this haughty one leave unregarded.

In the riddle, taken largely from the Latin one of Aldhelm,
De Creatura,[2] we get the puzzle element still more pronounced
in the conflicting aspects given of the same object :—

He (God) wrought me wondrously in the beginning
when He first set in place this globe,
He watching bade me long remain
and that I should never after sleep—
and straightway sleep comes on me,
and my eyes are closed in haste.

[1] Riddle LI.　　　　　[2] Riddle XLI, v. 6.

I am so timid that boldly may
a softly passing phantom fright me ;
and I am everywhere bolder than the boar,
when he in anger turns to bay.
I am greater far in fragrance
than incense or a rose may be
that, peerless, on earth's greensward,
grows beauteous. I am more delicate than it.
Though the lily be beloved of men,
and bright of blossom yet am I better still.
So likewise do I surpass the scent of spikenard
with my sweetness always and in every place,
and yet I am fouler than this black mud,
which here in evil wise stinks with its filth.
I am more wide than earth in every place,
extending farther yet than these green plains.
But still a hand may hold me and three fingers
with ease enclasp the whole of me.

Many further examples could be given, showing ingenuity
or poetic charm or both, such as the description of the
making of a codex or the various uses of the horn ; and for
a knowledge of the collection in all its aspects one example
should be given of those riddles which have certainly no
poetic quality and little ingenuity. The answer which is
now accepted for this riddle is " a one-eyed garlic seller ".[1]
It goes :—

> A being came where men were sitting,
> many in the meeting place, wise in heart ;
> he had one eye, two ears,
> and two feet, but twelve hundred heads,
> a back and a belly and two hands,
> arms and shoulders, one neck
> and two sides. Say what he is called.

These riddles were long attributed to Cynewulf. The
first to assert his authorship was Leo, because, as we have
seen,[2] he included in them the preceding poem, " Wulf and
Eadwacer," which he interpreted as a sort of charade on
his own name with which the poet introduced the set. This

---

[1] Riddle, LXXXVI (Grein, 86).
[2] See Chap. III, p. 49, Note 2.

view was accepted and worked out further by Dietrich. He considered that in a Latin riddle in the second set, to which the answer is Lupus, Cynewulf was referring to himself, and that in the last one, which he interpreted as " a travelling singer ", the poet was rounding off the whole series by describing his own life, just as he had introduced it by a charade on his own name. When, however, Leo's charade was shown to be no riddle at all, but an independent poem, the theory of Cynewulf's authorship lost its chief support, and its destruction may be said to have been completed when it was proved a few years later from the language that certain of the riddles were too early to have been by Cynewulf. As we have them in the Exeter Book, they are in a W.S. copy, but there exists an old Northumbrian version of one at Leyden, the so-called " Leyden Riddle ", a translation of Aldhelm's " De Lorica ", which cannot on linguistic grounds be dated later than the first half of the eighth century, and may even be by Aldhelm himself, whereas we have seen that Cynewulf belonged to the second half. Traces of this earlier date remain in other riddles also. Maddert [1] may be said to have given the theory final burial, when, in 1900, he pointed out that there were no marked characteristics of style or phraseology shared by the Riddles and Cynewulf's proved works, which could not be found elsewhere in O.E. poetry.

Cynewulf's authorship of the Riddles is therefore to be considered as definitely disproved. Linguistically it is impossible for many of them [2]; the poem on which the theory was chiefly based is not a riddle at all ; the solution of the last as a wandering minstrel has not found general acceptance, and therefore has no value as a proof, and the presence among them of a Latin riddle on a wolf could obviously never do more than corroborate an otherwise likely theory. It has been necessary, however, to dwell to some extent upon the question, because they are still attributed to Cynewulf in early accounts of O.E. literature,

---

[1] Die Sprache der altenglischen Rätsel des Exeterbuches und die Cynewulffrage, Marburg, 1900.
[2] Sievers, Anglia, XIII, pp. 19–21.

such as still, from their many excellencies, are largely used by students.

The question then arises, if not by him, are they necessarily by any one writer or are they a collection merely ?

The invention of riddles would appear to have been a general exercise of ingenuity with primitive man, for we have some so widely spread that they may be called world riddles. It would appear to have been also a favourite amusement of the scholar, and riddles may be divided, therefore, into two classes, the popular and the literary, according to their origin. Thus in the literary class we have the riddle questions of the Vedas [1] and probably the questions propounded to Solomon by the Queen of Sheba. In Greece they were sufficiently important for Aristotle [2] to interest himself in their character. In Latin we have a collection of a hundred by Symphosius, each of three hexameters, and these had a considerable influence and set a fashion for other collections in Latin and the vernacular. In England we have a set of a hundred riddles composed in Latin hexameters by Aldhelm, Bishop of Sherburne (+ 709), which, unlike those of Symphosius, are of varying length ; another set by Tætwine, Archbishop of Canterbury (731–4), is shorter, containing forty only, also of varying length, but the hundred is completed in the same MS. by a third collection of sixty by Eusebius, who may have been a contemporary of Tætwine. These are mostly in four hexameters.

Thus it will be seen that the composition of Latin riddles was flourishing in England in the late seventh and eighth centuries, and this fashion may have spread and led to the writing of similar series in English at the same time. This would agree with the date given above for our riddles. Since the sets of Latin riddles were known to be each the work of one poet, it was perhaps natural to assume at first, as earlier scholars did, that the English would also be from one pen. Greater familiarity with them has, however, raised doubts on this point. It is a question which it is difficult to solve. Attempts to detect differences of date from syntactical usage have not led to any definite results,

---

[1] Tupper, p. xviii. [2] Rhetoric, III, 11, ii, and xi, 6.

tests of language only prove that some go back to the early eighth century, while other may be later, since they afford no such tests. The real ground for doubting unity of authorship is in the character of the poems themselves. When it is considered how greatly they differ in style, to what entirely different types of mind they point for the writers, it seems more reasonable to conclude [1] that we have to do with a compilation from various sources.

The collector may have written some himself and perhaps have modified others, even using folk riddles occasionally and he may have given, by his skill in versification, a certain superficial similarity to all, without altering to any extent their fundamental dissimilarity. Metrical consideration show that he was an Anglian, and, since he was clearly a scholar, he was probably a Northumbrian rather than a Mercian. The suggestion may be hazarded that the author of the finer poems, such as that on a storm at sea, would, had he been the collector, have hardly cared to include the inferior ones in his collection. It is more likely that the compiler was a poet of mediocre ability himself, but yet able to appreciate the work of a better man, and who therefore incorporated the finer poems in his collection.

Before leaving the subject it must be pointed out that these O.E. riddles differ from most of those of modern times. The term enigma is perhaps more suitable for them than that of riddle. Following Aristotle's view that metaphor is its germ, we may accept Gaston Paris's [2] definition of a riddle, as a metaphor or group of metaphors, the employment of which has not passed into common use and the meaning of which is not self-evident. The O.E. riddle is an obscure saying, rather than a catch, as in the usual modern type. It is in character more like such popular ones as

> A team of white horses upon a red hill,
> now they go, now they go, now they stand still.

Or better still like Miss Fanshawe's riddle on the letter " h ", so long attributed to Byron :

---

[1] Brandl, Geschichte der ags. literatur, Pauls Grundriss, II, p. 971. Trautmann, Kynewulf, p. 41.

[2] See Tupper, Riddles of the Exeter Books, Introd., xiii.

'Twas in heaven pronounced, and 'twas muttered in hell,
and echo caught softly the sound as it fell ;
on the confines of earth 'twas permitted to rest,
and the depths of the ocean its presence confessed.
'Twill be found in the sphere when 'tis riven asunder,
be seen in the lightning and heard in the thunder.

CHAPTER IX

JUDITH : LATER HISTORICAL LAYS AND OTHER POEMS

The habit of composing lays in honour of heroes and their achievements, out of which in earlier times the epic was developed, seems to have lingered on during the O.E. period, and to have been aroused to new activity, though in a somewhat modified form, under the stimulus to national feeling given by the struggles with the Scandinavians in the ninth and tenth centuries. In one instance it is possible that, as in earlier days, one of these lays was expanded into an epic. It is possible that this is the origin of the fragment of 350 lines which follows Beowulf immediately in the MS., telling of the final triumph of the Hebrews over the Assyrians, a triumph assured by the horrible and treacherous murder of their king, Holofernes, at the hands of Judith. It is based chiefly on the Apocryphal Book of Judith, in its Latin translation, but the poet has used his source very freely. It is divided into Fittes, or sections, in the MS., and our passage begins in the ninth Fitte in the middle of a sentence. The original length of the whole poem may be surmised by a comparison with the Latin version. Professor Max Förster [1] has computed that we have about a quarter of the original which must have been a work on a large scale, epic in theme and breadth of treatment. Our passage, fragment though it is, is sufficiently important to be given almost fully here. It begins by emphasizing Judith's faith, and telling how, because of it, she found protection in her deepest need, the favour of the highest Judge, so that He shielded her from her greatest enemy.

Then the poet goes on to describe in the style of the native poetry a magnificent banquet to which Holofernes summoned his chief thanes, and at which " altogether wondrous dainties "

---

[1] Die Beowulf Handschrift, p. 88.

were served ; he tells us how they went to sit down at the
feast, and deep bowls were borne frequently along the benches,
full cups and flagons, and how they were all the time doomed,
though of that Holofernes had no presentiment. Holofernes
is represented here as the boisterously hospitable host.
We read that he shouted and laughed so loudly that the
sons of men might hear from afar how the boldhearted
one " stormed and yelled, bold and flushed with mead, and
urged on frequently those sitting on the benches to play
their part well too ". This revelry went on till nightfall,
by which time all lay unconscious, as if struck down by
death, except the king himself, who then bade Judith
be fetched to his tent.

A description follows of the royal tent, in which a curtain
of gold meshes was hung round the bed, so that Holofernes
could see anyone who entered, but himself remain invisible.
Brought in here by his attendants, he fell unconscious on
to the bed while the men hurried away. Then was the
handmaid of the Lord sternly intent, considering how she
might most easily deprive the terrible one of life, ere he, evil
and defiled, should awake. Then she took a sharp sword,
hard in storms of battle, and, drawing it from the scabbard
with her right hand, began to call upon the Lord of Heaven,
the Saviour of all dwellers in the world, in these words :—

I pray to Thee, God of Creation, Spirit of Consolation,
Son of the Almighty, for Thy mercy to me in this my need,
O glorious Trinity ! Cruelly now is my heart inflamed,
and my mind filled with gloom. Bestow on me, Lord of
  Heaven,
victory and true faith, that I with this sword may
cut down this giver of death. Grant me success,
O stern-hearted Ruler of men ! never had I greater need
of Thy favour. Avenge me, mighty Lord,
glorious bestower of fame, because I am thus angered in my
  mind,
thus hot in my heart. . . .
                  Then was her heart lightened,
the hope of the holy one renewed. Seizing the heathen man
firmly by his hair, she drew him with her hands towards her,
in ignominious fashion and disposed the evil one

skilfully, the hostile man,
in such a way as she, the wicked one (Holofernes) most easily
might overpower. Then the woman, curly-locked,
struck the evil foe with glittering sword,
the hostile-minded one, so that she cut half through
his neck and he lay in a swoon,
drunken and wounded. He was not dead though yet
quite lifeless. Fiercely then she struck,
this woman strong in courage, a second time,
the heathen dog, so that his head leapt forth
on to the floor, and the foul corpse lay
lifeless behind ; the spirit passed elsewhere
under the dark earth and was there abased,
bound in torment for ever after,
encompassed by worms, chained in torture,
cruelly imprisoned in hell fire
after his going hence. Nor might he ever hope,
o'erwhelmed in darkness, that he thence might flee
from out that house of worms, but there must he dwell
for ever and ever, henceforward without end,
in that dark house, without the joy of hope.

Here the more individual part of the poem ends. What
follows is entirely on the model of the old native poetry.
Taking the head with them, Judith and her attendant set
out for their own city, Bethulia. We are told how the
warriors were sitting there keeping watch as Judith had
bidden them before she set out on her dangerous undertaking and how she called to them to let her in, saying that
she had important news for them, that they need no longer
mourn, for the Lord had been gracious to them. It would
be known far and wide that fame was at hand for them in
the place of the wrongs which they had long endured :—

At this the army was full of joy,
towards the fortress gate the people hurried,
men and women together, in bands and multitudes,
in troops and crowds, onwards they pressed and ran,
towards the handmaid of the Lord, in thousands,
both young and old. The heart of each man
in the mead city was cheered
as soon as he perceived that Judith was come
back to her native city.

As soon as she was let in, Judith showed the head of Holofernes, " that most hateful heathen, now no longer living," who of all men had done them the most harm, and she bade them prepare for fight :—

> As soon as the God of Creation,
> the faithful King, shall send from the east
> His bright light, bear ye forth your linden shields,
> your bucklers before your breasts and your corslets,
> your glittering helmets, into the army of the foes.
> Fell the leaders with your bright swords,
> the doomed chieftains. For your enemies
> is death decreed but ye shall have glory,
> fame in the fight, as God has signified to you
> by my hand.
> Then was the band of the bold ones quickly prepared,
> the keen ones for the fight, very fierce, they went forth,
> men and comrades, they bore their triumphant banners,
> marched to the battle, going straight forwards,
> the men beneath their helmets, from out the holy city,
> at the very dawn. Shields clashed,
> loudly resounded. At that the lank one rejoiced,
> the wolf in the forest and the black raven,
> the carrion-greedy bird. . . .
> And behind them flew
> the hungry eagle, dewy-feathered,
> black-coated, curved of beak, it sang a battle song.

Then follows a very fine description of the fight :—

> The warriors marched onwards,
> the men to the battle, covered by their shields,
> their curved linden shields, those who for a while before
> had endured the twitting of the strangers,
> the insults of the heathen ; to them all was that
> sternly repaid in the play of spears,
> to all the Assyrians, as soon as the Hebrews
> beneath their banners had reached
> the encampment. They there with zeal
> sent forth flying showers of arrows,
> snakes of battle, from their bows of horn,
> arrows firmly bound ; loudly stormed
> the angry battle wolves, sent their spears
> into the crowd of the bold ones, the men were enraged,

the dwellers in the land against the hostile race.
Stern of mood they pressed on, strong of heart,
urgently they awakened their old foes
heavy with mead ; with their hands they snatched,
these men, from their sheaths, the bright bladed swords,
choicest of edge ; resolutely they attacked
the warriors of Assyria,
the hostile-minded, no one did they spare
of all that army, mean or high,
of the living men whom they might overcome.

Here the scene shifts to the Assyrian camp and we are
taken back a little. As soon as they were roused and had
armed themselves, the poet goes on :

Then I learnt
that the doomed men started up from sleep,
and towards the pavilion of the evil one
the warriors gloomy-hearted, thronged in crowds,
to the tent of Holofernes ; they were minded at once
to announce the battle to their lord
before the terror should be upon them,
the might of the Hebrews.

But for some time none durst awaken him, though the
Hebrew army was coming ever nearer, avenging their old
wrongs as they came. At last, however, one was hardy
enough to venture in, where he found Holofernes, pale and
lifeless on the bed. Tearing his hair and raiment he uttered
these words to those waiting anxiously outside :

Here is revealed our own fate,
our future predicted ; that we must all perish together,
be destroyed in battle. Here lies our lord
cut down by the sword, beheaded.

Dismayed by the loss of their leader, the Assyrians turned
to flee :

They then, sad of mood,
threw down their weapons, turned them heavy hearted,
to take to flight. In their track men fought,
the mighty army, till the greatest part
of the hostile host lay overthrown in battle,
on that plain of victory, cut down with swords,
to the joy of wolves and also to the pleasure

of carrion-greedy birds. Those who lived fled
from the weapons of their enemies.
Then the Hebrews. . . .
. . . with glittering swords
cut themselves a battle path
through the crowd of their foes.

Thus the Assyrians were overcome and the Hebrews
turned back through the " shell " of the battle amid the
reeking corpses, plundering as they went. For the space
of a month they carried on this work ; from Holofernes
they took all his armour and weapons, sword, blood-stained
helmet, and broad corslet, adorned with gold, and these
were adjudged to Judith as her reward :—

For all of which Judith gave
glory to the Lord of Hosts, who had granted her honour,
fame in the kingdom of the earth, and also a reward in the
heavens,
triumph in the splendour of the skies, because she had had
true faith,
ever in the Almighty, and verily in the end she doubted not
of the reward which she had long desired.

And so with a final ascription of praise to God the episode
and perhaps the whole work ends.

This poem of Judith is not only in the same MS. as Beowulf,
one of about the year 1000, but it is in the same handwriting
as the second part of that work. On metrical and linguistic
grounds it must, however, have been composed much later
than Beowulf, well on into the tenth century ; that is to
say the poem cannot be much earlier than the MS. which
contains it. Whether this warlike outburst was due to any
particular event it is impossible to say, or whether the
dramatic quality of the story itself recommended it in those
troubled times. Several attempts have been made to find
a special source of inspiration. Of these by far the most
plausible surmise, indeed the only possible one, is that
Judith was written in honour of Æþelflæd, Ælfred's famous
daughter, the widow of Æþelred of Mercia.[1] After her

---

[1] Judith, T. G. Foster, Strasburg, 1892.

husband's death she herself led her forces against the Danes and recovered many cities from them, her greatest victories being between 915 and 918. The reputation which she gained for herself and the position she occupied may be gathered from the fact that the Chronicle constantly calls her "the Lady of the Mercians", and that elsewhere she is frequently termed "queen". The patriotic enthusiasm roused by her triumphs may well have found expression in verse, and lays celebrating her victories would no doubt have been composed soon after their occurrence, as the Lay of the Battle of Maldon was written almost immediately after that disaster. Some time, however, must be allowed to have elapsed before the patriotic deeds of Æþelflæd could have led to her association with Judith, who also saved her country by a deed of bravery, and before the story of the Hebrew heroine would receive epic treatment under the inspiration of the deeds of Æþelflæd. The epic cannot therefore be dated before 940 or 950. This date would fit in well with that suggested by considerations of syntax [1] and vocabulary.[2]

It will be seen that this association with Æþelflæd is possible, though rather remote. Other suggestions made are less easy to accept.[3] Judith may therefore be taken as

---

[1] This is not the place for an investigation of the syntax of the poem, but mention may be made of one feature, since it plays a considerable part in determining the date. This is the frequency of the occurrence of demonstrative pronoun, weak adjective, and noun together, as, for instance, in the phrase " æt þæm mæran þeodne ", *from the famous prince*. This is a construction which may be found at any time in Old English, but which only came gradually into frequent use; it is therefore only logical to conclude that a work in which it is of common occurrence is late.

[2] Vocabulary points to the same conclusion. The words " hearra " for *lord* (German *Herr*), and " gingra " for *disciple* (German *jünger*) were not found in Old English before the translation from Old Saxon of the Later Genesis (Genesis B). Outside that work they occur only in Judith and the Battle of Maldon, which latter poem is known to be late, for it commemorates a battle fought in 993. It is probable therefore that these words were introduced into English in that translation and that their application to Holofernes and Judith's attendant respectively is a further proof of later date.

[3] Because the poet treats a Biblical subject, earlier scholars assigned the poem to Cædmon, on the strength of Bede's assertion that he turned the whole of the Old and New Testaments into alliterative verse. It is not necessary, however, to go further into this view, for it has long been given up. Hardly more probable is the suggestion of Professor Cook in his first edition of the poem, that it might have been written in honour

representing O.E. literature in its later development. In it may be seen combined the original Germanic characteristics with the various elements and influences which had entered during the O.E. period. We have in it a variety of treatment and a richness of vocabulary which are not to be surpassed anywhere else in Old English. While it owes its theme to the widened knowledge introduced with Christianity, the old Germanic spirit is to be detected in the choice of that subject and its manner of treatment. Judith is no Christian martyr and, as far as it is possible to tell from a fragment, the main story is as warlike as any Germanic epic could have been. Nowhere have we a finer, more vivid description of a battle with the attendant figures of wolf, raven, and eagle. Germanic, too, is the grim realism of the murder, but the scene of Judith's shrinking before the terrible deed, the description of her doubt-torn soul, the passion of her prayer and perhaps the details of her preparations are new. Conflict of emotion is implied, and that very definitely, in the earlier poetry, but the detailed working out, the analysis of it, as here, is not found till later, and may no doubt be traced in part to the influence of Genesis B, in which, as we have seen, the psychological element is considerable and the workings of Satan's mind are far more prominent than the story. The anachronism of Judith's prayer to the Trinity need not surprise us in a poem of this date.

The poet of the Judith has known how to use to the full the means at his command. He has selected a good subject for treatment, one in which he could blend the characteristics of the older and the later periods. His gift of vivid description is unsurpassed, whether in his picture of Judith, in that of the actual murder, or of the later battle scenes ; he knows how to give reality by a definite detail here and there, as in the picture of the Assyrians standing, hesitating before

of Judith, daughter of Charles the Bald, on her marriage to Æþelwulf, father of king Ælfred, in 856. Apart from the consideration that the subject is hardly one to commend itself for a marriage song, and that the Chronicle contains no evidence that the marriage was regarded with any special enthusiasm in England, the date indicated by syntax and vocabulary is too late for this background.

Holofernes' tent and trying to awaken him by coughing. But the detail is never allowed to obscure or interfere with the main action.

The epic vocabulary as seen in Beowulf was in no need of enrichment ; the Judith poet has an equally large one at his command and he has admitted into it new words as they were useful to him. His kennings, too, deserve attention. Some, such as " hildenædran " (*snakes of battle*) and " scildburh " (*phalanx*) are good, but they occur elsewhere. " Wælscell," however, for *battle field*, the field or shell containing the bodies of the slain, is equally picturesque and apparently all his own. He has accepted, when he wanted it, the older mode of construction without demonstrative or preposition, for the sake of its vigorous terseness, as in phrases like " dēaðe geslægene " (*struck down by death*), or " Olofernes, goldwine gumena " (*Holofernes, goldfriend of men*) and he has adopted the newer, freer movement of the demonstrative or preposition when it helped to the easier flow of his line as in such phrases as " wiþ þæs hēhstan brōgan " (*against the highest terror*), or " drencte mid wīne " (*plied with wine*).

In his metre, too, he has shown the same independence and appreciation of possibilities. He alone among O.E. poets has seen and made a systematic use of the rival possibilities of the long and short line. For the narrative passages he has retained the more general short line, which had probably been involved for its suitability for epic ; but elsewhere he has used the long line with great effect. This appears specially in Judith's prayer. She begins on the short line in her invocation to the Trinity, but, as her passion rises, the verse is allowed to swell out into the long line with not only the three feet in each half, but a great freedom in the matter of unaccented syllables. Then as she ends her prayer and prepares for action, the metre drops back, in marked contrast, into the short line. So, too, our poet has shown his independence in another point in his metre. Hitherto, noun and adjective had been looked upon as the most important words in the sentence and had carried the alliteration before any other part of speech. In later O.E. poetry we find, however, that the importance

of the verb was beginning to be realized, and the old rule
to be modified by allowing it to take precedence. The poet
of Judith has accepted this modification. For instance,
we get such a verse as :

On þæt dægred sylf ; dynedan scyldas, *in the very dawn, shields
resounded.*

In the dim morning light it would be the sound of the
warriors arming themselves which would attract attention,
they themselves would be scarcely visible. This idea the
poet conveys by making the verb " resound " alliterate
instead of the noun. Our poet shows, too, that he was
moving with the times in the frequency of his end-rhymes.
An example of this would be :

dryhtguman sīne drencte mid wīne, *his warriors he plied with wine.*

It is a usage which we have already seen in Cynewulf
and the Phoenix, and employed more systematically by
them, but which is very little found before their time.

Further in considering the poet's skill in technique, the
manner must be noticed in which he has rounded off his
episode by ending on the same note on which it began,
namely Judith's faith. Our fragment is, we know, but part
of a longer poem, it is, however, complete in itself. In this
feeling for form, the Judith poet stands alone in O.E.
poetry.

Before leaving this poem, attention must also be drawn
to the skill with which the crowds are handled, whether
they are Hebrews hurrying out to meet Judith, Assyrians
fleeing, or Hebrews pursuing them. In this the writer has
only one rival in O.E. poetry, in the author of the Exodus.
Like him, he is the forerunner of Langland with his " faire
feld full of folk ". There is another point also of resemblance
between the two poems of Exodus and Judith. In both we
have Biblical subjects, which from their manner of treatment
appear to have been chosen for their own sakes rather than
for any purpose of edification, though both begin and end
on the orthodox didactic note.

To sum up. In Judith we have an admirable subject
selected and developed in the tenth century by a poet who

could treat it in a manner to compare favourably with the
finest of the earlier epics, but could also make use of all
later modifications of thought, words, and metre. In common
with the writers of poems already considered, he has no
idea of local colour or chronology.   Holofernes's feast is
a Germanic drinking bout, more barbarous by far than
the dignified banquets of Beowulf ;   the armour worn is
that of the Germanic warrior ;   Judith prays to the Trinity.
It is thus by using a medium with which he was familiar
that the poet has been able to give us such a vivid picture.

But whatever the origin of the Judith fragment may have
been, whether it was expanded out of a lay or not, it is
clear that hero lays continued to be composed during the
O.E. period.   We have no direct survival of the earlier
ones, but their existence may be inferred from the entry
in the A.S. Chronicle for 755.   The first entries met with in
that Chronicle are, as a rule, brief, but for that year five
out of the six MSS. give us a full and vivid account of the
death of Cynewulf of Wessex and the vengeance taken by
his followers on the murderers. As the entries for some years
before and after are noticeably short, this amplitude is
remarkable, and it is probable that the chronicler had some
special source of information from which to draw for this
event.   From the nature of the narrative that source would
seem to have been a lay or lays.   There are two fights, one
in which Cynewulf falls, the other in which the murderer,
the nobleman Cyneheard, is slain.   In both fights families
are divided, each force having kinsmen on the other side,
in both, according probably to the etiquette of the times,
the attackers offer to let their kinsmen go before beginning
the assault, and the offer is refused, and in both fights all
are killed except the one surviver necessary to tell the tale.
Such an obvious similarity of framework can only point
to a regular tradition for the composition of these
" occasional " poems, and therefore to a regular practice
of making them.   Unfortunately all that have survived
in their proper form belong to later O.E. literature.   First
among these is the Battle of Maldon.   The MS. of this poem
perished in the fire in Ashburnham House, that disastrous

fire in which the Beowulf MS. was injured, but happily
it had been transcribed a few years earlier by Hearne and
his copy is the source of our knowledge.

The subject is the battle fought between Byrhtnoþ the
" ealdormonn " of Mercia, and the Danes under Anlaf in
993 at Maldon, where the Pant (O.E. Panta) and the Chelmer
flow into the Blackwater. The Danes appear to have left
their ships and taken up their position between the two
converging streams, while the English were to the north of
the Pant. The story is told in a series of scenes, only two
words remaining of the first sentence, but from what follows
we must conclude that Byrhtnoþ and his companions
were surprised at a hunting party by the news of the landing
of the Danes :—

Then he bade each of the warriors give up his horse,
drive it far away and go forth,
look to his arms and be of good courage.
As soon as Offa's kinsman discovered
that the "Earl" would not tolerate cowardice,
he sent his favourite hawk
flying to the wood and went forth to the fight.
By this might be seen that the youth would not
flinch in the strife with weapons in his hand.

Another young warrior, Eadric, acted in the same way,
fulfilling, we are told, an old vow.

The next scene gives us Byrhtnoþ reviewing and encouraging his band as they stood arrayed for battle and a Viking
herald on the opposite bank of the river shouting his challenge
across it :—

Bold seamen have sent me to thee,
have bidden me say that thou must send at once
treasure in exchange for protection. It will be better for
    you all
to buy off this attack with tribute
than that we should fiercely join in battle.
No need is there for us to harm each other if you are good
    for that,
for we will in exchange for the gold make a treaty,
if thou wilt counsel this, thou who art mightiest here

and thou wilt redeem thy people
give to us seamen, at our own decree,
money in exchange for our protection and accept peace at our
  hands,
we with the treasure will betake us to our ships,
journey back across the sea, and hold our pact with you.

Byrhtnoþ was not behind the herald in the boldness of
his words :—

Dost thou hear, seaman, what this army saith ?
They will give you spears for tribute,
poisoned spear points and old swords,
wargear which will not profit you in the fight.
Messenger of the seamen take this answer back,
tell thy people in far more hostile words,
how here stands undismayed a noble midst his band,

    .   .   .   .

the heathen shall fall in the fight,

    .   .   .

nor shall ye so easily obtain our treasure.

This ended the parley, but for a while no action followed
for the tide prevented one army from attacking the other,
except when an occasional arrow felled a foe :—

too long it seemed to them
till they might bear their spears together.

But when the tide was out Byrhtnoþ bade a warrior,
hard in battle, hold the bridge. This was Wulfstan, son of
Ceola, and with him were the dauntless pair, Ælfhere and
Maccus, who held it steadily against the foe as long as they
could wield their weapons.

Finding it thus impossible to take the bridge, the Danes
began to try strategy, the poem says, though the strategy
seems fairly simple. They asked to be allowed to cross by
the ford, and Byrhtnoþ, in his arrogance, permitted it. " Too
much land he gave," the poet says. " Now you have space
enough," he cried, " so come quickly to us. God alone
knows who shall prevail on this battle-field." And now the
fight began in earnest :—

Then trod the wolves of war, they recked not of the water
this band of Vikings, westward, across the Panta,
over the bright water they bore their shields,
the sailors bore their linden shields to land.

At this point the tone changes somewhat, the exultation
in the fight is still there, but a note of foreboding begins to
make itself heard :—

Then was battle nigh,
glory in fight. The time was come
that doomed men should fall.
Then was clamour raised, the ravens circled,
and the eagle eager for the feast.
There was uproar on the earth.

The description of the battle which follows is given in
cinema fashion. We have a series of short accounts of the
deeds of prowess of one warrior after another till at last
Byrhtnoþ fell. He was, however, avenged by the young
thane Wulfmær, who snatched the spear from the wound
and hurled it back again at the Viking who had sent it.
Then Byrhtnoþ, like the earlier hero Beowulf, made a last
speech, but there is the difference of three centuries in the
character of the two utterances :—

I thank Thee, Ruler of the nations,
for all the joys which I have known on earth.
Now I have, O gracious Lord, the greatest need,
That Thou shouldest show mercy to my soul,
that my spirit may journey to Thee,
into Thy keeping, Lord of Angels,
may pass in peace. I pray Thee
that the fiends in hell may not injure it.
Then the heathen knaves cut him down,
and both the warriors who stood beside him,
Ælfhere and Wulfmær, both lay dead,
giving up their lives beside their lord.

At this some lost courage and turned from the fight,
Odda's sons, Godrinc and Godwig, being the first to flee,
and many more followed them than was, as the poet says,
seemly. But the rest of Byrhtnoþ's comrades, when they

saw their chief was slain, declared their intention to avenge their lord or to lose their lives in the attempt.

At this point comes a second series of pictures. The warriors are represented, one after the other, as raising their shields or brandishing their spears, declaring their own determination to fight to the death and encouraging their followers to stand firm, till at last all have fallen. Alfmær, son of Ælfwine, reminded them of boasts made by them at the feasts. Now might be seen who was really bold. The thanes should not twit him among his clan, saying that he had desired to seek his home, now that his lord lay slain. Æþelric, Offa, Leofsuna, Dunnere, and others all make similar speeches ; even the hostage Æscferþ of Northumbrian race did not waver, but sent forth arrows enough. After him, Byrhtwold, an old comrade, shook his spear and exhorted the men thus :

> The mind must be the sterner, the heart the bolder,
> the courage the greater, as our might grows less.
> Here lies our lord all hewn down,
> the valiant one in the dust. Ever may he mourn,
> who thinks now to turn from this battle-play.
> I am old in years, I will not hence,
> but I think to lay me beside my lord,
> beside one so loved.

Finally Godric, not, the poet explains, he who had fled before but another, encouraged his comrades till he fell, and the poem, as we have it, ends, though probably one or two lines have been lost.

It is clear from its style that this lay was composed soon after the battle which was its subject. The events must have been fresh in the minds of the people, from the way in which many of the warriors are introduced simply as son of so and so, or merely by their own names. Moreover the poet was not far enough away from the event to see it in any perspective, he has hardly shaped his theme at all. It is true that Byrhtnoþ is given greater prominence than the other warriors, but their deeds are told independently, they are merely grouped loosely round him. In fact, the poem may be said to tell the story of the death of certain heroes in a battle, greater prominence being given to their leader, rather than that of the death of one hero, set off against the background of a fight in which many others fell. Such a lay would need much remoulding before it could develop into an epic, as did the lays of the earlier centuries. Very noticeable is the rapidity of the action, which is in marked contrast to the dignified sweep of the epic. It almost gives a sense of breathlessness, hence we do not find the poet stopping often for the parallel phrase. He had no time for the descriptions for which that method was so admirable. Neither does he make much use of the kenning, he has only such as had no simpler equivalent in the language, as for instance, bordweall or scildburh for the phalanx. Nevertheless without the kenning he has a large and brilliant vocabulary at his command, his narrative is vigorous and he has contrived to get a good deal of variety into his single fights.

The Battle of Maldon, coming as it does at the end of the Old English period, illustrates well the development of culture during the centuries since the writing of Beowulf. It is as warlike in spirit as Beowulf ; the virtues held up for admiration in it are, as in that poem, loyalty, courage, and gratitude rather than brute force or recklessness. The most despicable of vices are treachery and ingratitude. But Christian teaching has penetrated much deeper. This comes out in Byrhtnoþ's dying prayer if compared with that of Beowulf. While the latter congratulates himself that he has not been guilty of treachery nor has failed his people, Byrhtnoþ appeals to the mercy of God with no thought of his own merits. The ethical standard of Beowulf has been replaced by definite Christian teaching.

So, too, the classical influence to be traced in the epic in a general way only, may be seen more definitely in this later lay. It appears in details as in the holding of the bridge, and perhaps in the individual challenges, but the Finnsburg Fragment shows a similar usage in the description of the fight.

Besides the Battle of Maldon, there are five short lays in the Anglo-Saxon Chronicle. Of these it is thought that the last may have been written for the Chronicle, while the others were most probably composed independently and inserted afterwards, not turned into prose as in the case of the story of Cynewulf and Cyneheard,[1] but simply incorporated as they were. While most have little literary quality, the first is, however, a poem of some merit and of greater importance than the others. In 75 verses it celebrates the victory at Brunanburh in 937 of Æþelstan of Wessex and Mercia, supported by his brother Edmund, over a combined army of Danes, Scots, and Britons from Strathclyde. The battle was part of a general attempt to overthrow the power of Wessex, but had also the special object of supporting the claims of two Dublin kings, Anlaf, son of Sictric, and his cousin of the same name, the son of Godfrey, to earlier possessions of the family in Northumbria. The author of the lay has made the two Anlafs into one. The Anlaf Sictricson, also known as Anlaf Cwiran, has probably provided in part the historical background for the figure of Havelok in the M.E. romance of that name.

The O.E. lay begins :

In this year (937) Æþelstan the king, lord of nobles,
ring-giver of men, and his brother also,
Eadmund the Æþeling, lifelong glory
gained in fight with the edges of swords,
by Brunanburh. The shields they clove,
hewed the battle shields, the leavings of the hammers,
these sons of Eadweard, as became the race
of these bold kinsmen, who oft in fight
against every foe protected their land,
their treasure and their homes. The enemy fell,
the people of the Scots and the pirates
being doomed.

Then the poet goes on to say that the battle lasted from sunrise to sunset, there lay many a man slain with the spear, men from the north, wounded over their shields, and Scots too, battle-sated. The men of Wessex pursued the hostile races through the livelong day, the Mercians did not refuse fierce fight to any of those who had, with Anlaf,

---

[1] See pp. 220 and 278.

sought their land in their ships over the surging of the sea. Five young kings and seven " earls " of Anlaf lay on the battle-field, put to sleep with swords, and a countless number of pirates and Scots. The prince of the Northmen took refuge in his ship with a small band and departed over the " fallow " flood to save his life. The Scottish king, too, the aged Constantine, a hoary warrior, also escaped, fleeing northwards to his people. His kinsmen were slain in the battle, his friends in the fight, and his young son was left on the field of slaughter.

Neither he nor Anlaf with their war remnant had cause to boast of this meeting of men, of this exchange of weapons in which they had been active against the sons of Eadweard. The Northmen departed, the sad leavings of the javelins, to seek Dublin again, the land of Ireland, over the deep water. The brothers also, king and æþeling, sought their native land of Wessex, exulting in their victory, leaving behind them the black raven, dark-plumaged and curved of beak, the grey-coated eagle, white of tail, and the greedy battlehawk, to tear the corpses, and the grey beast, the wolf of the forest, to enjoy the feast. Never yet had there been greater slaughter, as the books and old chroniclers tell us, since Angles and Saxons sought Britain over the wide seas and, overcoming the British, acquired this land.

This lay has been given almost in full. It will be seen that unlike the Battle of Maldon, it gives no names of individual warriors ; the leaders only are mentioned, and, with the O.E. love of depicting the sombre side of life, the emotions of the vanquished are treated first and at greater length than the exultation of the victors, though it is the English who have the victory. The poet is viewing his story from a greater distance. He gives it in general outline, and he apparently knows no details. The other four lays are much shorter. The second gives a brief account of Edmund's successes in which he gained from the Danes the five cities of Leicester, Lincoln, Nottingham, Stamford, and Derby. It tells us that, " In this year (942) Eadmund, lord of the English, protector of his kinsmen, a valiant leader, overran Mercia as bounded by Dore, Whitwell, and the waters of the Humber, that great stream. The five cities had been Danish before under the rule of the Northmen, held long in the bonds of captivity by the heathen, until King Eadmund, son of Eadweard, freed them to his own glory." This is little more than alliterative prose. At the best it reads like the first sketch of a lay, in which the points to be emphasized and elaborated are indicated by the use of the parallel phrase, these points being the glory of the king and the humiliation of the five towns under alien rule, with which it is contrasted. Or it might have been intended for the introduction to a longer lay never finished or since lost.

The third lay gives us an equally brief account of the coronation of Edgar at Bath in 973. The subject is admirable, but again we seem to have either an outline only for an intended lay, or possibly an introduction to a longer poem. We have, moreover, here no indication of the points to be emphasized as in the lay just discussed. It runs :

In this year was Eadgar, ruler of the English,
in a great concourse, hallowed as king,
in the old city of Acemannes ceaster,
which men by another name
call Bath. There was great joy
come to pass for all upon that blessed day,
which the sons of men name and call
the Day of Pentecost. There were many priests,
a great company of monks, as I have heard,
and of the learned, gathered together.
It was ten hundred years since the birth of the Saviour,
save for seven and twenty, so nearly had the thousand passed,
when this happened. And Eadmund's son,
hard in battle, had lived nine and twenty winters
in the world when it came to pass that he was
hallowed king in his thirtieth year.

The Beowulf poet could have made a fine picture of the scene, but as it stands it reminds the reader of the introduction to the Elene in which the facts are stated before the poet throws himself into the interest of his story.

The fourth lay laments the attitude of Edward towards the clergy, and is more than a mere chronicle of events. The poet has not produced a work of much merit but he has a subject and a point of view, he can suggest pathos and he can use the poetic vocabulary with some effect, but he has missed his opportunity over the appearance of the comet.

This lay comes immediately after the third in the MS., but the two are too unlike to have been by the same writer. It begins with the death of Edgar, how he came to the end of earthly joys and in the old poetic phrase " chose another light," glorious and lovely, and gave up this feeble transitory life. It was in the month called July by men who have been rightly instructed in the art of numbers, on the eighth day, that the young prince departed this life, the ring-giver of men, and his son Eadweard, a child still, succeeded to his kingdom. After this the writer goes on to lament the decline of religion throughout Mercia. " Many were driven away," he says, " of the servants of God. That was great sorrow to those who bore in their breasts, burning love, in their hearts, for the Creator " :—

Then also was banished the noble hearted man,
Oslac from the land, over the raging of the waves,
over the gannet's bath, the grey haired man,
wise, and prudent of speech, over the tumult of the waters,
over the home of the whale, bereft of a home.
Then was shown, above in the skies,
a star in its place, which the bold-hearted,
wise-minded men call far and wide,
a comet by name, men skilled in science,
wise soothsayers. Then was throughout the nation
the vengeance of the Lord widely made known
in hunger (sent) over the earth. This afterwards the
    Guardian of Heaven,
the Prince of Angels bettered, and gave joy to each
of the dwellers in this isle, through the fruits of the earth.

The fifth of these lays tells of the death of Edward the Martyr, in 979 at the gate of Corfe Castle, through the treachery of his stepmother. In this we are reminded of some of the Riddles, especially the one known as " De Creatura ",[1] or on a larger scale, of the Dream of the Rood, in the use of antithesis.

> Never was a worse deed done in England than was this,
> since the Angles first sought the land of Britain.
> Men martyred him, but God gave him fame.
> He was in this life an earthly king,
> he is now after death a heavenly saint.
> Him his earthly kinsmen would not avenge,
> but him hath his heavenly Father sternly avenged.
> His earthly murderers would fain wipe out his name in the
> world,
> but his heavenly Avenger hath his memory
> spread abroad in heaven and on earth.
> Those who would not before
> bend before his living body,
> now in humility
> bow the knee to his dead bones.

Now we may perceive that human wisdom and councils and their projects are of no avail against the purpose of God.

As might be expected, the best of these lays, the only two of real value, the Battles of Maldon and Brunanburh, are due to the patriotic feeling aroused by the incursions of the Danes. If some of these passages seem wanting in poetic quality, there are others in the Chronicle yet nearer the borderline of prose and poetry, over which authorities differ, some taking then for lays, others for rhythmical prose only, with alliteration sometimes, and sometimes with rhyme.

One of these may be mentioned here because while having little claim to attention on its own merits, it is noticeable for the frequency with which the two halves of the long line are made to rhyme. It is for the year 1036 and tells how Ælfred, son of King Æþelred, wished to visit his mother at Winchester, but Godwine prevented him, imprisoning him and scattering his comrades, slaying some and selling others for money, while yet others he imprisoned. Of the twenty

[1] p. 204.

lines of the whole, ten rhyme more or less perfectly. They
run :

> Ac Godwine hine gelette, hine on hæft sette,
> his gefēran todrāf, sume mislice ofslōh,
> sume hī man wiδ fēo sealde, sume hrēowlice ācwealde,

and so on, showing how the use of end-rhyme was becoming
more and more common by this time.

This chapter on later O.E. poetry may be concluded with
a mention of certain minor poems of very different kinds,
which have little literary value but are of interest in other
ways. One, the Rune Song, marks the dying out of the older
alphabet of the Germanic tribes before that of Latin-trained
scribes ; some, like the Dialogue of Salomo and Saturn show
English writers sharing in European literary developments,
as we have seen them beginning to do in the Riddles and
Physiologus ; others show developments in subject, treatment, or form which lead on to M.E. literature, as in the
Address of the Soul to the Body, the little poem on the
Doomsday and the Rhyming Song. Yet others widen our
knowledge of English life and thought, such as the Gifts
of Men and the Fates of Men.

The Rune Song referred to already on p. 19 is in its
matter somewhat reminiscent of the Gnomic verses. In it
each rune in turn is named and explained. Thus of the
Þ, (w), called *joy* or according to some *hope*, we are told :

> He feels no need of joy, who knows little of woe,
> of pain or sorrow, and himself has
> wealth and happiness and cities enough.

Or for the symbol for " i " we read :

> Ice is overcold, exceedingly slippery,
> It glitters brighter than glass, most like to gems.

Such verses remind one of Calverley's rhymed alphabet,
" A was an angel of blushing eighteen," or of the more
prosaic instructions in the Telephone Directory ; they must
have been meant as a help to the memory. The metre shows
the poem to have been of Northumbrian origin, but the forms
of the language give no clue as to date. While most scholars

assume it to be late, written when the use of the runes was being preserved artificially, it is just possible that it, like other Northumbrian poems, was an early effort composed for the benefit of the monks in their attempts to learn the native alphabet. The explanation of the rune for " f ", called " feoh ", *property*, has been thought to indicate a minstrel as the writer. It runs, " Money is a consolation to every one ; each man must deal it out freely if he is to gain honour before his lord ". But this theory is difficult to support in the face of a curious mistake made elsewhere. The runic symbol for " o " was called " ōs ", which is the O.N. " āss " meaning *god*. But in O.E. the word survived only as the name of the rune and was apparently not known to the writer of the poem for he has taken it as the Latin " ōs " and explained it as " the mouth, the leader of the speech, the home of wisdom, the comfort of the wise ". Such a mistake would hardly have been made by a minstrel, but easily by someone to whom Latin was more familiar than English.

The preservation of the Rune Song with its valuable information upon the original alphabet used by our ancestors, is one of the debts which we owe to Hickes. The MS. was one of those destroyed in the fire of 1731 at Ashburnham House, but fortunately he had already copied it and published it in his Thesaurus in 1705. From his copy the MS. seems to have been of the eleventh century, whatever the date of the poem may be.

The curious Dialogue of Salomo and Saturn exists in two MSS. both at C.C.C., Cambridge. The first, which is the earlier and the longer, is unfortunately very defective, but the gaps can be filled in in some cases from the second MS., short though it is. The poem is in two parts. First comes a dialogue between Salomo and Paternoster, the personification of prayer. This is chiefly filled with a long account of what prayer can do. Each letter of Paternoster is taken in its runic form and represented as the initial of some agent in its victories. Then comes an inserted prose passage and finally the second part of the poem. This consists of a series of riddle-like questions asked by Saturn, who represents the wisdom of the East. Salomo, standing here for Christian wisdom, sometimes answers, sometimes propounds similar difficulties, and sometimes merely agrees.

This is a literary form which was widely spread over Europe and may go back to very early times. The O.E. version and an Old French one stand apart from the others in offering a serious treatment ; later the name Saturn was replaced by that of Marcolf and the treatment became full of rough, even coarse, humour, more in the medieval spirit, than in the dignified O.E. manner.

Another work which is of interest in the history of literature is the Address of the Soul to the Body. This is the first representative in English of a class of poems which became more popular afterwards, though it must be a side development rather than the exact source of the Debates between Body and Soul which appear in M.E.

Two copies exist of this work, one in the Exeter Book and the other in the Vercelli Codex. In it we learn that every seven nights for three hundred winters the soul shall revisit the body in which it formerly lived, unless the end of the world come first. In the O.E. text the soul is the only speaker and for 108 verses it reproaches the body. It could not free itself, and the time that it dwelt in it seemed like thirty thousand winters. While the body feasted and revelled, the soul starved, though it had been sent by God. Now the body has neither gold nor silver, ornaments nor any other possessions. Now it is dumb and deaf, with bones and sinews decaying. What will it answer at Doomsday ? Then shall soul and body together endure such misery as the body has earned for them on earth.

The address of a soul in bliss to its body is a rarer subject to find treated, but the Vercelli Codex does afford one example. The theme, however, has not stirred its author as has that of the " damned soul ". He has treated it far more shortly. " Alas ! " the soul says, that it could not have taken the body with it into the Father's keeping. While the body fasted, was poor and humble, the soul was feasted, with every wish supplied, and exalted to eternal joy. At the last day they will have no need to fear.

Doomsday was a favourite theme. Besides the fine poem already considered,[1] which follows Cynewulf's Crist, and is by some believed to be part of it, and allusions elsewhere, we have a short poem in the Exeter Book which is of interest because of the unusual nature passage with which it begins and which shows a new spirit coming into O.E. literature, a spirit faintly foreshadowed in the Seafarer, but not fully developed till Middle English. It is quite distinct from the exotic treatment of nature as seen in translations like the Phoenix :—

> Lo ! I sat alone within a grove,
> under the shelter of the tree-tops, in the middle of the wood,
> where the springs of water murmured as they flowed,
> through the middle of the meadow, as I tell.
> There pleasant plants too grew and flowered
> in among them on that peerless plain.
> Then the woodland trees began to move and sway
> through the violence of the wind, a cloud arose,
> and my sad heart was troubled.

The sudden overcasting of the peaceful scene leads the speaker on to the consideration of the last judgment.

The increasing frequency in the employment of rhyme, which we have traced, is seen most fully towards the end of the O.E. period in the Rhyming Song.

In this poem of eighty-five lines the poet represents the regrets of a rich man for all his former happiness and prosperity, now that he has fallen on evil days, or perhaps the poet means to represent him as already in hell. He has maintained rhyme and alliteration all through, not, however, apparently without allowing himself to sacrifice meaning sometimes to the exigencies of his metre. A few lines will be enough to illustrate this work :—

> Me lifes onlāh, sē þe þis leoht onwrāh,
> ond þæt torhte getāh, tillice onwrāh.
> Glæd wæs ic glīwum, glenged nīwum
> blissa blēoum, blostma hīwum.

Minor poems dealing with points of belief or doctrine are

[1] See p. 189.

those on the Gloria, the Creed, the Lord's and other prayers,
some hymns, a poem on the Wonders of Creation, which
tells of the dividing of the earth and sky, and of the land
and water, but none of these require detailed notice. Short
poems of a didactic character are those dealing with the
various gifts bestowed on men, " the Gifts of Men " ; with
the various fates to which they are liable, " the Fates of
Men " ; and the various dispositions with which they are
endowed " the Moods of Men ". We also have a little poem
in which a father gives advice to his son on various points,
" the Counsels of a Father."

These also are of little literary value. No plan of arrangement is to be traced in the first mentioned, the Gifts of
Men ; for instance, skill in deciphering runes and swiftness
in running are mentioned in the same line. The gifts treated
at greatest length are those of skill in building and in seamanship. We are told, " One man can think out the glorious
work of some lofty building, his hand is trained, wise, and
controlled, as is right for the maker, in order that he may
set up a hall. He is able to join together firmly a wide
dwelling, so that it shall not suddenly fall." Of seamanship
we read :

> One man on the dark waves can guide the ship, he knows
> the course of the currents, a leader of the band across the
> wide ocean when bold seamen with quick strength row with
> their oars at the edge of the ship.

The gifts for the religious life are dealt with more shortly
and are more varied. One man turns over in his mind the
needs of the spirit, chooses the grace of the Creator above
all earthly riches. Another is valiant in strife with the devil,
in the fight against wickedness. Yet a third has skill for
the services of the Church, can loudly praise in hymns the
Lord of Life. He has a clear voice. Among those gifts to be
expected, such as riches, prowess in war, or eloquence, are
some rather surprising ones. These include being able to
shoot straight, to run quickly, being a good butler, or keeper
of the beer, as it is called, and being swift in feats of activity
for entertainment, presumably in juggling.

The Fates of Men is worked out more thoroughly and with more originality. To be eaten by wolves is mentioned as a possible fate as simply as to die of hunger, be drowned at sea, or destroyed in battle. Some must pass their lives without sight, groping with their hands; some lament their pain, infirm in movement, suffering sinew-wounds (rheumatism?) One may fall from a high tree, he has no wings, yet he flies, moving through the air, until the (growth) of the tree comes to an end, and he sinks, lifeless to the roots, falls to the ground. Another must wander on distant paths, bearing his food with him, treading the dewy track of strangers; the friendless man is unwelcome everywhere, because of his destitution. One shall be burnt in a speedy death, others killed in a brawl. One who has wasted his youth, may yet in his old age regain happiness and riches.

After these "fates" follows a list of the various gifts bestowed on men, which overlaps the poem on that theme already mentioned, except that in it we get one gift not found before, that is, skill at draughts or chess.

"The Dispositions of Men" deals chiefly with the arrogant and the humble.

CHAPTER X

EARLY PROSE : ÆLFRED : GREGORY'S DIALOGUES

The prose of the O.E. period offers many points of contrast with the poetry. In the first place its importance is rather for its place in the history of English literature, or, in the case of the Chronicle, for English history, than for its own intrinsic value as prose. In Beowulf, the lyric poems, and Judith, for instance, we have a literature in its maturity and full of character. It is at its highest point of development, and can hardly be called decadent, as is so often done, since it was not too stereotyped to accept such modifications in form as the time required. In prose, while there is much that is good and much that is of extreme interest, we have no great height of attainment and most of it is too much under foreign influence to have developed any very individual English character. As long as everything has to be handed down by word of mouth, some form such as rhyme or alliteration is necessary as a help to the memory. Prose literature is only possible when a nation has advanced far enough in culture to possess the power of writing with comparative ease. Among the English this ease did not come till Latin culture through the channel of Christianity had replaced the old materials of stone, ivory, bone, and wood by the more easily manipulated parchment, and the angular runic symbols by its own more flowing script. Consequently O.E. prose is later than O.E. poetry. While some of the finest poems date from the late seventh and early eighth centuries, we have to wait for the ninth for any considerable prose work, for though it is true that Bede was engaged upon a translation of the Gospel of St. John at the time of his death, no trace of it has come down to us.

O.E. literary prose may be said to have arisen through Latin influence upon the vernacular, an influence coming first through translation and fortunately constantly modified by that of the native poetry. At first the monks began to prepare Latin-English glosses for the services of the Church and for the books used in the monastic schools; thus we have, to mention the most important, the Erfurt-Epinal glosses of the seventh century, the Corpus glosses of the eighth, and later in the ninth, the interlinear glosses of the Vespasian Psalter; some names appear in English form in Bede's Ecclesiastical History of the early eighth century, and in the Durham Book or Durham Liber Vitæ, a list of benefactors to the Church at Durham, of the ninth century, and the same century gives us English genealogies. But these provide material for historical and linguistic study, they are not literature.

For the beginnings of prose, faint beginnings indeed, we must look to the Laws. Though the extant MSS. are later, the Laws were early written down in English, those of Ethelbert of Kent about 600, our copy being about 1125; those of Ine of Wessex between 688–694, our copy being of the tenth century; while those of Offa of Mercia, which were written down sometime during his reign (757–796), are now unfortunately lost. The prose in those preserved is of a very elementary character, as in the following example : " If any one fight in the king's house, let him pay as fine all his property, and let it be at the king's discretion whether he keep his life or do not keep it."

Since the codes written down were based on older ones, which must have been in verse, it is not surprising that they often show the alliteration and rhythm of a poetic line. Take for example : " Gif féorrcund mon oððe frémde butan wége geond wúdu gonge," that is " *if a man from a distance or a stranger go through a wood without (keeping to) the path.*"

English had also begun to be used in part in charters, the first example being in that of Ethelbert of Kent, of the early seventh century, granted to the Church of St. Andrew at Rochester. The first charter wholly in English was written in 743.

The same simplicity of construction as in the Laws is seen in the earlier entries into the Anglo-Saxon Chronicle, the same limitation of conjunctions and economy in the use of pronouns. But the Anglo-Saxon Chronicle will be considered later by itself.

Thus prose began first to take the place of verse for laws and official documents, but for its use for literature we have to wait for Ælfred's time (848–889, or 900),[1] who in the midst of his great work for England as soldier and administrator yet found time to give her a new form for literature. While encouraging the preservation and study of the old poems, he laid the foundation of the whole later structure of English prose. When the obstacles are considered with which he had to contend, the degree of success to which he attained is surprising. In the first place, as we have seen, he was working in a medium (English prose) whose possibilities had been as yet little explored, and in his translations he was further hampered by not too good a knowledge of the language of his originals. He says himself [2] that he translated the books as he understood them and could most intelligibly render them, which seems to suggest a certain amount of difficulty with the meaning of the Latin and in finding fitting English in which to convey it. It is therefore from the independent additions to his works, in which he is free from, at any rate, one of these hindrances, that he can best be judged.

A further point of contrast between O.E. prose and poetry is that, whereas most of the latter is anonymous, we know not only the names of the most important prose writers but a good deal about them. For Ælfred we have various sources of information. In the first place, we have his own statement about the condition of England at the beginning of his reign and his plans for the education of his people [2] ; then we have the entries in the Chronicle, which were doubtless inspired, if not, as Professor Earle has suggested,[3] actually written, by him. Finally we have the life of him written by his friend and biographer, Asser,[4] later bishop of Sherborne. This last source of information must, however, as Mr. Plummer has shown, be used critically and with caution ; partly because the text we possess is apparently

[1] Plummer, Two Saxon Chronicles, Note to the year 901.
[2] Preface to Cura Pastoralis.
[3] Alfred the Great, ed. by Alfred Bowker. King Alfred as Writer, p. 202.
[4] Asser's Life of King Alfred, ed. by Stevenson.

corrupt and we have always to be alive to the possibility of later interpolations, and partly because the writer's fertile imagination was perhaps apt to run away with him in an age which was not given to examining its evidence too closely. Still we may accept his story of the way in which Ælfred's interest in the native literature was aroused. He tells us how he had English poems read to him constantly, (Asser says by day and by night) until he could read them for himself and thus gain the precious book offered as a reward by his mother, Osburh, not his stepmother Judith, as in popular tradition. This must have been before 856, the year in which his father Æþelwulf married Judith, that is before Ælfred was eight years old, not thirteen as Asser says. The other popular story of the burning of the cakes, also told by Asser, may be dismissed as absolutely without corroboration and as a not too intelligent invention.

A certain amount is known of Ælfred's childhood. He was born in 848.[1] At the age of five he was sent to Rome, and we possess the letter written by the Pope, Leo IV, to announce his safe arrival there. Two years later, in 855, he paid a second visit, this time with his father, and he was probably still with him when Æþelwulf, on his return home in the following year, stayed at the court of Charles the Bald, and there married Charles's daughter, Judith, a child of twelve or thirteen. Whether the primary object of Ælfred's visits to Rome was educational or not, they, and that to the French court, must have exercised a great influence on the mind of a boy under ten. After this little is known of him till, on the accession of his brother Æþelred in 866 to the throne of Wessex, Ælfred was associated with him in opposing the Danes. The year 871 was marked by many battles, in one of which Æþelred fell and Ælfred succeeded him on the throne of Wessex. In 878 came his enforced withdrawal of his troops to Athelney, where he spent his time in planning his next campaign and not in burning cakes, and near which the famous Ælfred Jewel was found in 1693. By 879 Wessex and the west of Mercia had been cleared of Danes. But alas! only for a time ; from 892 to

[1] See Plummer, Life and Times of Alfred, p. 70.

896 Ælfred was involved in a continuous and desperate struggle with them till at the end of that time the Danish host broke up, " some to East Anglia, some to Northumbria. And those who had no property got them ships and fared over the sea to the Seine ". No wonder that Ælfred made himself the idol of his people and gained for himself the title of England's Darling as well as that of the Great, and that after his death stories collected round his memory, as they had done round those of earlier heroes. Such a story would be that told by William of Malmesbury of his going disguised as a minstrel into the Danish camp, and entertaining the soldiers with his music until he had found out their strength, a story told of others than Ælfred. Ælfred cannot have begun his series of writings much before 896, nor can he have had much opportunity for learning Latin until he became king. He tells us in the Introduction to the Cura Pastoralis that there were very few this side the Humber who could turn one epistle from Latin into English, indeed he could not think of a single one south of the Thames when he came to the throne. Nor could he till then have collected round him the group of scholars he mentions, the Mercian, Plegmund, later Archbishop of Canterbury ; Grimbold the Fleming, later Bishop of Winchester ; John the Saxon, Abbot of Athelney ; and last, but not least, the Welshman, Asser, later Bishop of Sherborne, his intimate friend and biographer. It is interesting to note that Charlemagne had, a century before, in the same way gathered round him a group of scholars from different lands, among them being his biographer, Eginhart, and the Northumbrian Alcuin.

Ælfred's first work was a commonplace book, his Handbōc. Asser tells that one day the king was struck by a passage in a book which he was reading to him, and begged him to write it down in the little volume of psalms and prayers which he (Ælfred) carried about with him. Asser suggested that it would be better to have a separate sheet, as the little book was full and so the Handbōc was begun. Unfortunately it is lost but its existence may be taken as certain, for William of Malmesbury [1] writing in the twelfth century

[1] De Gestis Pont., p. 333.

mentions it among the other works, and Florence of Worcester,[1] rather earlier speaks of it as the " Dicta " of King Ælfred.

As in the case of the poets Cædmon and Cynewulf, there is some doubt as to how many of the works usually attributed to Ælfred are actually by him, but it may be taken as certain that the translation of the Pastoral Care of Pope Gregory the Great is his, and that it began the series. He has written for it a preface which is obviously meant as an introduction to all his works. In it he begins after the formal greeting by contrasting the state of learning in England at his accession with that happy time before, when men from abroad came here to seek wisdom and learning, whereas an Englishman must now go abroad if he would acquire them. Then too, before England had been ravaged and burnt, the churches throughout the country had been filled with jewels and books, though the congregations who also filled them had little use for the books because they were not written in their own tongue. He wonders why no previous scholars had thought of translating any of these works, but he answers himself that it must be because they never believed that men would become so careless and allow wisdom to decline so greatly. They would not translate because they wished that other languages should be learnt and the books read in the tongue in which they were written. He himself wishes all sons of free men to be set to learning till they can read and are old enough for some occupation ; after that some should go on to Latin, for whom it is desirable, and who are destined for higher positions. Therefore, he says, he has begun in the midst of the manifold occupations of the throne to turn into English the Cura Pastoralis, in English, the Hiérdebōc, or Shepherd's Book, sometimes word for word, sometimes meaning by meaning, helped by the four scholars mentioned above, and he intends to send a copy to each bishopric with a valuable " æstel ".[2] These books are not, he goes

---

[1] Chron., I, 272.

[2] The meaning of the word " æstel " is not certain. It may mean a book-marker or it may be the binding but, whichever it was, it was to be very costly.

on, to be moved from their places except under special conditions.

This is the first piece of original prose of any length. In the translation of the Cura Pastoralis which follows, in which Ælfred begins his educational work by providing instruction for the clergy as the teachers, he has kept close to his text, too close sometimes for his English, which is rather clumsy. Take for example this sentence : " And yet many are very severely to be reproved when they themselves will not perceive their guilt, that they then may hear, reproving (being reproved) from the mouth of the teacher, how great a burden they have in their guilt, when they will too greatly make light of the evil which they have committed, that they then may fear because of the reproaches of the teacher, lest they should make it heavier for themselves." In the rendering of such passages Alfred no doubt found difficulty, but the whole of Gregory's work was too valuable and too apt for him to wish to omit or change anything in it, though now and again he has put in an explanation of some word or phrase for the benefit of his readers. He has explained, for instance, that " manna " was a sweet food that came down from heaven, the cities of refuge he has compared with the Germanic " friþstow ". Now and again we get a glimpse of his personality. Like the O.E. poets, he has made no attempt at local colour ; for him all councils are " witan ", and all followers are " thanes ".

Two of the MSS. sent round to the bishops are in existence still. These are, first, the Hatton MS. in the Bodleian Library, which is probably the one promised to Wærferþ in the preface, and, secondly, all that has been left by the fire in Ashburnham House of a Cotton MS. Of this last we have also a copy made by Junius.

The needs of the teachers being thus supplied, Ælfred went on to provide for the pupils. For this he translated, or caused to be translated, the books which he thought most necessary, as he says himself, for all men to know. These were " The Compendious History of the World " by Orosius, the textbook of the day on geography and history ; Bede's Ecclesiastical History ; the Consolations of Philosophy of Boethius, the textbook of the time on philosophy ; and part of the Soliloquies of St. Augustine. The order in which these works were written is disputed, though the Soliloquies must come at the end and Orosius is generally taken as being the first. This is a work by Orosius, a Spanish priest, who lived at the end of the fifth and beginning of the sixth century. It was undertaken at the instigation of St. Augustine of Hippo, to whose City of God it was meant to be some sort of a sequel. The object of the book was to refute the accusations made against Christianity as the cause of the suffering which followed the sack of Rome by Alaric the Goth in 410, the Goths being Christians of the Arian branch.

Accordingly Orosius made his book a survey of the earlier history of the world with its sufferings from war, earthquakes, pestilences, and fire, but especially from war. He began by dealing briefly with the early conquests such as those of the Assyrians, Persians, and Amazons, going on to narrate the wars of the Greeks and Romans in greater detail. He has frequently interrupted his story with a phrase like " think on those times, and then on these, and see which is to be preferred ", when he wanted to point his moral, and show that the sufferings of such times were far greater than those of the moment, even those from earthquakes and pestilences.

The gist of the matter is given fully in the following passage which comes after the account of the Amazons. " And now when the Goths have come from the bravest men of Germany, whom Pirrus the fierce king of the Greeks and Alexander and the mighty emperor Julius all feared lest they should attack them in battle, with what excess do ye Romans complain and declare that it is worse for you now in these days of Christianity than it was for those (earlier) nations, because the Goths have harried you a little and taken your city and slain a few of you. And because of their power and valour they might have seized you yourselves . . . who now are asking only for friendship and peace at your hands and a portion of land in order that they may be a help to you."

Orosius's work is not of any literary value in itself, it is merely a chronicle of events in which some entries are of considerable length, especially in the later Roman history, and into which some interesting or marvellous details have been inserted. Thus we are told how the Romans stampeded the elephants in the army of Pyrrhus by means of bundles of lighted flax which were fastened to the ends of poles furnished with sharp nails at the points. The terrified animals when attacked with these turned back and did more harm to the army of Pyrrhus than to the Romans. In another place we have an early version of the sea serpent story. We read how Regulus encountered a sea serpent off the island of " Bagrada ", whose scales were so hard that nothing less than the spiked instruments with which fortress walls were broken down could pierce them. With one of these, however, one of its ribs was fractured, an injury as fatal, we are told, to a serpent as the harming of a foot to other creeping things. Ælfred has allowed himself a good deal of freedom in this work, for it is no translation in the modern sense of the word. He was not concerned with its original purpose, the tenets of Christianity were fully established by this time, indeed he has apparently rejected all responsibility of that kind, by inserting " said Orosius " whenever the latter has introduced one of his didactic disgressions. It was in the teaching in the school that he had himself founded, and in others, that Ælfred was interested, and he therefore has sometimes cut out anything which seemed to him unedifying, such as references to heathen divinities, but more often he has enlarged or put in explanations and comments in order to bring his matter up to date or to make it more intelligible to his readers. For instance, he has suggested that the defeat of Regulus was due to a simulated flight on the part of the enemy, a stratagem from which he may have suffered himself in his fights with the Danes. He has also inserted the well-known saying of Titus, that he had wasted a day on which he had done no good deed, and he mentions the fact that the world was at peace at the time of Christ's birth and the temple of Janus therefore closed.

Ælfred's great contribution, however, is a passage dealing

with the geography of that part of Central and Northern
Europe included under the name Germania, in which he is
extraordinarily exact and valuable for our knowledge of
the positions of the various Germanic tribes at that time.
At the end of this passage comes an account of two voyagers,
one of whom was the first to round the North Cape, while
the other had travelled from Schleswig to Dantzig and
now describes some of the habits of the peoples he had come
across. Both were apparently Scandinavians, though
Ælfred gives their names in English form, calling them
Ohthere and Wulfstan. It is a tribute to Ælfred's fame that
they should have come to England to him, to recount
their adventures. In this interpolated passage Ælfred
had free scope. For most of the account a simple form of
construction was all that was wanted, but at the end is
a description of the funeral rites among the Esthonians
in which something more was needed, and here he has
shown some skill as a narrator.

"There is a custom among the Esthonians," he says,
"that when a man is dead, he lies in his house among his
kinsfolk, and friends for a month and sometimes for two,
the kings and men of high rank lying thus longer in proportion as they have more wealth. Sometimes it is for half
a year that they remain unburnt and lie above ground
in their houses. And all the while that the body is within
there must be drinking and games until the day when it is
burnt. Then on that same day . . . they divide up his
property, anything that is left over after the drinking and
games, into five or six portions, according to the amount
of it. Then they lay it out in perchance a mile, the largest
share (being farthest) from the homestead, then the second,
then the third until it is all laid out within the one mile. . . .
Then must be assembled all the men who have the swiftest
horses in the land, perchance five miles or six from the
property. Then they all gallop towards the property,
and the man who has the swiftest horse comes to the first
and largest share, and so each after the other, until it is all
taken, and he gets the smallest share, who reaches the
property next to the homestead. . . . Then . . . they carry

him out and bury him, with his weapons and raiment,
and almost all his possessions they squander (thus)."

While in the translated part of the work Ælfred has not
learnt to manage his long sentences well, nor realized that
a phrase which was quite clear in the Latin was not so
in O.E. with its weakened system of inflections, here he
could make his sentences as simple as he liked. In spite
of this advantage, however, it will be seen from the above
passage that his constructions are not always clear and that
he is content with very little variety of conjunctions. But
his story has life, in spite of deficiencies in technique.

The preface to the Pastoral Care was a much more
difficult undertaking, thoughts as well as constructions
were more complex, and Ælfred has not always extricated
himself satisfactorily from the difficulties of either. But there,
too, he has been able to convey his meaning effectively.
We may assume for the moment that Ælfred's next book
was the translation of Bede's Ecclesiastical History. Bede
begins his work after a mention of his authorities with a
description of Britain, or Albion as he tells us it used to be
called. He speaks of its position, its size, its products,
animal, vegetable, and mineral, and its climate, the number
of large towns and the five languages spoken in it, British,
Scottish, Celtic, Saxon, and Latin, the last having become
common, he says, through the study of the Scriptures, and
he ends up this introduction with a short account of Ireland
where no snake could live and everything was efficacious
against poison. After this, he goes on to trace the history
of England from the time of the invasion of Julius Cæsar
down to his own day. As his title implies, he dwells most
upon those events which concerned the Church, the
gradual spreading of Christianity into the various kingdoms
of England and the merging of the two Churches, the Roman
introduced by St. Augustine, and the Celtic, brought in
by St. Columba and his monks from Iona, and he mentions
the early attempts at missionary effort outside England.
As he unfolds his story, he deals with the lives of the great
saints and martyrs, with the Arian and Pelagian heresies
each in its own time, and more fully with the special

English difficulty in the differences in practice between the two Churches, especially in the matter of the fixing of Easter and the form of the tonsure. He also lets fall interesting bits of information, here and there, about the development on the Roman model of the music in the church services. The value of this book for Ælfred's educational aims is obvious. As a source of historical knowledge it supplemented Orosius. The stories of learned and pious men it contained supplied Ælfred and his scholars with many models of good living, and as the work of the great English saint and scholar it was sure to be received with reverence. But equally obviously some parts were more valuable than others, and these Ælfred has translated very closely, while the others he has cut down considerably. Dr. Plummer says, " It (this book) needed no recasting, beyond a few omissions, to make it suitable for English readers".[1] Thus the introduction, with its description of Britain, Ælfred keeps. The next chapters of the early history of the country till the coming of St. Augustine he cuts down greatly, but he gives the account of the martyrdom of St. Alban, and the despair of the Britons after the departure of the Romans. He even gives their message of appeal, " The barbarians (Picts and Scots) drive us to the sea, and the sea drives us back to the barbarians, between them we are exposed to two sorts of death ; we are either slaughtered or drowned," and he tells us of Vortigern's invitation to the Angles to come over to his aid, and of the advantage which the Angles took of the position.

After the coming of St. Augustine some chapters are still summarized only, as of little importance at the time ; the Arian and Pelagian heresies, for instance, are merely mentioned, they were no longer questions of the day. The dissensions between the Roman and Celtic Churches, however, affected England more closely, and more attention is paid to them. Ælfred even gives an account of the great Conference held at Whitby in 664, in the hopes, vain as they proved, of a final settlement.

Of the whole matter some passages only can be referred

[1] Life and Times of Alfred, p. 157.

to or given here. The coming of St. Augustine and Pope Gregory's instructions to him for the organization and government of the newly founded Church are of course recounted in full, but the advice to the abbot Mellitus [1] to be patient with his converts is not mentioned, as perhaps liable to be thought untactful. The life of Pope Gregory is told at length, with the familiar story of the English boys exposed for sale at Rome, Gregory's puns on the names and his great desire to come to England himself. Later we have the conversion of Edwin of Northumbria, with the speech of the noble at the Council meeting at which the acceptance of the new religion was discussed. "Thus it seems to me O king ! that this present life of men on earth, as compared with that time which is unknown to us, is as if, when thou wert sitting at meat with thy nobles and thanes in the winter time with the fire kindled and thy hall warmed, while it rained and snowed and stormed outside, a sparrow should quickly fly through the house, coming in through one door and going out through another. Lo ! for the time that he is inside he is not touched by the winter storm, but that is for the twinkling of an eye only ; soon he must from winter pass into winter again. So this life of men appears for a short time only, but what went before or what will follow we know not." We are told how in Edwin's reign, as far as his dominions extended, a woman with her new-born babe could walk throughout the island from sea to sea without receiving any harm. The virtues of Oswald of Northumbria are dwelt upon and the story told of how, when sitting at dinner on Easter Day with Bishop Aidan, a silver dish laden with rich food was served to them. But at the same moment a servant came hurrying in to say that there were crowds of poor men collected and waiting in the street, having come from all parts. Whereupon Oswald commanded the food to be taken out and given to them and the dish also to be cut up and distributed with the food. Then Aidan seized his right hand, crying, "May this hand never decay !" And when after his death in battle his hand and arm were cut off, they did remain uncorrupted till Bede's

[1] Chap. I, p. 5.

own time. The holy life of Aidan is described, his gentleness, self denial, and charity which caused him to give away to a beggar a noble horse, presented to him by King Oswin for his own use. The beautiful description of the passing of Bishop Ceadda is worthy of mention. We are told that it was due to a pestilence, which " by means of the death of the flesh, translated the living stones of the Church from their earthly places to the heavenly building ".

The story of Hild and her monastery at Whitby is told and how Cædmon learnt to write his poems ; we read how Eðelwald calmed the sea with his prayers and how Wilbrord was sent to convert the Frisians. We have the vision of Dryhthelm and his return from the dead. We are told how, being apparently dead, he was taken to Purgatory where he found scorching flames on one side of the path and biting winds and storms on the other, and from whence he looked into the mouth of Hell. Afterwards, however, the story goes on, he was allowed a vision of Heaven before he was taken back to earth to resume his earlier life.

A book like this would have appealed to Ælfred from its scholarship, its piety, its justness, and generosity of thought. Whatever we may think now about the stories of miracles, it is clear that Bede did not accept such tales lightly, and that he has given those only for which he believed himself to have good evidence, and which Ælfred, too, would have been ready to accept. It is difficult now to understand how a difference of opinion about the rule for keeping Easter could be considered a serious sin, though it must have caused a great deal of inconvenience. But if Bede condemned the errors of the Celtic Church with no uncertain voice, he was generous in his praise of the virtues of its saints. Such a combination of liberality and fairness of outlook and sternness of principle would have been after Ælfred's own heart.

We possess four MSS. of the Ecclesiastical History and some fragments. Two of these MSS. are at Oxford, one in the Bodleian Library, the other at Corpus Christi College ; the other two are at Cambridge, one in the University Library and the second at Corpus Christi College there.

The fragments are in the British Museum. It has been questioned whether we have here Ælfred's own work or one entrusted by him to someone else. The most definite argument brought forward against his authorship is that Mercian forms are to be found in the text.[1] But, as it is generally agreed that we do not possess the original MS. among the four, such dialect forms as there are may have been introduced by a later copyist, or even by Bishop Wærferth or some other Mercian scholar helping Ælfred.[2] Had any one of the Mercians whom Ælfred attracted to his court been the original author, we should expect to find many more such dialect forms surviving in spite of later scribes.

In his translation of this book (if it is his), while Ælfred shows a greater skill in handling his Latin than in the Cura Pastoralis or Orosius, he allows himself certain Latinisms, such as the use of the dative absolute, for the Latin ablative.

From the translation of Bede's Ecclesiastical History we may pass on to that of the De Consolatione Philosophiæ of Boethius. This is perhaps the most important of Ælfred's works, it is certainly the one in which his personality makes itself most vividly felt. The original is a work in prose with metrical passages inserted (the Metra) written between 522 and 525 by the philosopher Boethius, during his imprisonment by Theodoric the Great at Pavia. After occupying the high position of a Senator at the court, Boethius became suspected of treason, he was thrown into prison and put to death in 525. To beguile the tedium of his long captivity, he wrote this work, in which he represents Philosophy as appearing to him in human form, upbraiding him for having forsaken her teaching and comforting him with her discourse on the nature of true happiness and similar subjects.

Boethius was probably a Christian, at any rate by profession, the medieval tradition was to that effect, but his philosophy is essentially pagan. It is to Aristotle and

---

[1] Dr. Miller, Introduction to Nos. 95 and 96 of E.E.T.S. Publications.
[2] Schipper, Vol. IV, of Bibliothek der ags. Prosa., pp. xl ff.

Plato that he refers and not to Christ. His reputation for learning and wisdom was high among his contemporaries, and, in later times, his book has been widely read and frequently translated into many languages. In England it has been translated not only by Ælfred, but also by Chaucer and by Queen Elizabeth. Other translations which may be mentioned are an early French version, made by Jean de Meun, and an O.H.G. one by the monk Notker of St. Gall. And not only was it translated, Latin commentaries were also early written upon it, and Ælfred certainly knew and used these.

This well-known work Ælfred has treated with remarkable independence, even for those days. He has omitted some passages, added many more and entirely recast his material, giving a definite Christian character to the non-Christian philosophy, and adapting it to his own public. Thus he has prefixed an introduction in which he explains the circumstances under which the Consolation was written. He tells his readers that Theodoric the Gothic king, having succeeded to the kingdom of Rome, at first promised the Romans his friendship, but kept his promise very ill for, among unnumbered crimes, he slew Pope John. Then a consul, whose name was Boethius, sent letters privily to the Cæsar at Constantinople, who was of the kin of their ancient lords, praying him that he would help him to retain their Christianity and ancient rights. But Theodoric heard of this and commanded Boethius to be thrust into prison.

Then follows the work itself, which is in the form of question and answer between Philosophy, which Ælfred renders by Wisdom or Reason, and the Mind. Boethius tells how, while lying in his dungeon, sorrowing over his fate, there came in to him Heavenly Wisdom and sought to comfort him, for she perceived that he was in need of cheering, rather than of woeful words. When the Mind, still sorrowstruck and uncomforted, asked why the Creator of Heaven and Earth, who controls sun and moon, stars and all nature, had allowed Fortune to be thus unjust, leaving the wicked to sit on high seats and to trample the holy under their feet, Reason reproved him for believing that Fate rules the universe.

In the long discussion which followed, Wisdom asked Boethius whether those things seemed to him really precious, which are neither constant to possess nor easy to relinquish. She pointed out that the wealth and honours bestowed upon him came from her and that he should rather be thankful for having enjoyed her gifts for a time than deem that he had lost aught of his own. He should mount up in mind with Wisdom. "When I soar aloft," she said, " with my servants, Knowledge and Skill, then we look down upon this storm-tossed world, as the eagle does, when he passes above the clouds and their storms, so that they cannot injure him." As Boethius's former happiness had come to an end so would his present unhappiness. Much comfort was still left to him in his family. None had all they desired. Riches and power and worldly weal are men's lords and masters, not they theirs. In Mind's excuse for his grief for his lost happiness, which follows, we may hear Ælfred's own feeling towards earthly riches : " O Reason ! indeed thou knowest that covetousness and the greatness of this earthly power never well pleased me, nor did I ever much endeavour after earthly authority. But I was never-theless desirous of materials for the work which I was commanded to perform, to the end that I might honourably and fitly direct and exercise the power which was committed to me. . . . This then is a king's material and his tools with which to reign, that he have his land well peopled. He must have men for prayer and men for fighting, and men for work."

Then Wisdom went on with her argument, pointing out that riches make enemies for a man, power is not necessarily a good thing, and fame is of no value. The earth is but a small point compared with the heavens, and a small part of it only is habitable ; it is foolish for a man to labour to spread his fame over so small a space, in which, too, seventy-two tongues are spoken The fame of great men may endure many years, it is nevertheless a short time compared with that which never ends. Where are now, she asked, the bones of the celebrated and the wise goldsmith Weland, or where is now the illustrious and patriotic consul of the Romans, who was called Brutus? All men desire to attain happiness, and the highest happiness is God. But in vain they seek to reach it through fame, wealth, or power. True happiness does not lie in such things, but in God, Who is the Supreme Good. A man must seek happiness within himself, not from outward circumstances if it is to be permanent. A man must be master of himself. Evil does not exist. God is not able to do evil; if evil existed God could do it, therefore it cannot exist.

In the latter part of the book considerable space is given to this question of the presence of evil in the world. Why, Boethius asked, do folly and wickedness reign over all the middle earth and wisdom and virtue have no praise or honour? Wisdom answered that it is not so. If he could fly with her above the high roof of the heavens, he would have his share in the true Light, and if he should then visit once more the darkness of this world he would be able to see that unrighteous kings and the haughty rich are feeble and poor, for every man desires to reach the highest good; the good man is able to do so, for he goes by the right way; but the wicked cannot attain his desire for he seeks it amiss. Therefore it is beyond doubt that the good have always power, while the wicked have none.

Some philosophers say that Fate rules the happiness or misery of every man, but (Ælfred puts in) I say, as do all Christian men, that it is Divine Providence and not Fate.

The last book treats of the question of Free Will and Predestination. Wisdom, when asked about Fate and Providence, explained that "Providence is the Divine Reason and lieth fast in the high Creator that knoweth how everything shall befall ere it come to pass. Fate is God's working day by day, both that which we see and that which is not seen by us. Some things are subject to Fate, but Fate is subject to Divine Providence."

How many of the additions in Ælfred's version are his own cannot be determined with certainty. Several of those earlier ascribed to him have since been discovered in the commentaries or appear to have been suggested by one or other of them, and further research may find such a source for more. Even the simile of the earth being surrounded by the sea and enclosed in the heavens, like an egg, in which the yolk is surrounded by the white and encased in the shell, is now known to have been suggested by a commentary. But still many additions remain which do appear to be Ælfred's own, and these are of great interest for the light they throw on his opinions and aims. Thus, in order to bring his pictures home to his island readers, he has added to the phrase in the original " riches in number as the grains of sand ", the words, " by these sea cliffs ", or in speaking of the small amount of the world which is habitable he puts in, " and the greater part of that is taken up by the ocean ". He has emphasized the happiness of the former age to a Dane-ridden England, with the words, " no man had then heard tell of the pirate host ". Elsewhere he has made his work more intelligible to the English by adding explanations to names of places or people, or to customs, which would have been familiar enough to Roman readers. Thus when hell is compared with the mountain called Ætna, Ælfred has explained that this mountain is in the isle of Sicily and is ever on fire with brimstone. He has added for the benefit of his readers that the Scythians dwelt on the other side of the Caucasus, and that in Rome only the worthiest might sit in gorgeous carriages, such as those he has just described. In the same way he has amplified the allusions to classical stories, such as those of Busiris, Ulysses, and Eurydice, since they would not be well known to those for whom his book was intended.

More interesting still are the passages which show Ælfred's own views, in which we see the man himself. Such are : " For whatsoever a man begins untimely, hath no perfect ending ", " Surely good respect and good esteem are for every man better and more precious than any wealth " ; or again, " All that is needful, I tell thee, is meat and drink, clothes and implements wherewith to exercise the powers thou hast, and that are natural to thee, and may be rightly used," or " Now true high birth is of the mind, not of the flesh ".

Of especial value is a long passage of which a few lines have already been given, in which Mind is excusing himself if he has valued his former prosperity too highly. " But I desired instruments and material." [1] Here Ælfred was undoubtedly thinking of his own responsibilities in the use of his position, and he has ended, " To be brief I may say that it has ever been my desire to live honourably while I was alive, and after my death to leave to them that should come after me a memory of me in good works." And he must have been thinking of the way in which ill health had interfered with his own activities when he wrote, " Though bodily sloth and infirmities often vex the mind with a dullness and lead it astray with a mist of delusion, so that it cannot shine as brightly as it would ". He has clearly given his own social views when he makes Boethius answer Wisdom's question, in connection with Free Will : " How would it please thee if a very rich king had no friends in his kingdom, but serfs only ? Then said I, It would not appear to me right, nor in aught seemly, if serfs alone should serve him."

A feature of Ælfred's style which is very characteristic of this work in his use of similes. Many of the additions which he has made are of the nature of explanations of the Latin by means of a simile. Very noticeable is the one already quoted, " When I soar aloft with these my servants, as does the eagle, etc.[2]

Worthy of note also is the comparison of the way in which all kinds of happiness proceed from the highest happiness and return to it, with that in which all water proceeds from and returns to the sea. " No brook is too small to seek the sea ; afterwards it passeth from the sea into the earth and so it goeth winding through the earth till it cometh again to the same spring from which it flowed at first and so again to the sea." This use of springs and rivers to illustrate a point occurs more than once. Elsewhere the statement that the forms of good which issue from God are many and various is illustrated by adding, " Even as all stars receive their light and brightness from the sun, yet some

---

[1] See p. 253.   [2] ibid.

are more, other less bright. Likewise the moon shines
according as the sun illumines her, when she is fully lighted
up by him she shines with all her brightness". More matter
of fact is perhaps the comparison of the gradual perception
of an idea with the opening of a door, " Now I confess to
thee," he says, " that I have found a door where before
I saw but a little crack, so that I could just spy out a very
little gleam of light from out of this darkness," and that of
the connection of good with God, " as the walls of every
house are firmly set on the floor and in the roof." The
elaborately worked out comparison of the movement of the
universe with the way in which the wheels of a wagon
turn upon its axle, the axle being still and yet bearing all
the waggon and guiding all its movements, is not wholly
Ælfred's, but suggested in a commentary, and worked out
by him.

Partly no doubt from the congenial nature of the subject
but partly also from increased skill in handling his matter,
Ælfred's prose here shows a great advance on that in
Orosius. The thought is more complex and the constructions
are more difficult to render than in the narrative matter
of the latter work, but he has succeeded with both. The
remodelling of the material does not suggest that it was
due to the wish to escape difficulties in translating, but rather
to the freedom which comes from power. As elsewhere
a few Latinisms are retained, and Ælfred's translation is
not always right, as in his curious rendering of " ossa
Fabricii " by the bones of Weland (the famous smith) in
which he has apparently confused Fabricius with fabricator.

Several passages have already been given in as close
a translation as possible, but the following may be added
to bring out the advance in skill in treating a complex
passage since Ælfred's writing of Orosius :—

" Then he began to smile and said to me. Thou dost lead
me on to a great subject for discussion, and one most
difficult to explain, this explanation all philosophers have
sought and toiled most mightily over, and hardly has
anyone come to an end of the subject. For it is the nature
of discussion and questioning that when one doubt is settled

then are countless more aroused; as men say in the old story, that there was a serpent with nine heads, and if one were cut off then grew up seven on that one head."

Boethius has been preserved in three MSS. The most complete is in the Bodleian Library. It is on vellum with coloured initials at the beginning of the chapters, in a hand of the twelfth century. Less complete is the Cotton MS. in the British Museum, having suffered badly in the fire in Ashburnham House. It is on vellum, and written not later than the middle of the tenth century. The third MS. is a mere fragment, discovered in 1886 by Professor Napier; it is of the first half of the tenth century and also in the Bodleian. There is also a transcript made by Junius from the Cotton MS.

As in the case of the Ecclesiastical History, doubts have been raised as to Ælfred's authorship, on the strength of certain dialectal forms, this time Kenticisms, which occur in both complete MSS., but not in the fragment. But as neither MS. is believed to be the original, and the dialect forms may have been introduced by later scribes, such an argument is not conclusive. On the other hand, Ælfred's authorship is vouched for by several early writers, notably by Æthelweard [1] and William of Malmesbury,[2] and it is expressly stated in the proem, which reads as if it were the king's own work. Further, so many passages, such as those already given, suggest an author with an experience of kingship and are so characteristic of what is otherwise known of Ælfred that most critics now attribute the work definitely to him.

Whether he is the author of the verse Metra is much more open to question. The chief argument against their being by him is their poorness of quality, but they are in the same MS.[3] in the British Museum and a proem is prefixed to them in which they are definitely attributed to Ælfred, whereas quality is a vague criterion.

Finally we come to Ælfred's translation of the Soliloquies

---

[1] Chron. for 901, Liber IV, Cap. 3.
[2] de Gestis Regum, Liber II, Cap. IV.
[3] Otho, A. VI.

of St. Augustine. He himself calls his work "Blostman" or Blooms, because in it he has, he says, collected the flowers of thought of the original.

This is almost certainly his latest work, for in it we have an echo of thoughts and ideas found in Boethius and probably suggested by that translation. It also shows the same wealth of similes as that work, as though Ælfred in his last two books had developed a definite, picturesque style of his own.

The O.E. work is in three books, the first and second of which are based almost entirely on St. Augustine's Soliloquies while the third is from various sources. The title of Blooms applies better to the later part of the second book and to the third than to the rest, for in these Ælfred has selected and rejected freely. In the first book and earlier part of the second he has, on the other hand, kept fairly close to his original and given the whole plant rather than the blossoms only. The whole shows an increased independence of treatment even greater than that in Boethius. In the third book, which is much shorter than the others, he has brought his heterogeneous material together with considerable skill, throwing all into dialogue form in order to make it harmonize with the others. This increased skill in handling his material again suggests a later work. Of special interest is the introductory passage. Though nominally a preface to the Blooms, it must have been meant as an epilogue to the whole series of translations. In the preface to the Pastoral Care Ælfred has told us what he intended to do ; here he tells under the figure of a woodcutter choosing trees in a wood, what he has done. In it we have the simile, which has given vividness to his other writings, expanded into a parable in order to present a living picture to his readers.

He begins :—" Then I gathered me staves, props, bars, and helves for each of my tools, and boughs ; and, for each of the works which I would work, I chose the fairest trees, as far as I might carry them away. Nor did I ever bring any burden home without longing to bring home the whole wood if that might be ; for in every tree I saw something of which I had need at home. . . . But He who taught me to love that wood, He may cause me to dwell more easily both in this transitory dwelling and also in the eternal home." The Blooms have been preserved in one MS. only, and that is in a very imperfect state. It is of the twelfth century and is bound up now with the Beowulf MS. There is also in the Bodleian Library a copy by Junius. At the end of the MS. comes the sentence, "Here end the sayings which King Ælfred gleaned from the book," and the work is now generally accepted as the king's own, though doubts were raised at one time.

William of Malmesbury [1] tells us that at the time of his death Ælfred was engaged on a translation of the Psalms. No certain trace of this is left, though it has been conjectured that a prose translation of the first fifty psalms, known as the Paris Psalter, may be this work. This must, however, remain an unsettled question.

No better illustration can be found of the development of English prose in Ælfred's hands than in a comparison of the preface to the Cura Pastoralis with that to the Blooms. His prose always lives, and as one goes on from one work to another it can be seen to be gaining in finish and literary charm. When it is realized how much he did achieve in spite of the difficulties with which he had to contend, the question suggests itself whether, with all the advantages which Ælfric enjoyed, Ælfred would not have been the greater writer. The grace and ease of Ælfric, writing a century later, was impossible in the then state of English prose, but Ælfred has a freshness which is sometimes lacking in Ælfric, his similes are as poetical and his use of words from the poetic vocabulary as effective as in the later writer. The artistic feeling is there, only the imperfect nature of his tools prevented the accomplishment of a finished work of art.

Finally Ælfred's Will and his collection of Laws must be mentioned, though their chief importance is for the study of law rather than literature. He begins the latter with a long preface, which he concludes by stating that his collection is based on those of Ine of Wessex, Offa of Mercia, and Ethelbert of Kent, from which he has taken those which

[1] Gesta Regum, Liber II, Cap. IV.

he considered most just, but this work need not detain us further here.

Ælfred's services to literature were not, however, confined to his own writings. The nature of his contribution to the contemporary entries in the A.S. Chronicle will be considered in a later chapter in dealing with that work,[1] whether these are actually from his own pen, or the result of stimulus from him, either general or by a definite commission to some scholar at his court. But besides this, before he could free himself from other matters sufficiently to begin his own translations, he gave his first encouragement to prose literature by commissioning Bishop Wærferþ of Worcester to turn the Dialogues of Gregory the Great into English. He himself wrote a preface to it, which is of value from the additional light which it throws on his personality. In it he says that he has seen fully and often heard that those to whom high positions in this world have been given have great need, in the midst of their worldly business, to relax and turn their minds to divine and spiritual matters. Therefore he goes on :—" I besought my trusty friends to write for me out of God's Book [2] of the lives and miracles of the saints . . . so that I may, amid the troubles of this world, sometimes think on the things of Heaven." A second preface follows by Bishop Wærferþ himself. The work is, as the name implies, in the form of a dialogue between Pope Gregory and the deacon Peter. While Gregory is mourning for the lost calm and opportunity for meditation of his former monastic life, Peter comes in to him and asks the cause of his sorrow. Gregory tells him that his life is now as a frail ship, hard pressed in the waves of a great sea, " so am I now tossed about with the disturbances of this world, and beaten about in the storms of its tempestousness." His sorrow, he goes on to say, is increased when he thinks of those holy men who have renounced the world and its evils and are living the life for which he longs. Peter then asks to be told about them, that the knowledge of their

---

[1] See Chap. XII, p. 280.
[2] Dr. Plummer, Life and Times of Alfred the Great, p. 142, would read Gregory's for God's.

examples may be a help to others, and so Gregory goes on to narrate anecdotes of the saints and the miracles which they had been able to perform through their holiness.

Wærferþ was no more prepared to criticize the miraculous in these stories than was Ælfred in the case of those told by Bede, and he evidently endorsed Peter's opinion that examples of holy lives were often more useful than teaching.

A characteristic story is one in the second book. During a time of severe famine, in which St. Benedict had insisted on the last drops of oil being given by the monks to the needy folk outside, as he knelt in prayer among the brethren, the cover of an empty oil vessel which stood near suddenly began to rise up because of the flow of oil into it. The oil went on increasing in amount until it overflowed on to the floor, but, as soon as St. Benedict became aware of it and rose up, it ceased to flow. A fine example of loyalty is given in the story of the monk Libertinus, though in other respects the moral is open to criticism. Libertinus was once so badly beaten with a footstool by his abbot about the head and face, that they were all bruised and swollen. When, however, he was asked next day by his friends what had happened to him, he declared that he had stumbled over a footstool and so accidentally bruised himself. Whether his friends accepted such a lame tale, we are not told. Better known is perhaps the story of the nun and the lettuce. A nun while walking in the convent garden saw a lettuce and greatly desired to eat it. But she began to bite it without stopping to make the sign of the cross over it. Now a little devil had been sitting upon it and was swallowed with it, whereupon the nun fell at once to the ground in great affliction. When St. Equitius was summoned to heal her, the devil cried out with pardonable indignation, "What did I do to her? I was only sitting on the lettuce when she came and bit me."

The two existing rescensions of this work differ so so much that it has been suggested that they are independent translations, though that view is not now accepted. There are two MSS. of the first rescension, one at Corpus Christi College, Cambridge, and the other a Cotton MS. in the British Museum, which is incomplete, having suffered much in the fire at Ashburnham House. One MS. only exists of the second rescension, and that is very imperfect. It must be somewhat later than the first, since it seems to have been based upon it, but with much left out, and other passages modified.

In point of date, Wærferþ's book is the first example of any length of O.E. prose, since it preceded Ælfred's own writings, but it is too close a translation to be representative. It is the work of a Latin scholar, who while he did not suffer from one of Ælfred's difficulties, an insufficient knowledge of that language, got out of the second, that of the inadequacy of English for literary prose, by keeping Latin constructions, especially that of the dative absolute (Latin ablative), which he uses very frequently through the whole work. This is a construction which, as has been said, Ælfred uses too, but very sparingly. It is still to the king's original passages that we must look for the beginnings of O.E. prose in its natural character.

In spite of the Bishop's adherence to classical forms, the influence of the native poetical diction is to be seen in the frequent use of the parallel phrase, of alliteration, and to some extent in vocabulary. This applies specially to the first rescension. An example of alliteration may be seen in the following sentence of the introduction :—

" bideþ þe se bisceop, se þe þas bōc beȝeat." *The bishop who acquired this book, prays thee.*

CHAPTER XI

LATER PROSE: THE BLICKLING HOMILIES: ÆLFRIC AND WULSTAN

Towards the end of the tenth century were written nineteen homilies, known as the Blickling Homilies, because till lately they were in the library of Blickling Hall in Norfolk. These sermons are not all complete but there is sufficient left to show a stage of prose between those of Ælfred and Ælfric. They are nearer in date to Ælfric than to Ælfred and, on the whole, they are nearer to him in style.

While the unknown preacher has not yet attained to the simple grace of the best of Ælfric's prose, he shows some advance in ease of expression over Ælfred. The following passage from the familiar story of St. Martin and his cloak, which is given as literally as possible, will show this.

It happened on a certain occasion that St. Martin journeyed with others of the king's thanes into the city called Ambinensus. And it was in midwinter. The winter that year was also so severe that many a man lost his life for the cold. Then there sat there a beggar at the gate of the city; he sat there naked and begged for clothing and alms for God's sake. Then they all passed by him and no one of them would turn to him or show any mercy. Then the man of God, St. Martin, perceived that the Lord had kept the beggar for him, that he should take pity on him, since none of the others would show mercy. He did not know, however, what he ought to do, because he had nothing else than a single garment; all else that he had had, he had already disposed of in similar deeds and had given away for God's sake. However he drew his knife and took the cloak which he had on him and cut it in two and gave half to the beggar and in half he wrapped himself. Then there were many men, who saw this, who blamed and mocked at him because he had cut up his single garment!

The writer has some versatility, and his lively description of the astonishment of the devils at the Harrowing of Hell, when they ask Satan what he is going to "do about it", shows him in another style. "Whence is this one so strong, so shining, so terrible? The world has long been subject to us, and Death has paid us much tribute; never has it been before that Death has been brought to nought. Nor has ever such terror been appointed before for us in hell. What is this man, who thus undaunted, comes into our domain? Not only does he not fear our tortures for himself, but he will redeem others from our chains. We believe that this must be he of whom we expected that, through his death, all the world should become subject to us. Dost thou hear, Lord? This is that same for whose death thou hast long been active, and at which thou didst promise us much plunder at the last. But what wilt thou do with him now? And what of this mayest thou avert? Now hath he put to flight thy darkness with his bright light, and all thy prison hath he broken open, and all whom thou before didst hold in bondage hath he set free and their lives hath he turned into joy, and those mock us who before lamented in our chains." Further the homilist has something of the power of the poets in describing scenes of horror, as in a passage in the Sermon for Michaelmas Day, which is strongly reminiscent of the mere in Beowulf. "While St. Paul was looking towards the northern part of the earth, where all the waters pass downwards, he saw there beyond the water a certain hoary and rocky cliff, and north of the rock grew groves thickly covered with rime, and black mists were there, and under the rock was the dwelling-place of water monsters and accursed things; and he saw also that over the cliff, on the ice-covered boughs, hung many black souls bound by their hands, and devils in the likeness of sea monsters were seizing hold of them like greedy wolves. And the water under the cliff was black, and it was about twelve measures (?) between the cliff and the water, and when the boughs broke, then the souls fell which had been hanging to them, and the monsters seized them."

Less gifted than either Ælfred or Ælfric, the writer of
these homilies has at his disposal a more perfect instrument
than had Ælfred and he has some skill as a prose writer
and some variety of style as the above passages will have
shown. His sermons also illustrate the way in which
the simile used so strikingly by Ælfred was replacing more
and more in prose the kenning of O.E. poetry.

From the writings of Ælfred and the Blickling Homilies
we may pass on to the works of Ælfric, a pupil
trained in the monastic school at Winchester, novice master
at Cernel (Cerne Abbas in Dorsetshire), and later Abbot of
Eynsham, near Oxford, in whose hands O.E. prose attained
its highest development. A greater contrast could hardly
be found than that between the lives of Ælfred and Ælfric,
or, indeed, between the two men themselves. In Ælfric
we have the scholar with a classical education behind him,
who could write with equal ease in Latin and English,
instead of a man, to some extent self educated, to whom
the reading of Latin was, at any rate, for a time, a difficulty ;
we have the churchman, not the statesman, a man whose
life was spent in the peaceful seclusion of the cloister instead
of on the battle-field or in the midst of the turmoil of public
life. Both, it is true, were interested in education and
both wrote for edification, but while Ælfred was concerned
with the general needs of the people, Æfric's interest was
chiefly in theological teaching. While Ælfred translated
the works of others and only interpolated passages of
practical explanation or personal knowledge, Ælfric's
writings, while also largely translations, show a deep and
independent learning, used with discretion.

The exact date of Ælfric's birth is not known, but cannot
have been later than 957. He was a pupil in the school
at Winchester, at a time when, under Bishop Æthelwold's
fostering care, it had become a centre of education for a large
part of England. In 987 he was sent as novice master to
teach the monks at the restored monastery of Cernel, and
in 989 he seems to have returned to Winchester, and to
have remained there till, in 1005, he was appointed abbot
of the Abbey recently founded by Æthelmær at Eynsham.

He died some time soon after 1020, but the exact year is not known.

Such are the meagre outlines of his life. Uneventful in itself, it, however, left him leisure for a rich literary activity, the importance of which can hardly be realized without some reference to the time at which he lived. Ælfred's efforts had, no doubt, done something to improve the deplorable state of learning in England, of which he gives us so graphic a picture, but it was not till the second half of the tenth century that any great advance appeared in matters of education or in the monastic discipline, which, as the poem Guþlac shows us, had deteriorated, together with learning, in the disturbed state of the country. But then began the movement for reform associated specially with the names of Dunstan (924 ?–988), Abbot of Glastonbury and later Archbishop of Canterbury, and of his disciple, Æthelwold (+ 984), Bishop of Winchester and rather later with the Benedictines. One outcome of this movement for monastic reform was a translation of the Rule of St. Benedict, which has been attributed to Æthelwold,[1] and it was this movement with which Ælfric became involved. His ready pen was constantly at work in the service of others for educational purposes or to help with the theological questions of the day, as well as in the composition of his own works. Indeed much of his writing seems to have been in response to a demand from some prominent personage in Church or State.

Ælfric is best known by his sermons and translations of certain books of the Old Testament. His earliest works were his Homiliæ Catholicæ, written between 990 and 994 ; that is, after his return to Winchester. These are a collection of homilies intended for Sundays and the great festivals of the Church. They are in two sets, with a Latin and an English preface to each set. They are based on works of earlier writers, principally on those of Augustine, Gregory, and Bede, and they are dedicated to Sigeric, Archbishop of Canterbury. In the English preface to one (added later) Ælfric speaks of them as translations ; he says : " I, Ælfric, monk and mass-priest, although weaker than befits such a position,

---

[1] Schröer, Bibliothek der ags. Prosa., Bd. II, Vorwort.

was sent in the days of King Æþelred by Bishop Ælfege to a certain monastery called Cernel, at the petition of the thane Æþelmær, whose nature and virtues are known everywhere. Then it came into my mind, I trust through the grace of God, that I should turn this book from Latin into English, not through the pride of great learning, but because I saw and heard many errors in many English books, which the unlearned in their innocence took for great wisdom. And it grieved me that they should not know or have the gospel teaching in their writings, except those alone who knew Latin and except for those books which King Ælfred in his wisdom had turned from Latin into English, and which are to be had." He goes on to say that such books were specially needed at this time when the end of the world was so near, and, after a description of the present evil state of the world, he ends, " Much evil ever does he do, who writes what is false, unless he correct it. It is as if he should turn true doctrine into false error. Therefore must every one put right that which he before twisted into wrong, if he is to be guiltless before the judgment seat of God."

Ælfric's next works were of a different character and undertaken, no doubt, for the benefit of the pupils in the school. They were a Latin Grammar and Glossary, based on Donatus and the Institutiones Grammaticæ of Priscian. These he followed up with a Colloquy (Colloquium Ælfrici), a discourse in Latin between teacher and pupil, as a method of learning the more difficult and technical terms necessary for conversation. In one of the two MSS. which have been preserved, an English interlinear version has been added of which the following passage may be taken as illustration. After the " discipulus " had declared his readiness to be beaten into knowledge rather than have none, but his determination to render that method unnecessary, the teacher asks, " What work hast thou ? " and is answered, " I am a professed monk. I sing seven times a day with the brethren, and I am occupied with reading and chant ; but, none the less, I would learn between whiles to speak in the Latin tongue."

Then the teacher asks : " What are these comrades of thine able to do ? "

" Some," he is answered, " are husbandmen, some shepherds, some oxherds, others are hunters, fishermen, fowlers, merchants, shoemakers, saltworkers, and bakers." The husbandman tells the teacher, " Alas ! lord, I labour cruelly. At dawn I go out driving the oxen to the field and yoking them to the plough. Be the winter ever so hard I dare not lurk at home for fear of my lord, but, having yoked the oxen and fastened share and coulter to the plough, each day I must plough a full acre and more." And so the book goes on through the other callings.

These school books, though they do perhaps teach us more about Ælfric himself, do not tell us more about him as a writer of prose ; for that we must go on to his next work, in which he returned to his earlier theological subjects. In 996 he wrote another set of forty homilies, his Passiones Sanctorum, intended this time for the use of the monasteries, rather than, like his earlier sermons, for that of the whole Church, for they deal with the lives and sufferings of individual saints venerated in special monasteries. They were written at the request of the " ealdorman " Æþelweard and his son Æþelmær. The preface begins : " Ælfric humbly greeteth Æþelweard and I tell thee this, beloved, that I have now brought together in this book such passions of the saints as I have had leisure to put into English, because that thou and Æþelmær earnestly prayed me for such writings, and took them from my hands, for the strengthening of your faith by means of this history, which ye never had in your tongue before."

Ælfric's next important works were translations of the Bible ; first, again at the pressing request of Æþelweard, the earlier part of Genesis, to be prefixed to an already existing version of that book from the story of Isaac onwards ; then extracts from, or rather perhaps epitomes of, Numbers, Deuteronomy, and Joshua. Already, in his Lives of the Saints, he had given outlines of the Books of Kings and of the Maccabees, and at some time he dealt with the Judges, Esther, Job, and Judith. It has been doubted whether the

Books of Exodus and Leviticus are by him or not, but in his "De Veteri et de Novo Testamento", as Professor Crawford [1] has pointed out, he distinctly lays claim to them and to a translation of the whole of Genesis. His next work, the Canones Ælfrici, was in Latin and does not therefore concern us here.

In 1105 he was appointed Abbot of Eynsham and while there among other things, he wrote at the request of Sigweard, thane of East Healon in Mercia, an original treatise on the Old and New Testament, a sort of introduction to the study of the Bible, another treatise entitled "Emb Clǽnnysse", emphasizing the necessity of chastity for the clergy, and an English version of the Latin Sermo ad Sacerdotes, which he had written between 1014 and 1016 for Wulfstan, the Archbishop of York, in which he repeats largely what he has already said in his Canones. Other homilies have been attributed to him from similarity of style, but those already mentioned, which are certainly his, are sufficient to illustrate his work.

A glance at any of Ælfric's writings will show what strides English prose had made since Ælfred's time. In the first place we have got away from the long involved sentence in which Ælfred sometimes lost himself, when trying to work out some argument or more complicated line of thought. Ælfric's sentences are always as clear as were Ælfred's when telling a simple story. He is using a tool over which he has complete control, and a tool whose capabilities have been much developed. Like Ælfred he can tell an anecdote well, and, with less variety of theme, he has a greater range of tone than his great predecessor ; he can play upon the whole gamut of emotion ; he can be tender or pathetic, as when telling of the slaughter of the Innocents ; he can be indignant or stern, he can work out an argument or follow an abstruse line of thought with clearness ; he can rise almost to eloquence upon occasion. His style is easy, limpid, graceful, with well balanced sentences ; like Ælfred in his later, freer, writings, he gives us beautiful similes,

---

[1] Crawford, Heptateuch, p. 425.

as when he compares the infant martyrs to blossoms killed by an untimely frost.

The following passage from the Sermon on the Nativity of the Innocents may perhaps be given as characteristic of Ælfric as any one example could be. It goes : " Christ did not forget His young warriors, though He was not present in the flesh at the slaughter of them, but He sent them from this life of misery into His eternal kingdom. In a happy hour (gesæliglice) were they born, that they might for His sake suffer death. Blessed is their age, which might not yet confess Christ, but might yet suffer for Him. They were witnesses to the Saviour though they did not know Him yet. They were ripe for the slaughter, but, nevertheless, to their own happiness (gesæliglice) they died unto life. Happy was their birth, because they found eternal life at the entrance to this present life. They were torn from their mothers' breasts, but they were entrusted straightway to the bosoms of the angels. Nor might the evil persecutor have benefited these little ones by any service as greatly as he did by the hatred of his fierce persecution. They are called the flowers of the martyrs, because they were like flowers growing up in the midst of the cold of unbelief, and cut by the frost of this persecution." It is however impossible in a translation to show the skill with which Ælfric uses for instance the word " gesæliglice " in its various O.E. senses and thus gives a certain character to his narration. Like Ælfred he appreciates and uses well poetic terms, such as " goldfatu ", or " hordfatu " for *coffer* or *treasury*.

It is this style which is Ælfric's strong point ; he is not original, though, as in Genesis, he can translate with vigorous freedom ; there does not seem to have been a compelling force within him which obliged him to write. He did so gracefully and carefully, but on the initiative of others.

And he has the defects of his qualities. The ease in writing, the feeling for the poetry of the time, led Ælfric from what was at first an effective use of alliteration and a telling rhythm for his sentence to a sort of prose in which both were as regular as in verse. This alliterative prose is found sometimes in his first set of sermons, it becomes more and more frequent in his later work. Though it must be admitted that we sometimes get good rhetorical effects in this way, as in the account of the Fall of the Angels, more often what we find are tedious passages of prosaic verse, rather than the poetic prose which must have been in part his object. No doubt, he intended also to attract the attention of hearers accustomed to listen to the native poetry and to popularize his sermons. Certainly Ælfric tried to treat his saints as the native poets had treated their heroes in order to recommend them to his public. Still, however he may be criticized in detail, Ælfric must be considered on the whole as the greatest prose writer of the O.E. period ; he is certainly the most finished. And the student of Old English owes him another debt.

The dates of the MSS. of his works show that those works continued to be read for some time after his death. Indeed he was long looked on as the authority on certain questions of theology or discipline, especially on those concerning transubstantiation and the marriage of the clergy. At the Reformation the renewed concern for these questions brought his writings again into prominence. The interest in them which arose from their theological importance was extended to their antiquarian value and thus brought about the revival of O.E. studies under the leadership of Archbishop Parker and others.

The Wulfstan for whom Ælfric wrote his " Sermo ad Sacerdotes," was also a great preacher, though his sermons were very different in character from those of Ælfric. As Bishop of Worcester from 1002 to 1016 and Archbishop of York from 1002 to 1023, he was called upon to take his part in public affairs and the few sermons which he has left us reflect the troubled times in which he lived. There is a collection of thirty-five Homilies preserved in many MSS. which were long looked upon as Wulfstan's, but Professor Napier's thorough investigation of them, made in 1883, has shown that four only are certainly by the Archbishop. Among the others of the collection we have sometimes the same sermon with different headings, in other cases a heading by Wulfstan has apparently been prefixed to a sermon by some other writer. Four are, however, signed with his name in the Latinized form Lupus, which he affected. These are very similar in character, and from them a definite idea of the writer can be formed. The most important and the best known is the " Sermo Lupi ad Anglos " which is dated 1014 in one MS. This date is confirmed by internal evidence. In the sermon the preacher speaks of Æþelred as having been driven out of the country, which happened in 1013, but does not know of his recall which took place during the year 1014. The special characteristics of Wulfstan's style are to be seen perhaps even more strikingly in this sermon than in the others and it may well be used, therefore, to illustrate that style.

It was written when the people were suffering most cruelly from the ravages of the Danes and it gives us a vivid picture of the condition of England at the time. For many years before, the entries in the Chronicle are largely concerned with these ravages.

In 1001 the Danes had harried even Devon and Somerset, and, in the following year, the king bought them off for £24,000. In 1004, they plundered and burnt Norwich and Thetford after fierce fighting. In 1006, they were again in Wessex, plundering Reading and Wallingford. The Chronicle says that " they had cruelly marked every shire in Wessex with burning and harrying ". The following year a larger sum, £36,000, was paid them. By 1011, they had overrun all the east of England south of the Wash and had extended their raids as far west as to include Northampton, Oxfordshire, and much of Wiltshire. When they had done the most evil, the Chronicler tells us, " then a truce and peace was made with them. And nevertheless, they went everywhere in flocks, and harried our miserable people, and robbed and slew them ". The next year, 1012, they had to be paid a still larger sum, £48,000, before they could be persuaded to leave the country. In 1013, we read " they wrought the greatest evil that any army could do ", getting as far west as Bath ; Swein was accepted as king of all England, and Æþelred the Unready fled overseas. In 1005

T

there had been such a famine throughout England, as no man before remembered.

From other sources we learn that in the eleventh century, " the people of Bristol had an odious and inveterate custom of buying men and women in all parts of England and exporting them to Ireland for gain . . . nor were these men ashamed to sell into slavery their nearest relatives, nay even their own children."

Such was the state of England when Wulfstan wrote, the state which he describes. He says : " We know full well where the shameful thing has come to pass that, for a payment, a father has sold his child and a son his mother, and one brother, another, out of this land into the power of strangers " ; or, again, he says elsewhere : " There has long been no goodness anywhere, but there has been harrying and enmity in every part oft and frequently, and the English have now been for long without victory and too greatly discouraged through the wrath of God ; and pirates have been so strong through the permission of God that often in fight one has put to flight two, and two, often, twenty, sometimes less, sometimes more, and all for our sins . . . often two seamen, or three, drive the drove of Christian men from sea to sea through this nation chained together, to the public disgrace of us all if we could seriously feel shame or understand what is right."

Wulfstan was a priest first and a statesman afterwards ; he was, too, a man of his times, and he looked upon all these calamities as punishments sent upon the country for the sins of its people. He therefore denounced in no measured terms other great evils of the time, revealing the inner corruption of Church and State. Perhaps he was thinking of the treacherous massacre of the Danes on St. Brice's Day when he wrote : " For there are in this land great treacheries in the eyes of God and man, and many traitors in this country." He mentions other evil deeds, the murder of Edward the Martyr in 979 outside Corfe Castle, the harm done by bad appointments to great positions in the Church, and the general neglect of religion and law since the days of Edgar of Mercia (957–975). He implies that

Æþelred's departure overseas was a forced one due to treachery, a detail to which the Chronicle makes no reference. But while urging his hearers to penitence and amendment, as the first steps towards remedying these evils, the Archbishop had some idea of the futility of trying to buy off the Danes. He says : " But all this ignominy, which we so often endure, we repay with honour to those who put us to shame. We pay them tribute constantly and they put us daily to shame ; they harry and they burn ; they plunder and rob and carry away their booty to their ships."

Wulfstan is the orator rather than the scholar ; he appeals to the emotions rather than the intellect ; his style is rhetorical with all the force and energy which Ælfric's perhaps lacked, but with none of his grace and finish. He has a strikingly rich vocabulary, without rival in the language of any other O.E. prose writer, and in poetry only in that of Beowulf, the Battle of Maldon and Judith. A few Old Norse words had come in by this time, and Wulfstan uses some, but his native vocabulary had no need of any foreign enrichment. He gets his effects sometimes by the use of antithesis, but more often by that of doublets, which may alliterate, as in " here and hete ", *harrying* and *hatred* ; " byrne and blōdgyte ", *burning* and *bloodshed* ; " swutol and ʒesēne ", *clear* and *visible*, or they may rhyme, as in "stalu and cwalu", *stealing* and *murder*. And these repetitions give no impression of redundancy, in Wulfstan they make for emphasis.

Very effective, too, when thundered from the pulpit must have been passages with long lists of the evil happenings of the time, such as the following : " But there have been harrying and hunger ; burning and bloodshed, on every side often and frequently ; and robbery and murder ; sedition and pestilence ; disease of cattle and of men ; calumny and hatred ; and the plundering of ravagers has cruelly injured us ; excessive taxation has oppressed us and storms have often caused failure of crops."

Equally impressive must have been other passages with similar lists of sins and sinners such as this : " Here are, as we said before, murderers and slayers of kinsmen and priests ; despoilers of monasteries and betrayers of lords ; open apostates ; swearers of false oaths ; doers of deeds of violence, and of breaches of law and order, and many are guilty of all kinds of wantonness."

A hearer who remained unimpressed by such denunciations must have been phlegmatic indeed.

Wulfstan has mannerisms by which a sermon of his may be recognized. He is fond of phrases like " gecnāwe se þe cunne ", *let him recognize it who can*, or " gelȳfe se þe wille ", *believe it who will*. And it is not surprising to find a writer of such vehemence making great use of the adverb " too ", either by itself or reinforced by " ealles ", as in " tō swīþe ", *too greatly*, or " ealles tō gelōme ", *all too often*. Like Ælfric, he has borrowed from the poetic language in his use of alliteration and the poetic compound ; generally with both that use is discreet and effective for their different styles. But, as we have seen, Ælfric tends, on the one hand, to use the poetic device of alliteration in a way unsuitable for prose, and, on the other hand, he has not quite shaken off the shackles of Latin syntax. With Wulfstan, alliteration is used occasionally and for special effects only. We have very little of Wulfstan's from which to judge but, from what we have, it would seem that, if his syntax is faulty, it is not due to anything in O.E. prose, but to the impatience of the writer.

Thus in the hundred years after Ælfred began to write, English prose had developed into a literary medium capable of expressing every kind of mood. It could now be used with equal success for all shades of emotion, ranging from the pathetic, the calmly reflective, the pleasantly narrative, to the fiery and passionate.

CHAPTER XII

LATER PROSE (*cont.*) ; THE A.S. CHRONICLE AND MINOR WORKS

Important in the history of English prose as is the position of Ælfred as its founder, and that of Ælfric, whose writings illustrate the highest stage in its development during the pre-Conquest period, no work of either is of such outstanding importance in itself as the one we now pass on to consider. The greatest prose work of the O.E. period and the best known is the Anglo-Saxon Chronicle. Based as are the earlier entries on the records made from the time when the monks first began to jot down the chief events of each year, and continued into the Middle English period (the latest entry is for 1154), it affords a complete illustration in itself of the development of O.E. prose, as well as examples of fine prose writing, while, even if some statements have to be accepted with caution, it will always remain one of our principal historical documents for those times. It may be said that the Chronicle takes a place as prominent in O.E. prose as Beowulf does in the poetry of that period.

We possess seven MSS. of this work which differ considerably among themselves, but in all the Chronicle proper begins with the Roman conquest of Britain. In front of this three MSS. have put a description of that country, with an account of the five races inhabiting it, the English, the British, the Welsh, the Scottish, and the Pictish, an account based apparently on that in Bede's Ecclesiastical History, while another, the Parker MS. at C.C.C. Cambridge, has prefixed a genealogical table in which Ælfred's descent is traced back to Cerdic, who landed in Britain in 495. Similar tables are inserted elsewhere in the Chronicle ; for instance, under the year 855, the genealogy of Ælfred's father Æþelwulf is taken back not to Cerdic only, but to Adam, and we are told that one member,

Sceaf (mentioned in Beowulf also), was the son of Noah and was born in the Ark. Elsewhere the descent of King Ceolwulf of Wessex is traced back to Wodan.

The earlier entries are very meagre. Even as late as 705 one as short as the following is found: " In this year Aldferþ, king of Northumbria, died, and Seaxwulf, bishop, died." This may be taken as typical of a large number, though occasionally even earlier we get more detail, as in the description of the coming of Hengest and Horsa in 449 : " In this year Martianus and Valentinus succeeded to the kingdom and reigned seven years, and in their days Wyrtgeorn invited the race of the Angles hither and they came in three keels hither to Britain, at the place Ebbsfleet. King Wyrtgeorn gave them land in the south of this country, on condition that they should fight against the Picts. They fought against the Picts, and had the victory wherever they went. Then they sent to the Angles, and bade them send them supports, and bade them be told of the worthlessness of the Britons and of the excellence of the country. Then they sent at once a larger band to the help of the others. Then came men from three tribes of Germania," and so on. The primitive nature of the prose and the poor vocabulary need no comment. The first entry of any real fulness, however, is that for 755, in which year we have a graphic account of a vendetta between Cynewulf of Wessex and an " æþeling " Cyneheard, whose brother, Sigebryht, Cynewulf had supplanted on the throne, driving him out with the support of the " Witan " for his injustice. The story goes : " Then Cyneheard learnt that the king was with a small retinue only, in the company of a woman at Merton, and he rode up to him there and surprised him in the lady's bower, before the men who were with the king (and were in the hall) discovered it. And when the king became aware of it, he went to the door and defended himself nobly till he perceived the ' æþeling ', and then he rushed out at him and wounded him severely and they all continued to assail the king until they had slain him ; and when the king's thanes discovered the disturbance from the woman's screams, they ran thither, ' whosoever was soonest ready,'

Brittene igland is ehta hund mila lang.
⁊ twa hund brad. ⁊ her sind on þis
iglande fif geþeode. englisc. ⁊ britt
isc. ⁊ wilsc. ⁊ scyttisc. ⁊ pyhtisc. ⁊
boc leden. Erest weron bugend þises
landes brittes. þa coman of armenia. ⁊ ge sætan
suðewearde bryttene ærost. Þa ge lamp hit þ pyh
tas coman   suþan of scithian. mid langu scipu
na manegum. ⁊ þa coman ærost on norþ ybernian
up. ⁊ þær bædo scottas þ hi ðer moston wunian. ac
hi noldan heom lyfan. forðan hi cwædon þa scottas.
we eow magon þeah hwaðere ræd ge læron. we witan
oþer egland her be eastan. þer ge magon eardian gif
ge willað. ⁊ gif hwa eow wið stent. we eow fultumiað. þ
ge hit magon ge gangan. Ða feredon þa pihtas. ⁊ ge
ferdon þis land norþan weard. ⁊ suþan weard hit hef
don bryttas. swa we ær cwedon. And þa pyhtas heom abæ
don wif æt scottum. on þa ge rad þ hi ge curon heora
kyne cyn aa on þa wif healfa. þ hi heoldon swa lange
syððan. ⁊ þa ge lamp hit ymbe geara ryna. þ scotta
sum dæl ge wat of ybernian on bryttene. ⁊ þer lan
der sum dæl ge eodon. ⁊ þes heora heretoga reoda ge
haten. from þam heo sind ge nemnode dæl reodi. Six
tigum wintrum ær þa þe crist were acenned gaius iuli
romana kasere mid hund ehtatigum scipu ge sohte
bryttene. þer he þes ærost ge swenced mid sumum um
ge feohte. ⁊ micelne dæl his heres forlædde. ⁊ þa he

"Opening lines of A. S. Chronicle from MS. Bodl. Laud 636"

and Cyneheard offered each of them money and life, but not one of them would take it. And they continued fighting till all lay dead except one British hostage and he was severely wounded." Then on the morrow the king's thanes, who had been left behind previously, heard that the king had been slain and rode up and (in their turn) surrounded the whole place, thus imprisoning in it Cyneheard with his murdered victim, Cynewulf, and the same series of events followed with the rôles reversed. Again Cyneheard tried to bribe the loyalists, telling them, moreover, that they would be fighting against their own kinsmen if they attacked, for he had some among his troop. They, in their turn, refused the bribe but offered their kinsmen a safe conduct out first, as they said had been done in the fight before, in which a similar situation had arisen. This offer was rejected and they fought to the death except that one, Cyneheard's godson, escaped with his life, but not till he had received many wounds.

After this the entries are for some time of the same terse character as before, and the question naturally forces itself on the reader, how has this vivid anecdote made its way in among the other records ? The resemblances between the two fights, in the offer made, as we are told, in both cases, to let the kinsmen of the besieging force escape before the attack began, the resolute loyalty on both sides in the refusal of all bribes, and the fight to the death, all suggest an accepted tradition as to how such a story should go, and make it probable that, in revising the earlier entries in Ælfred's time, an old lay was used, turned into prose, but with none of the spirit of the poem lost in the process. That the story was inserted later from another source is to be inferred also from its being interpolated under the date of Cynewulf's accession. The event itself took place nearly thirty years later. So true has the chronicler been to his original that he has kept the early character of the constructions, using chiefly short sentences connected by " and ", or sometimes by " oþ " (until), as has been done as far as possible in the modernized version above. The obscurity, too, as to the part played by the different personages, which demands some consideration from the modern reader, would be explained if the story was taken from a lay composed so soon after the event, that no introductions were necessary. But it will be observed that the style, with all its imperfections, is already less clumsy than that in the earlier account of the landing of Hengest and Horsa.

The next entries of any length occur in Ælfred's time. In 871 we are told of the death of Æþelred and the succession of his brother to the throne of Wessex, and for some years after that we get stirring accounts of the battles between the Danes and the English. So vivid are the entries between 893 and 897 that Professor Earle suggested that they, at any rate, were by Ælfred himself ; he could, he said, hear the king's own voice in them.[1] Among so much that is good, it is difficult to select, but perhaps the following passages may afford a fair illustration of these records.

In 893 the Danes had invaded Kent and were in two armies, one under Hæsten at Milton, near Sittingbourne, and the other farther south at Appledore. In the entry for the next year we read : " Then the king gathered his levies and marched to where he could take up his position between the two Danish armies, as near as he could find space for woodfastness and waterfastness, so that he could reach either band if it should seek the open field. Then the Danes marched afterwards along the wood in bands and flocks, by whichever edge was free from the English army and they were attacked almost every day or by night, both by the English levies and also from the cities. The king had divided his army into two, so that they could always be half at home and half out, besides the men who had to hold the cities." Later, however, the Danes managed to leave their encampments and march northwards with much booty, and the chronicler goes on : " Then the English caught them up and fought against them at Farnham and put them to flight and rescued the booty, and the Danes fled over the Thames, without waiting to find a ford, and up the Colne to an island. Then the English army besieged them there as long as they had food, but when they had

[1] Alfred the Great, ed. by Bowker. King Alfred as Writer, p. 202.

finished their term of service and consumed their provisions,
the king was (still) on the road thither with the division
which marched with him. Then he was on the way thither
and the other division was on its way home but the Danes
remained behind (on the island) for their king had been
wounded in the fight and they could not carry him away."

The second passage is for the year 897. We read how after
the Danes had harried the coast of Wessex with their ships
called " æscas ", Ælfred's navy shut up a fleet of six of them
either in Southampton Water or in Poole Harbour.   The
Chronicle goes on then to tell us that : " Then King Ælfred
bade long ships be built against the æscas. They were well
nigh twice as long as the others ; some had sixty oars,
some more, and they were swifter and steadier and higher
than the Danish ships, and they were shaped neither after
the Frisian model nor the Danish, but just as it seemed to
him that they would be most useful. Then at a certain
time of the next year came six (Danish) ships to the Isle
of Wight and did much damage there, both in Devon and
everywhere along the coast. Then the king bade (his men)
go up with nine of the new ships and they blockaded the
mouth into the outer sea against them. Then they (the
Danes) went with three ships out against them (the English)
and three remained higher up in the mouth on dry land,
the men having gone away up on shore. Then they (the
English) seized two of the three ships at the outer mouth
and slew the men, and one ship escaped : on it also the
men were slain except five, and these got away because the
ships of the others (English) were aground. These were
stranded too in a very awkward position, three on the side
of the deep inlet where the Danes were aground, and the
others all on the other side, so that they could not get to
each other. But when the water had ebbed away many
furlongs from the ships, the Danes went from their ships
to the other three which where left stranded on their side
and there they fought."

So noticeable is the contrast between these vigorous
descriptions and the entries which precede and follow them,
that again some explanation must be sought.   If it is

difficult to accept Professor Earle's view, given above, that Ælfred, at this overwhelmingly busy time, yet contrived to write an account himself of these happenings, his influence was no doubt at work, possibly only in the general stimulus which he gave to national feeling and enterprise, but more probably in a direct commission to one of the "learned clerks" around him to record such important events. It will be seen that the style, vigorous as it is, has still some of the weak points to be seen in the earlier passages, as, for instance, in the ambiguity in the use of the pronouns. The matter to be expressed is simpler than that in Ælfred's later works of about the same date, and the writer has, therefore, succeeded better, but he has not attained to the graceful, lucid style of Ælfric. For that we must wait for the next passage, the death of Archbishop Ælfeah.

After Ælfred's death the Chronicle resumes its old character, with fuller accounts, it is true, than those for quite early years, but with no entries of special literary interest till 937. For that year most of the MSS. have inserted a poem in praise of Æþelstan's victory over the Danes at Brunanburh. Four other short poems occur between 937 and 979. These, however, with the exception perhaps of the last, are not thought to have been written primarily for the Chronicle and they have therefore been considered under the later lays.[1]

About the year 1000 the entries become again rather fuller in describing the luckless attempts of Æþelred to form a navy to protect the country, and telling how the land army which he raised was nearly as destructive to the country districts as those of the Danes, and of the sums levied in order to buy off the Danes.[2] The treacherous murder of the Danes on St. Brice's Day is, however, told quite shortly. These later entries are not only somewhat more consistently full than the earlier ones, but a new note has crept into them. The passages from Ælfred's reign are filled with war news, the means taken to defeat the enemy, and the details of the fights, but as time went on a more human element is to be detected ; the sufferings of the

[1] Chap. IX, p. 226 ff.
[2] Chap. XI, p. 273.

people are realized and in the account of the murder of Archbishop Ælfeah we get a touching note of pathos.

The story runs thus : " In this year (1011) between the feast of the Nativity and Michaelmas, they (the Danes) besieged Canterbury and entered it through treachery, for Ælfmær, whose life Archbishop Ælfeah had saved before, betrayed Canterbury to them. Then they took there the Archbishop Ælfeah and Ælfweard the king's reeve and Leofwine the Abbot and Godwine the Bishop, but they let Abbot Ælfmær go free. And they took therein all the religious orders, men and women—it was incredible how many people there were—and they remained in the city afterwards as long as they wished. And when they had searched all the town, they turned them to their ships and led the Archbishop away with them." The next passage suggests a poem on the subject :

> Then was he a prisoner, who before had been
> the head of England and of Christendom.
> There might be seen misery
> where before had been seen bliss,
> in the wretched city, from whence came first
> Christianity and joy before God and the world.

After a few lines the story goes on : " Then on the Saturday (after Easter) the army was greatly stirred against the Archbishop because he would promise them no money and forbade that any ransom should be paid for him. They were also very drunk, for wine had been brought there from the south, and they took the bishop and led him to their ' hustings ' on the eve of the Sunday of Easter week, and there they pelted him with bones and heads of cattle and one of them struck him on the head with an iron axe, so that he sank under the blow and his holy blood fell on the earth and he sent his holy soul to the kingdom of God."

It will be seen that the change in outlook is here begun which was further developed in the M.E. period, as, for instance, in the account of the attack on the monks at Glastonbury, and of the state of England in Stephen's reign, which we have added here, though they, of course, do not belong to our period. In this year (1083) arose the discord at Glastonbury between the abbot Thurstan and his monks, in which the abbot called laymen to his aid.

" And then the monks were greatly afraid of them and knew not what they should do, but fled in all directions ; some ran into the church and locked the doors after them, and they (the soldiers) went after them into the monastery and would have dragged them out as they durst not go out, and a rueful thing happened there on that day. The Frenchmen broke into the choir and rushed towards the altar where the monks were ; and some of the young ones went up to the upper floor and kept shooting downwards with arrows towards the sanctuary, so that in the rood that stood above the altar there stuck many arrows. And the wretched monks lay about the altar, and some crept under and cried earnestly to God, imploring His mercy, seeing that they could obtain none from men. What can we say, but that they shot cruelly ? Others brake down the doors and went in and slew some of the monks and wounded many therein, so that the blood flowed down from the altar upon the steps, and from the steps down on to the floor."

This change of treatment and point of view is even more marked in the description of the sufferings of the people in Stephen's reign. " Then they took the men whom they believed to have any wealth, both by day and by night, men and women, and put them into prison for their gold and silver, and they tortured them with unspeakable tortures, for never had martyrs been tortured as they were. They were hung up by the feet and smoked with foul smoke, they were hung up by the thumbs or by the head and coats of mail fastened to their feet. Knotted cords were put round their heads and tightened till they penetrated to the brain. They were thrust into dungeons in which were adders and snakes and toads and killed in that way." Other tortures are mentioned equally " unspeakable ", but this passage is enough to illustrate the change in point of view, already noted in speaking of O.E. poetry, as well as the gradual increase in ease of expression in the course of the Chronicle. In short, the entries in the Chronicle confirm the evidence of the gradual development of O.E. prose which has already been afforded by the passages from the Laws, from Ælfred's works, and from those of Ælfric and Wulfstan, and give us a further glimpse into its later history.

Seven MSS. of the Chronicle exist, which are distinguished here by the letters adopted for them by Dr. Plummer in his edition of " Two Saxon Chronicles ".

A (1). The Parker MS. (C.C.C.C. 173) bequeathed by Archbishop Parker to C.C.C. Cambridge and preserved there. It comes down to 1070.

A (2). A MS. in the British Museum (Cott. Otho B XI) reduced in the great fire in Ashburnham House to a few charred remains. There is, however, a transcript previously made by Wheloc, which is an important source of information for the contents. This MS. comes down to 1001.

B. Another British Museum MS. (Cott. Tib. A VI), slightly injured in the same fire, which brings its records down to 977.

C. A third British Museum MS. (Cott. Tib. B I). Its records come down to 1066. It is in the same MS. as Ælfred's Orosius.

D. Also in the British Museum (Cott. Tib. B IV), where it is bound up in a MS. with other things. This brings us down to 1079.

E. The Laud MS. (Misc. 636), in the Bodleian Library, with entries down to 1154. This copy is often known as the Peterborough Chronicle.

F. A Cotton MS. in the British Museum (Cott. Domit. A VIII), extending to 1058.

For a full discussion and description of these MSS. the student should consult Dr. Plummer's exhaustive account.[1] Here, if it may be allowed to summarize his results, it may be said that in 892, or a little after,[2] a national chronicle must have been written, probably at Winchester, as the capital, under the stimulating influence of Ælfred, possibly

---

[1] Two Saxon Chronicles, Vol. II.

[2] The probability that this is the approximate date is to be inferred from the fact that the genealogical table prefixed to the Parker MS. comes no further than Ælfred. It is noteworthy that striking resemblances may be detected between the phraseology of the Chronicle and that of Ælfred's Orosius, and that one copy of the Chronicle is in the same MS. as that work.

under his personal supervision, possibly even at his dictation, the chronicler drawing for the earlier entries from sources such as the Northumbrian list of kings or Bede's Ecclesiastical History and other sources not yet traced.

From A (1) before it left Winchester several copies were made, one remaining at Winchester, another being sent to Abingdon, and a third to Ripon. A(1), after various wanderings came eventually into the possession of Archbishop Parker and so to Cambridge, and a copy of the transcript sent to Ripon made its way in time to Peterborough and so to Oxford.

Other prose writings of the O.E. period which must be mentioned briefly in conclusion as of interest in different ways are some Bible Glosses of the tenth and early eleventh centuries, the apocryphal Gospel of Nicodemus and the fragmentary story of Apollonius of Tyre.

The first of these glosses, known as the Lindisfarne Gospels, is a Latin text of about the year 700 [1] to which an interlinear English translation in the Northumbrian dialect was added about 950. The Latin is glossed word by word, so that the English is of no use for a study of literature or syntax, though it provides the philologist with an invaluable source of information for later Northumbrian forms, and the magnificent MS. is of very great general interest from the beautiful illustrations with which it is adorned. Excellent reproductions of the plates were published in 1923.

Secondly come the Rushworth Glosses, of about the same date, written by the priests Farman and Owun. This again is of value chiefly to the linguist, though Farman's work is in places more than a mere gloss. Rather later, of the early eleventh century, is a translation of the Gospels in W.S. by a certain Ælfric, but not the Ælfric of Eynsham. Of this six MSS. exist, bearing witness to the efforts made to place the Bible in the vernacular within the reach of all who could read.

In one of these MSS., in that in the Cambridge University Library, is the Gospel of Nicodemus, which is of importance as having first introduced into England the Legend of Joseph of Arimathæa, his imprisonment by the Jews and

---

[1] Brit. Mus. Cotton Nero, D 4.

miraculous deliverance. It also gives another account of the popular subject, the Harrowing of Hell. This is told by Karinus and Leuticus, sons of Simeon, who were among those raised from the dead. They are represented as writing down the story independently, and when all was written down, they rose up and gave the pages which they had written to the elders. " Karinus gave his to Annas and Caiaphas and Gamaliel, and in like fashion Leuticus gave his to Nicodemus and Joseph. . . . And when the elders and the priests read the writings which Karinus and Leuticus had written, then was each written, just like the other, so that there was nothing less or more in the one than in the other by a letter or even by a dot ! " There is another copy of this work in the Beowulf MS. in the British Museum and the Bodleian has a transcript made by Junius.

The last of these prose works mentioned, the story of Apollonius of Tyre, illustrates the widening of the themes treated in later O.E. as well as the increasing flexibility of the prose, for it is of Eastern origin, probably Greek, and of considerable antiquity. In it we get the first version of the story of Pericles, treated later by Gower and Shake-speare. The O.E. narrative is briefly this : Apollonius, fleeing from Tyre, is shipwrecked but escapes and drifts on to the land of Cyrene. There he is well treated and wins the affections of the daughter of the King Arcestrates by his skill in music and other gifts. They are married and set sail for Tyre, but on the way the princess appears to die in giving birth to a daughter, and the sailors demand that her body should be thrown overboard. She is, however, still living and is rescued ; the infant is given into the charge of guardians at Tarsus, but these prove false to their trust. Finally, however, after many adventures the three are happily reunited. A short passage may illustrate the style.

Apollonius is sitting sadly in the hall, thinking of his lost possession, and the king has just bidden him be of good cheer. Even as the king spoke these words, then came in suddenly the king's young daughter and kissed her father and those sitting around. When she came to Apollonius then she turned to her father and said, " Thou noble King and my dearest Father, who is this young man who is sitting opposite thee on such a worthy seat, but with so sad a countenance ? " Then said the king, " Dear daughter, the young man has been shipwrecked ; he pleased me best at the ball play and therefore I have invited him to our feast. I know not what he is, nor whence he is, but if thou wilt know what he is, ask him, because thou hast a right to know."

This influence from the East is also to be seen in two other works of this period, the " Letter of Alexander to Aristotle ", and " the Wonders of the East ", both in the Beowulf MS. in the British Museum.

Hitherto classical influence in O.E. times has been traced in literature in themes treated, to some extent in the form of the works, and later in a modification of the manner of treatment, especially in that of nature. But it is also to be seen in the pseudo-scientific writings of the late O.E. period. These are of great interest in other ways also. They give us an insight into the lives of those who produced the literature, into their customs and beliefs, and they are valuable as increasing our knowledge of their vocabulary. Some account of them should therefore be given here before leaving the subject of the literature of the O.E. period. Chief among these scientific works are the Enchiridion or Handbōc of Byrhtferþ,[1] the Herbarium, a work entitled Medicina de Quadrupedibus, and the Læcebōc or Leechdoms. The Enchiridion or Handbōc is in a MS.[2] of the later tenth century. The contents of this work are very varied. It touches upon many of the sciences, as they were then understood, but deals chiefly with mathematics and astronomy. Thus it treats, for instance, of the signs of the zodiac and the length of the sun's course through each ; of the method for finding Easter ; the symbolic properties of certain numbers and the correspondence between the four ages of man, the four seasons, the four elements, the four humours

---

[1] Byrhtferth's Manual, ed. by S. J. Crawford, B.A., B.Litt., for E.E.T.S., orig. series, 177.
[2] Bodleian, Ashmol., 328.

(choleric, melancholy, etc.), and the four qualities, dry, moist, cold, and hot. Thus the summer is to spring as adolescence is to youth and so on. The style of this book is as unlike that of a modern scientific work as is the matter. After the prologue comes the following passage : " We have stirred with our oars the waves of the deep pool. We have likewise beheld the mountains around the salt seastrand, and with outstretched sail and prosperous winds have succeeded in pitching our camp on the coast of the fairest of lands. The waves symbolize this profound art and the mountains, too, symbolize its magnitude. . . . Where we perceived the beauty of the lily, (that is the beauty of computation), there we scented the perfume of the rose, (that is we perceived the profundity of learning)." The whole work is illustrated with diagrams.

The Herbarium and Medicina are found in four MSS., of which one, Cotton Vitellius C III, and two others are in the British Museum and the fourth, Hatton 76, is in the Bodleian. Of these the first, to be dated between 1000 and 1050, is the finest. It is illustrated by drawings in colours of the plants described, and of some of the animals, and is further adorned with two large pictures, one of which represents Æsculapius between the Centaur Chiron and Plato. Some of the illustrations, though they may not help much towards our recognition of the plant described, are charming in the delicacy of their colouring. Unfortunately the MS. was injured in the fire in Ashburnham House. The first work, the Herbarium, consists, as Cockayne [1] has shown, of two parts, the first being based chiefly on the Latin Herbarium Apuleii, the second on the work of Dioskorides. In all 185 plants are named and the various medicinal uses of each given. As a rule each plant is allowed two or three such uses only, but some have more. We are told, for instance, that the wort which men name betony is produced on meads and clean downlands and in sheltered places ; it is of virtue whether for a man's soul or for his body ; it shields him against uncanny night visitants and terrifying

[1] Leechdoms, Wortcunning, and Starcraft in Early England, ed. by the Rev. Thos. Oswald Cockayne in the Rolls Series.

visions and dreams. "And this wort is very life-giving (?) and thus thou shalt get it in the month of August without use of iron tool. And when thou hast taken it, then shake off the mould until none is clinging to it and dry it in the shade very thoroughly and grind it to dust, roots and all. Then use it ; swallow it when thou hast need." The Medicina de Quadrupedibus treats of animals as the Herbarium does of plants. Thirteen only are mentioned, however, with the parts of each of value to medicine. For instance, the cure for a child with epilepsy is as follows : " Draw the brain of a mountain goat through a gold ring : give it to the child to swallow before it tastes milk. It will be healed." This work is based on that of Sextus Placitus.

Of equal interest are the three books of Leechdoms, to be found in MS. Reg. 12, D, XVII in the British Museum.[1] While the prescription in the Herbarium are arranged according to the plants used, and in the Medicina according to the animals required, here they are arranged according to the maladies to be cured, and remedies are given for every kind of ill of mind or body in men, women, or children, and even in horses. The first book has remedies for eighty-eight maladies, the second for eighty-seven, and the third for seventy-three, though headings are given for more. Usually there is a choice of remedies for each illness. Among the many alternatives given in the first book for pains in the head we have this prescription : " For pain in the head take rue and wormwood ; pound in a mortar and mix with vinegar and oil. Strain through a cloth and anoint the head therewith, or make a paste of the same and lay it on the head. Bandage it well when thou wilt go to rest."

But physical ills are not the only ones treated. We have a prescription for madness which is far more complicated. It runs : " Against madness and folly. Put into ale, marshmallows, lupins, betony, southern fennel, cat's mint, water agrimony, cockles, smallage, and then drink it."

The remedy for elf's disease is still more elaborate. It goes : " Take bishop's wort, fennel, lupins, the lower part of

---

[1] Cockayne (see above) has eked these out with a short passage from another MS., Harl. 55. See also Grein-Wülker, Prosa, Vol. VI.

enchanter's nightshade, and moss, or lichen from a hallowed cross, and incense, a handful of each, bind all the worts in a cloth, dip into a font with hallowed water three times ; let three masses be sung over it, an ' omnibus sanctis ' and a third ' pro infirmis '. Put gledes into a pan, lay the herbs therein, and ' smoke ' the man with the herbs before night ; sing a litany, a credo, and the paternoster and write Christ's mark on every limb. Then take a small handful of worts of the same kind hallowed in the same way, drop hallowed water thrice into it, and boil in milk. Let him sup it before his meat and he will soon be well."

In the last recipe we have a good example of the part played by charms in some of these leechdoms. Other prescriptions are much more nauseous. The O.E. physician had no idea of sugaring his pills.

Finally, may be mentioned a set of similar prescriptions, known as the Lacnunga [1] or Healings in which Latin ones are interspersed with the Old English.

[1] British Museum, MS. Harleiana, 585.

BIBLIOGRAPHY

SOME BOOKS RECOMMENDED

The MSS. in which the O.E. poetical and prose works are to be found are given in Chapter I or in speaking of those works. Authorities on special texts are mentioned in treating of them. It only remains, therefore, to give here a list of some of the editions, translations, and general works on O.E. literature which will be found useful.

Most of the prose and poetry will be found in the "Bibliothek der angelsächsischen Poesie und Prosa", edited by C. W. M. Grein (now out of print), re-edited and enlarged by Richard Paul Wulcker.

Other works are :

Ælfred. Alfred as a Writer, by the Rev. Professor Earle, in Alfred the Great, ed. by Alfred Bowker. 1899.
—— King Alfred's Anglo-Saxon Version of the Compendious History of the World, ed. by the Rev. J. Bosworth (with map). 1859.
—— King Alfred's Old English Version of Boethius, De Consolatione Philosophiæ, ed. from the MS., with Introduction, Critical Notes, and Glossary, by Walter John Sedgefield. 1899.
—— King Alfred's Old English Version of St. Augustine's Soliloquies, ed. with Introduction, Notes, and Glossary, by H. L. Hargrove, Ph.D., Yale Studies in English, XIII. 1902.
—— King Alfred's Orosius, ed. by Henry Sweet, M.A., No. 79 of E.E.T.S. 1883. There is also a useful little book of extracts by Sweet.
—— King Alfred's Version of Boethius. Done into Modern English, with an Introduction, by Walter John Sedgefield, Litt.D. 1900.
—— King Alfred's West Saxon Version of Gregory's Pastoral Care, with an English Translation, ed. by Henry Sweet, M.A., No. 45 of E.E.T.S. 1871.
—— Life and Times of Alfred the Great, by Charles Plummer, M.A. 1902.
—— Soliloquies of St. Augustine, ed. by the Rev. T. O. Cockayne, in the "Shrine". 1864-9.
—— The Legal Code of Alfred the Great, by M. E. Turk. 1890.
—— The Old English Version of Bede's Ecclesiastical History of the English People, ed. with Translation and Introduction by Thomas Miller, M.A., Ph.D., for the E.E.T.S. 1898.

Ælfred. The Whole Works of Alfred the Great, with Preliminary Essays illustrative of the history, arts, and manners of the ninth century, ed. by J. A. Giles, Jubilee edition. 1858.

Ælfric. Homilies of A.S. Church, ed. by Benjamin Thorpe for the Ælfric Society. Part I. 1844.

—— Selected Homilies of Ælfric, ed. by Henry Sweet. A useful little volume of extracts. 1885.

—— The O.E. Version of the Heptateuch, Ælfric's Treatise on the Old and New Testament and his Preface to Genesis, ed. by S. J. Crawford, B.A., B.Litt., E.E.T.S. Orig. Series, 160. 1922.

Andreas and the Fates of the Apostles, ed. with Introduction, Notes, and Glossary by George Philip Krapp in the Albion Series. 1906.

An Anglo-Saxon Verse Book by W. J. Sedgefield, M.A., Litt.D. This contains nearly all the shorter pieces, many passages from Beowulf, and some from the religious poems. 1922.

Anglo-Saxon and Old Norse Poems, ed. and translated by N. Kershaw. 1922. This contains the Wanderer, Seafarer, Wife's Complaint, Message of the Husband, Ruin, and Battle of Brunanburh.

Beowulf, and the Finnsburg Fragment. A translation into modern English prose by John R. Clark Hall, M.A., Ph.D. 1911.

—— and the Fight at Finnsburg, ed. with Introduction, Bibliography, Notes, Glossary, and Appendices by Fr. Klæber. This also contains also Deor, Waldere, and Widsith. 1922.

—— An Introduction to the study of the Poem with a discussion of the Stories of Offa and Finn, by R. W. Chambers, 2nd ed. 1932.

—— and Epic Tradition by William Witherle Lawrence. 1928.

—— ed. with Introduction, Bibliography, Notes, Glossary, and Appendices by W. J. Sedgefield, Litt.D. This contains also the Fight at Finnsburg, Waldere, Deor, and Widsith. 1913.

—— mit ausführlichem Glossar, herausgegeben von Moritz Heyne, besorgt von Levin L. Schücking. 1908.

—— with the Finnsburg Fragment, ed. by A. J. Wyatt. New edition revised with Introduction and Notes by R. W. Chambers. 1914.

—— Translated into modern English rhyming verse by Archibald Strong, M.A., D.Litt. 1914.

—— Article on Beowulf in Encyclopædia Britannica, by Henry Bradley.

—— Essays on questions connected with Beowulf by Knut Stjerna, translated and edited by John R. Clark Hall. 1912.

—— The Tale of Beowulf by W. Morris and A. J. Wyatt. Kelmscott Press. 1895.

Blickling Homilies, ed. by the Rev. Richard Morris, LL.D. 1880.

Byrhtferth's Manual, ed. by S. J. Crawford, B.A., B.Litt., for the E.E.T.S. orig. series, 177.

Cædmon. The Cædmon Poems translated into English by Charles Kennedy. The illustrations are reproduced. 1916.

Crist. The Christ of Cynewulf, ed. with Introduction, Notes, and Glossary by Albert S. Cook. 1900.

Chronicle, the A.S. The Anglo-Saxon Chronicle, ed. with a translation by Benjamin Thorpe. (All texts given.) 1861.

—— Two of the Saxon Chronicles, Parallel. A revised Text, ed. with Introduction, Notes, and Appendixes by Charles Plummer, M.A. 1892.

Dichtungen der Angelsachsen. A translation into modern German of most of the poetry by C. W. M. Grein, Dr. Phil. 1863.

Doomsday. Be Dōmesdæge, ed. by R. Rawson Lumby, B.D., in vol. 65 of E.E.T.S. 1876.

Elene. Cynewulf's Elene, ed. by Julius Zupitza. 1888.

—— Elene; Judith; Athelstan or the Fight at Brunanburh; Byrhtnoth, or the Fight at Maldon translated by James M. Garnett, M.A., LL.D. 1889.

—— The O.E. Elene, Phoenix, and Physiologus, ed. by A. S. Cook. 1919.

Exeter Book, ed. from the MS. with a Translation, Notes, and Introduction, by Israel Gollancz, M.A., for the E.E.T.S. orig. series 104. 1895.

Exodus and Daniel. Ed. by Francis A. Blackburn, Ph.D., in Belles Lettres Series. 1907.

—— Cædmon's Exodus and Daniel, ed. by Theodore W. Hunt, Ph.D. 1893.

Genesis. B. The Later Genesis and other O.E. and O.S. texts relating to the Fall of Man, ed. by Fr. Klæber. 1913, second edition 1923.

Judith. An Old English Epic Fragment, ed. by Albert S. Cook in the Belles Lettres Series. 1904.

Juliana, ed. by William Strunk, jun., in the Belles Lettres Series. 1904.

Junius MS., ed. by G. P. Krapp, Anglo-Saxon Records, Vol. I. 1931.

Laws of the Earliest Kings, ed. and translated by L. F. Attenborough, M.A. 1922.

Leechdoms, Wortcunning, and Starcraft of Early England, ed. by the Rev. Thos. Oswald Cockayne in the Rolls Series. 1864. A later edition in Grein-Wülcker, Prosa, Vol VI by Günther Leonhardi. 1905.

Maldon, Battle of, and short Poems from the Saxon Chronicle, ed. by W. J. Sedgefield, Ph.D., in Belles Lettres Series. 1904.

Nicodemus, Gospel of, ed. by S. J. Crawford, B.A., B.Litt. Edinb., 1927.

Riddles of the Exeter Book, ed. with Introduction, Notes, and Glossary by Frederick Tupper, jun., in the Albion Series. 1909.

—— The O.E. Riddles, ed. by A. J. Wyatt, M.A., in the Belles Lettres Series. 1912.

Three Northumbrian Poems; Cædmon's Hymn, Bede's Death-Song, and the Leiden Riddle, ed. by A. H. Smith, Ph.D. 1933.

Vercelli Book, ed. by G. P. Krapp, in Anglo-Saxon Records, Vol. II.

Wulfstan. Sammlung der ihm zugeschriebenen Homilien nebst Untersuchungen über ihre Echtheit. Heraus gegeben von Arthur Napier. 1883.

GENERAL WORKS

Early English Literature, Vol. I, by Bernard ten Brink, translated from the German by Horace M. Kennedy. 1877.

English Literature from the Beginning to the Norman Conquest, by Stopford A. Brooke. 1898.

Epic and Romance. Essays on Medieval Literature, by W. P. Ker. 1897.

Geschichte der altenglischen Literatur von Alois Brandl. Teil I. Offprint from Pauls Grundriss der Germanischer Philologie. 1908.

The Cambridge History of Literature, Vol. I, Chaps. I–XIV.

The Growth of Literature, by Hector Munro and Norah Kershaw Chadwick. Vol. I, 1932.

The Heroic Age, by H. Munro Chadwick. 1912.

The History of Early English Literature, by Stopford A. Brooke. 1892.

Widsith. A Study in Old English Heroic Romance, by R. W. Chambers. 1912.

English Literature before Chaucer, by P. G. Thomas. 1924.

INDEX

Printed in Great Britain by Stephen Austin & Sons, Ltd., Hertford.